Jews, Labour and the Left, 1918-48

Jews, Labour and the Left, 1918-48

Edited by

CHRISTINE COLLETTE and
STEPHEN BIRD

Ashgate

Aldershot • Burlington USA • Singapore • Sydney

Published by
Ashgate Publishing Limited
Gower House
Croft Road
Aldershot
Hants GU11 3HR
England

Ashgate Publishing Company
131 Main Street
Burlington
Vermont 05401-5600
USA

Ashgate website: http://www.ashgate.com

British Library Cataloguing in Publication Data

Jews, Labour and the Left, 1918-48.
    1. Labour movement—Religious aspects—Judaism. 2. Jews—
    Political activity—History—20th century. 3. Jews—History—
    20th century. 4. Socialism and Judaism—History—20th century.
    5. Labour Zionism—History—20th century.
    I. Collette, Christine. II. Bird, Stephen.
    322.2'089924

Library of Congress Control Number: 00-105496

ISBN 0 7546 0262 1

This book is printed on acid free paper

Printed in Great Britain by Antony Rowe Ltd., Chippenham

Contents

Notes on Contributors

Stephen Bird BA MSc ALA took BA Honours in History at the University of North London and his MSc at Birbeck College London in Politics and Administration. He was appointed Labour Party archivist in 1978. Since 1990 he has been archivist/librarian at the National Museum of Labour History in Manchester. He is a member of the Society for the Study of Labour History Executive Committee, the Co-ordinating Committee of the International Association of Labour History Institutions and is the Secretary of the United Kingdom Political Parties Archives Network. Established Labour Heritage, the Labour Party's history society in 1981.

Christine Collette BA (Oxon), MLitt (Oxon) is Reader in Class and Gender Studies at Edge Hill College of Higher Education. She is a member of the Society for the Study of Labour History Executive Committee and was a Founder member of Labour Heritage, the Labour Party's History Society. She is a member of the Labor and Working Class History Association (USA). Her publications in the fields of Labour and Women's History and feminist pedagogy include *The International Faith*, the first book in Ashgate's Studies in Labour History series.

David De Vries is a lecturer at the Department of Labour Studies, Tel Aviv University. He is the author of *Idealism and Bureaucracy in 1920s Palestine. The Origins of 'Red Haifa'* (Tel Aviv, 1999). His research interests focus on the social history of Palestine and in several articles he examined the interrelations of labour and nationalism. At present he is working on strikes and national identity in Palestine during the first half of the twentieth century.

Jason Heppell is a tutor in the Department of History, University of Sheffield. He is preparing a doctoral thesis on Jews in the Communist Party of Great Britain. In 1996-1997 he attended the Oxford Centre for Hebrew and Jewish Studies at the University of Oxford. He has presented papers at conferences in Britain and the USA.

Paul Kelemen teaches in the Department of Sociology, University of Manchester. He has published articles related to Zionism and the British Labour Movement in *Social History, International Review of Social History, Labour History Review* and *Economy and Society.*

Arieh Lebowitz is Director of Public Information as well as Program Associate at the Jewish Labor Committee. An activist for many years in Americans for Progressive Israel, a Socialist Zionist organisation, he is currently a Vice President of Meretz USA, API's successor body. He holds a

BA degree in Judaic Studies from Binghamton University. Together with Gail Malmgreen, he edited a volume on the Holocaust-era papers of the Jewish Labor Committee Collection at the Robert F. Wagner Labour Archives.

Gail Malmgreen is the archivist for the Jewish Labor Committee Collection at the Robert F. Wagner Labor Archive, New York University. She holds an MLS degree from Columbia University and a PhD from Indiana University and has published on both British and US Labour History.

Deborah Osmond graduated with her Masters in Labour History at Dalhousie University in Halifax, Nova Scotia and is now pursuing doctoral studies in British History at York University in Toronto.

Isabelle Tombs studied history at the Sorbonne and Cambridge, where she did her PhD on Socialist Politics and the Future of Europe. She is now a Senior Lecturer at South Bank University. She is the author of articles in France and in Britain on socialist exiles in Britain, on European identity, on trade union policies and on Jewish issues.

Irene Wagner emigrated to the UK in 1938. After working as a Labour journalist's au pair, she married and joined her husband in confidential war work. She took up her interrupted librarianship after the war and was librarian until retirement to the Labour Party. She is active locally in education.

Introduction

Christine Collette and Stephen Bird

There has been no history like that of the Jews. No other people can trace their chronicles back over thousands, let alone hundreds of years, nor, indeed, have influenced such a wide range of cultures during that time. The last hundred years have been especially significant in Jewish history. As one of their sons (albeit a prodigal one) remarked: 'There have been decades like centuries and centuries like decades'. Karl Marx could have added, in relation to the Jews of the twentieth century: 'and there have been centuries like millennia'.[1]

In 1900 there was hope for the Jews. Starting to be accepted in Western European society, they contributed to its political and economic development. Even those refugees crammed into transatlantic steamers, fleeing the pogroms of Eastern Europe, could aspire to a new home in a democratic republic, large enough to absorb them, with a constitution which allowed them to campaign for their further freedoms. Others, however, were not content to find a place of freedom but aspired, like other captive peoples, such as the Poles and the Irish, to have a nation of their own. Zionism was no longer a prayer but a nationalist dream that could be fulfilled in their lifetime.

It was natural that not only were Jews inspired by, but that they initiated revolutionary and socialist ideas; not only did they participate in, but they led the early left-wing movements. Their messianic culture and their constant experience of religious oppression made such ideas more meaningful to them. Not all were Zionists by any means and to many this nationalistic concept contradicted the very basis of socialism. However, this debate was to be overwhelmed by the most significantly tragic event of the twentieth century. Anti-Semitic persecution was an ingrained part of their history, but never had it been so systematically undertaken and with such cold ideological clarity, as in the Third Reich. Auschwitz and Buchenwald made anti-Zionism seem anti-Semitic.

The chapters in this book deal with the first half of the century, during this period of hope and despair. The book's timescale begins from the destruction of the old European empires at the close of the First World War, and covers the development of national self-determination, fascism and anti-Semitism in Europe, the creation of international socialist institutions and the British mandate of Palestine. War and insurgency in Palestine made new choices available. In one sense, the book is about the issues which arise from nation-building; territory, criteria for including and excluding people, ethnicity, the rights of ethnic minorities, class and the representation of workers in civil government, personal identities. Also apparent is the division of Labour movements into socialist and communist wings. Positioning here depended, to an extent, on whether one took a Zionist stance, Communist parties being anti-imperialist while the British Labour Party, of importance because of British mandatory powers, was Zionist. Much feminist scholarship has addressed the gendered nature of citizenship[2] and here, Deborah Osmond and Christine Collette consider this issue. Of the countries represented in the international socialist institutions, the minority had women's suffrage;[3] the franchise was generally not extended to women in Palestine. David De Vries shows that women were under-represented in the Palestinian Labour movement, which combated anti-Semitic stereotyping by emphasising the masculinity of the image of Jewish workers.

The book arose from a number of sources. At the 1994 North American Labor History Conference on International and Comparative Labor History, Gail Malmgreen critiqued the lack of coverage of anti-Semitism in inter-war Europe. At the Robert F. Wagner Labor Archives she contributed to the production of a video documentary, *They were not silent: the Jewish Labor Movement and the Holocaust*.[4] Here, she gives an account of the inter-war American Jewish Labor Committee, examining trades union interaction with Jewish activity. While Isabelle Tombs's and Christine Collette's route to addressing Gail's comments was through their ongoing work on British Labour internationalism, Paul Kelemen here represents those engaged in Jewish historiography.[5] Arieh Lebowitz has contributed, for this volume, a bibliographical listing of sources for studying Jewish interaction with the American and British Labour movements. Representing Israeli Labour movement historians, David De Vries gives an account of the symbiotic relationship between the Palestinian Labour movement and nation-building. A new generation of historians, of whom Deborah Osmond and Jason Heppell are examples, were meanwhile further researching the topic we have summarised as *Jews, Labour and the Left*. Cyril Goldstein, of Manchester University, was the motivator of a 1998 conference funded by Labour Heritage, the British Labour Party's historical affiliate, to mark the fiftieth anniversary of the state of Israel, which brought some of the contributors together. Irene Wagner, Labour Heritage Treasurer and a Jewish emigrée from Germany sixty years earlier, completes this book by an account of her 1998 return to her birthplace. Much of the editing of this book was carried out by email correspondence with contributors in New York, Tel Aviv and Ontario, and the editors thank all the contributors for their insights and willingness to collaborate.

The Labour Heritage conference marked the founding of the state of Israel as an historical event, but this in no way meant that participants necessarily took a Zionist stance. Indeed, it was the forum for lively debate on the politics and historiography of Zionism. A linked topic was whether Jewish people could/should be distinguished as participants in the politics of their country of domicile. These two debates lie at the heart of this volume's project to understand Jewish involvement in Labour movements outside Israel.

Inevitably, with an intercontinental remit and contributors, the editors have

2

been aware of terminological problems. In this case, these problems underlie some areas of passionate debate and controversy. We have been guided by American contributors in the appellation 'Jews' in the title, while we are more comfortable with 'Jewish people'. The terms 'Zionism' and 'Bundism' (the outlook of the followers of the Jewish Workers' group founded in Russia and based in Poland between the World Wars) are in themselves controversial and are explored in this volume. Isabelle Tombs uses the term 'Doykeyt' (hereness) to describe the Bundist position of seeking equal rights within the country of domicile.[6] Gail Malmgreen describes the Bund's position as 'a clear if idiosyncratic programme of socialist internationalism combined with vigorous Yiddish-based "cultural nationalism". They always supported the notion of a distinct national existence with autonomy over cultural institutions etc. for the Jewish people'.[7] A related controversy is that over the terms 'assimilation' and 'integration'. Paula E. Hyman has pointed to the different meaning of assimilation, both a project and a cultural process.[8]

The second half of the twentieth century has continued the tale of hope and despair. The State of Israel may be the ultimate refuge, where the Jewish nation has been continuously at war with its neighbours. It is itself being accused of imperialism and its people accused of racism, even genocide. Its socialist foundation is disappearing. Anti-Semitism may be outlawed in Western Europe (though it continues in Eastern Europe and the Middle East), but widespread assimilation by Jews into Western society is causing great consternation among traditionalists in their communities. These chapters in many ways foresee some of the problems that lie ahead. The debate goes on.

Notes

1. Karl Marx.
2. Representative is Ruth Lister (1997), *Citizenship: Feminist Perspectives*, London: Macmillan.
3. Christine Collette (1998), *The International Faith: Labour's Attitudes to European Socialism, 1918-1939*, Aldershot: Ashgate, ch. 6.
4. *They Were not Silent: the Jewish Labor Movement and the Holocaust*, executive producers Debra Bernhardt and Gail Malmgreen, Producer/Director, Roland Millman
5. Paul Kelemen (1998), 'Zionist Historiography and its critics: a case of Myth-taken identity', *Economy and Society*, **27** (4).
6. See Isobelle Tombs's chapter, fn. 2.
7. Gail Malmgreen, email message 23 March 1999.
8. Paula E. Hyman (1995), *Gender and Assimilation in Modern Jewish History: Roles and Representations of Women*, Washington: University of Washington Press.

CHAPTER ONE

Comrades and Kinsmen: The Jewish Labor Committee and Anti-Nazi Activity, 1934-41

Gail Malmgreen

The historical debate on the response of the US government and the American people, including American Jewry, to the rise of Nazism and persecution of Jews in Europe is tending more and more to oscillate between two extremes. Some have followed David Wyman, who presents a bitter indictment not only of the inaction and obstructive tactics of the Roosevelt administration, but also of what he characterises as the indifference of Americans in general, and the confusion and timidity of American Jewish organisations in the face of the greatest crisis in Jewish history.[1] At the other end of the spectrum we find the view most insistently expressed by W. D. Rubinstein, who holds that the barriers to Jewish emigration from 1930s Germany were far less severe than most historians have acknowledged, and that most East European Jews were not seeking to emigrate in the years before the Nazi occupation of their homelands. He further points out that a substantial majority of German Jews did find refuge abroad before the death camps went into operation, and that once the Final Solution was fully under way, roughly from 1942 onwards, there was no longer anything the Allied powers could have done to prevent the mass murder of Jews.[2]

The difficulty with both these lines of argument is that they ultimately take their stands on the dizzying heights of counter-factual history, with the inevitable consequences of overstatement. It should be useful at this point to take a more microscopic view, which may reveal some middle ground between blanket condemnation and wholesale exoneration. As far as American Jewish response is concerned, there is little reason to expect uniformity. When the Nazis came to power in Germany, American Jewry was divided along many lines: by place of origin, by geography, age, gender, language, religious belief (or lack thereof), economic status and politics. Throughout the first half of the twentieth century New York was home to the largest single community of Jews in the world. The largest sector of that community was concentrated on New York's Lower East Side, sharing the Yiddish-based, socialist-tinged culture vividly described by Irving Howe in his 1976 best-seller, *The World of Our Fathers*.[3] It is surprising that so little of the discussion of American Jewish response to Nazism and the Holocaust has directly addressed the history of that culture and that community.

In the USA, as in Britain, the great wave of Jewish immigration from Eastern Europe began in the 1880s and continued at a high level until it was interrupted by the First World War. In New York these immigrants created something hitherto unknown in Europe, a kind of Jewish metropolis. The Jewish population of Progressive Era New York cannot be measured with scientific precision, but by the end of the First World War it was already over a million, at a time when the largest Jewish community in Europe, that of Warsaw, numbered around 300,000.[4] Relative to the ghettos and shtetls of the East, New York offered prosperity, personal safety and freedom from legal constraints on access to education and employment, and on political expression.

The intellectual and political leadership of the New York Jewish immigrant community, relatively well educated and relatively urbanised, was modern in outlook from the moment of disembarkation at Ellis Island or Castle Garden. They came from all the political and religious tendencies of Jewish Europe, from Orthodox to Anarchist, but were overwhelmingly socialist, however, loosely defined. Of the prominent cultural and political leaders, the greatest number had their early political training in the Bund, the General Jewish Workers Union of Lithuania, Poland and Russia. Founded in Vilna in 1897, the Bund was legal in Poland, illegal in Russia, and was to be proscribed in the Soviet Union. Where legal, it functioned as a social democratic party, but with a revolutionary left wing – of whom a substantial number left to join the Communists, both in the Soviet Union and abroad, after 1917. In Poland, which became its main post-First World War centre, the Bund was the largest Jewish political entity in the inter-war years; its cadre led a network of Jewish trade unions and staffed Yiddish schools and cultural/fraternal organisations. The party also attempted to build links to non-Jewish socialist allies in Poland, and affiliated to the Labor and Socialist International. This distinctive political programme, combining socialist internationalism and cultural nationalism, was to find more fertile ground, in some respects, in the United States.[5]

Among notable New Yorkers who served their political apprenticeship in the European Bund before the First World War were: David Dubinsky, president of the International Ladies Garment Workers Union; Sidney Hillman, president of the Amalgamated Clothing Workers of America and wartime Labor adviser to President Roosevelt; Baruch Charney Vladeck, a New York City Councilman and Manager of the *Jewish Daily Forward*; Joseph Weinberg and Joseph Baskin, President and Secretary of the Workmen's Circle; and Nochum Chanin of the Jewish Socialist Farband. They came to the USA in their teens or early twenties and set out to build a New Jerusalem – or perhaps a new Vilna – on the Hudson.

The ranks of Jewish socialists in New York were also swelled by Mensheviks and other dissidents expelled from the Soviet Union in the 1920s and by victims of anti-Jewish outbreaks in Poland. Later there was a steady stream of refugees from Nazism.[6] The newcomers sustained links with comrades in Europe, and

5

with other émigré communities from Prague and Paris to North Africa and Shanghai. In New York they helped to build an overlapping network of organisations which would eventually provide a sturdy mass base for anti-Nazi activity.

These émigrés founded schools, libraries, theatres and societies for every political and fraternal purpose, among them many *landsmanshaftn* and the Workmen's Circle, which eventually claimed branches in every sizeable town and city of the USA. Within the Socialist Party of America, Yiddish-speakers formed the Jewish Socialist Federation, with its journal, *Naye Velt* (*New World*). The Federation split from the Socialist Party after 1917: some members, whose Yiddish daily was *Freiheit* (*Freedom*), left to join the Communist Party, and others to found the Jewish Socialist Farband, with its own journal *Der Wecker* (*The Awakener*). They built a Jewish labour movement several hundred thousand strong by the late 1930s.[7] Jewish socialists brought to the USA a new vision of trade unionism, based on the programmes of European socialist parties; it embraced housing complexes, health clinics, workers' education programmes, sports teams, theatre groups and summer camps.

The bedrock of this distinctive Jewish culture was Yiddish, not just the language of the 'greenhorn' but the vehicle of a sophisticated political and literary culture and a lingua franca which in the anti-Nazi struggle was to become crucial in sustaining links between centres of leftist Jewish activity around the world. New York was home to four Yiddish dailies in the inter-war years, as well as an array of weekly newspapers, monthly journals and a flourishing pamphlet press. Billing itself as the premier Yiddish paper of the world, the socialist *Jewish Daily Forward* (*Forverts*) produced 11 regional editions in the USA and claimed a circulation of a quarter of a million. The *Forward* maintained a large staff of correspondents in Europe, and it was widely read there, as the Eastern European Yiddish press was avidly read in New York. The debate over how the US press covered Nazi persecution and the Holocaust has generally not focused on the extent to which the immigrant communities, and especially the Yiddish-speaking Jewish community, had their own, very different, sources of information.[8]

When Hitler came to power in January 1933, mass protests and demonstrations began immediately in New York. Marches and meetings were sponsored by the Communist Party, Jewish unions and cultural groups, Jewish war veterans and followers of the popular Zionist leader, Rabbi Stephen Wise. The non-Communist Jewish labour movement joined in these protests, but there was a considerable sentiment in favour of creating a permanent co-ordinating committee, which would be structurally independent of the middle-class Jewish establishment, the non-Jewish labour and socialist organisations, and the liberal anti-fascist groups. Such a group could engage in separate fund-raising and agitation, and could also provide representation for Jewish socialist/labour interests in any joint activity that might be proposed. Preliminary discussions

6

about the new committee took place in the fall of 1933, under the auspices of the *Jewish Daily Forward* and led by Baruch Charney Vladeck. Wariness of Communist domination of anti-Nazi activity played a part in this decision. The political abyss between socialists and Communists had been steadily widening, from the earliest Bundist-Bolshevik struggles in Russia to the socialist-Communist labour wars of the 1920s over control of New York garment unions.[9] By the mid-1930s the abyss was, or seemed to be, unbridgeable; as if to confirm the impossibility of co-operation, a mass meeting at Madison Square Garden on 16 February 1934, called by the Jewish socialists to protest the suppression of the Austrian left by the right-wing Dollfuss regime, was forcibly broken up by the Communists.[10]

Soon after, on 25 February 1934, more than a thousand delegates gathered at Central Plaza on New York's Lower East Side, for the founding meeting of the Jewish Labor Committee (JLC).[11] They represented a wide spectrum of the non-Communist Jewish left: International Ladies Garment Workers Union (ILGWU), Amalgamated Clothing Workers, United Hebrew Trades, Workmen's Circle, *Jewish Daily Forward* Association, and a number of smaller groups, including the Left Labor Zionists and the Jewish Socialist Farband. Baruch Charney Vladeck was chosen president of the new organisation; David Dubinsky of the ILGWU, treasurer; Joseph Baskin of the Workmen's Circle, secretary; and Benjamin Gebiner, also of the Workmen's Circle, executive secretary. Of the founding (all male) Executive Board, most were foreign-born and all were Socialist or Bundist in political affiliation. In its declaration of principles the JLC declared that only a broad-based workers' movement could overthrow Hitlerism, and emphasised its labour orientation and non-sectarian philosophy. Its aims would be to support Jewish rights everywhere, support all progressive and democratic anti-fascist groups, aid refugees, and educate the American labour movement (and the general public) about the Nazi threat. In keeping with its Bundist origins, the JLC further stated that the 'Jewish question must be solved in the countries in which the Jews lived'.[12] This oblique rejection of Zionist principles lost the JLC the allegiance of the main body of Labor Zionists, but the more radical contingent, the Left Poale Zion (long-time allies of the Bund in Poland) continued a working (if junior) partnership with the Bundist majority.

The JLC was the brainchild of Baruch Charney Vladeck. A brilliant writer and organiser, known for the elegance of his Yiddish oratory, he was adept at navigating the perilous waters of New York immigrant politics and cultivated the friendship of William Green, president of the American Federation of Labor (AFL). He hoped, with reason, that Green would welcome the JLC as a trusted advisory body on Jewish affairs. Vladeck had persuasive power, but no independent power base or treasury at his disposal. Jewish Labor Committee treasurer, David Dubinsky, who exercised autocratic control over his 200,000-member union, was to provide the financial ballast for the new committee.

Toughened by bruising struggles with the Communists in his union, Dubinsky took over as ILGWU president in 1932. In 1934 he was appointed by President William Green to sit on the AFL's Executive Council. At age 42 Dubinsky was the youngest member of the Council and its only Jewish member. The JLC, relying on Vladeck's ingenuity and charm and Dubinsky's insider influence, decided to enlist the AFL officially in the anti-Nazi campaign. They would do it by obtaining the help of a prominent non-Jewish ally.

In July of 1934 Dubinsky had been approached by German socialist Martin Plettl, president of the German clothing workers union (who was arrested in the early weeks of Nazi power and later fled to Holland) with the suggestion that Walter Citrine, secretary of the British Trades Union Congress, be invited to speak at the AFL's October Convention to be held in San Francisco. Citrine, as President of the International Federation of Trade Unions, was a frequent traveller to Germany and well versed in the details of Hitler's assault on labour, the left and the Jews. Dubinsky secured William Green's approval, and he and Vladeck accompanied Citrine on a cross-country lecture tour, culminating in grandstand performances by both Citrine and Vladeck at the convention.[13] The outcome of this appeal was the establishment of an AFL-sponsored Labor Chest for the Liberation of the Workers of Europe.[14] The Chest bore the invaluable imprimatur of the AFL and provided a useful entrée into the none-too-sympathetic ranks of the non-Jewish labour movement. It was closely watched over by Green's chief adviser for foreign affairs, AFL vice-president Matthew Woll,[15] and top AFL officials appeared at Labor Chest rallies bringing a degree of press interest that the JLC could not have commanded. But the Labor Chest's offices were in New York, and its staff and programme were largely provided by JLC recruits. The Chest funded a host of JLC-inspired educational and aid projects, and it is probable that most of the money came from the Jewish unions. The JLC oversaw the Labor Chest News Service and helped produce many Labor Chest pamphlets and posters, including material in German, Italian and Polish, aimed at immigrant communities whose allegiance in the anti-fascist effort was in doubt.[16]

Another of the JLC's chief concerns was to build support for a boycott of Nazi goods.[17] At the urging of Dubinsky and Jewish union leaders, the AFL had already endorsed the boycott at its 1933 convention. The American Jewish Congress, under the direction of Rabbi Stephen Wise, had been a pioneer in the advocacy of the boycott strategy, emphasising appeals to consumers and retailers. The JLC added an element of industrial action, with energetic picketing by local unions, and organised refusals by garment workers and machinists to use German-made tools and equipment. The American Jewish Committee, B'nai B'rith, and other mainstream Jewish organisations hung back from the boycott, fearing either a backlash against Jews in Germany or an upsurge of anti-Semitism in America if Jews adopted such high-profile methods as picketing and public appeals. In February 1936 the JLC joined with the

American Jewish Congress to form the Joint Boycott Council; their representative to the Council would be newly appointed JLC executive secretary, Isaiah Minkoff.[18] Energetically led by Joseph Tenenbaum, a Wise appointee, the Council had some effect in the area of consumer goods, eventually enlisting Macy's, Gimbel's and other major retailers in the boycott. The JLC organised demonstrations on the shop floor by workers protesting the use of German supplies and equipment, and co-ordinated picketing by local unions and Workmen's Circle branches.

While the JLC pressed for unified action it also pursued an independent anti-Nazi campaign on several fronts. For example, when the US Olympics Committee declined to heed widespread protests against United States participation in the Berlin Olympics of 1936, the JLC held a World Labor Athletic Carnival, also known as the 'Counter-Olympics', at Randall's Island in New York City during August 1936.[19] Dozens of teams representing New York union locals competed, and the main events featured amateur athletes from across the country. Governor Herbert Lehman presented the prizes. Although it failed to attract masses of hardcore sports fans, and did not eclipse the Berlin events – in part because the JLC did not mount an effort to persuade Black and Jewish athletes to refuse to compete in Berlin[20] – the Carnival was something of a propaganda success. Press coverage was extensive, and the JLC repeated the event in the summer of 1937.

The Jewish Labor Committee and its constituent unions were keenly attuned to reports of persecution and in close touch with exiles, both Jewish and non-Jewish, in their places of refuge. They generously supported organisations offering emergency aid to political exiles, such as Kurt Grossman's Democratic Relief for Refugees, based first in Prague and later in Paris, the Labor and Socialist International's International Solidarity Fund, and smaller aid committees in many temporary havens.[21] At the same time they tried to assist East European Jews who were destitute or victims of pogroms, and to sustain the Jewish labour movement's schools, cooperative workshops, and clinics in Poland, Lithuania and Romania.[22] They sponsored lecture and fund-raising tours by prominent European trade unionists and socialists, including Martin Plettl, Toni Sender, Gerhart Seger, Giuseppe Modigliani, and many representatives of the Polish Bund. When Arthur Zygielbojm, who represented the Bund on the Jewish Council of the Warsaw Ghetto, was forced to flee Poland in 1940, the JLC brought him to the USA and sponsored a cross-country lecture tour, during which he addressed Yiddish-speaking audiences in dozens of cities and small towns, bringing the plight of Polish Jewry to life in vivid detail.

As anti-Jewish legislation and physical persecution intensified in Germany, growing numbers of Jews and other anti-fascists fled, seeking asylum wherever they could find it. The prospect of mass Jewish emigration, or any sizeable influx of refugees, was widely viewed with alarm in the USA, where strict immigration quotas had been in place since 1924.[23] With many thousands of Americans out of work and on Depression bread lines, there was no question of the American Federation of Labor modifying its traditional hostility to easing immigration restrictions. The organized Jewish community, too, hesitated to call for the adjustment of quotas, or for special measures on behalf of refugees. As they read and listened to the xenophobic rantings of Father Charles Coughlin and other far-right demagogues, Jewish leaders could easily imagine anti-immigrant hostility touching off a paroxysm of racial hatred. What was happening in Europe might also happen in the USA. Some, such as Rabbi Wise, feared that a declaration of support for Jewish emigration could be seen, in Germany and elsewhere in Europe, as a licence for Jews to be driven from their homelands.

Jewish-led unions, including both the International Ladies Garment Workers and the Amalgamated Clothing Workers, did introduce resolutions calling for special immigration measures on behalf of refugees at their own annual meetings and New York state labour conferences in the mid-1930s. After a similar resolution introduced by the ILGWU at the 1935 annual convention of the American Federation of Labor met with defeat, the JLC and its allies abandoned any attempt to secure a broad pro-refugee commitment from the AFL[24] There is, however, some striking evidence of the efficacy of behind-the-scenes lobbying by Jewish labour leaders in the AFL by the end of the decade. When, in 1939, Senator Robert Wagner and Congresswoman Edith Rogers introduced a bill which proposed bringing 20,000 German (mostly Jewish) children to the USA on special visas, both the AFL and the CIO sent representatives to testify in favor of the measure at preliminary hearings on the bill.[25] Against a backdrop of virulent anti-immigrant feeling across party lines in Congress, and in the face of the labour movement's unbroken tradition of staunch opposition to any loosening of immigration restrictions, this represents a significant lobbying achievement for Jewish labour. At the same time, the Jewish Labor Committee spoke out in opposition to various German proposals which offered to facilitate the emigration of Jews, in exchange for some financial benefit to the Nazi regime. The JLC's position was based not only on its distaste for any arrangement which would purchase the lives of Jews by dealing with the Nazis (and its distrust of Nazi guarantees), but also on the pragmatic consideration of there being no country willing to welcome and resettle the often penniless emigrants (a consideration which became even more weighty as Jews from countries other than Germany swelled the ranks of the displaced).[26] The JLC went further and financed some clandestine, illegal attempts to bring a few refugees to safety.[27]

The outbreak of the Spanish Civil War in the summer of 1936 posed a difficult challenge to the Jewish labour movement, Jewish socialists and the JLC. The Socialist Party (SP), hitherto the political rallying point for most of the non-Communist Jewish left, found itself in serious disarray at this point in its

10

history. Its left wing, highly factionalized and tempted by prospects of Popular Front alliances with Communists and Trotskyists, was inclined to support military aid to Spain. The right, including a great many who were soon to follow David Dubinsky into the Roosevelt camp through the vehicle of the newly formed American Labor Party, were inclined to stay clear of the Communist-tainted Spanish cause. To further complicate matters, the Party included a large contingent of committed pacifists, whose recollections of the First World War predisposed them to see any departure from anti-militarist purity as a betrayal of that hallowed tradition. Both Socialist Party standard-bearer Norman Thomas and Dubinsky himself were attracted to the Loyalist cause and saw it as a chance to stop Nazism and fascism short of an all-European war. To this end they were willing to defy the Roosevelt Administration's embargo on material aid or intervention. Thomas impulsively announced a campaign to assemble a 500-man Eugene V. Debs Column (bringing on himself more abuse from those who saw this as a desecration of Debs' well-known anti-war principles) and a 50,000-dollar fund to support the recruits. Only a handful of volunteers were forthcoming and fewer still made it to Spain. Most of them, along with Thomas himself who visited Spain in May 1937, were dismayed by the Communist political domination they observed there. The SP quietly gave up its recruiting effort, though Thomas continued to support the Republic and pressured the Administration to change its policy.[28] Dubinsky and the JLC continued to offer financial and practical support to non-Communist veterans of the war in every way they could, well into the post-Second World War period.[29]

The question of Zionism added another dimension of complexity to JLC activity. Jewish Labour Committee leaders tended to adhere to the traditional Bundist attitude that Zionist appeals were a distraction from the essential goal of ensuring the right of Jews to live as free and equal citizens in every country. There always were, however, Jewish labour leaders, such as Joseph Schlossberg of the Amalgamated Clothing Workers, Max Zaritsky of the Hat, Cap and Millinery Workers, and Max Pine of the United Hebrew Trades, who maintained close and cooperative relations with the JLC and also embraced the labour Zionist ideology. Even in Poland the Bund had developed a working relationship with the Left Poale Zion; despite elements of tension and mistrust, a shared devotion to Yiddish culture and to radical socialist principles provided a basis for some cooperation, especially during the years of crisis. The JLC continued this relationship in America, and the Left Poale Zion was eventually represented on its Executive Committee. The JLC also put out tentative feelers in 1939 to several labour Zionist groups, apparently in hopes of splitting them off from the middle-class Zionist movement epitomised by Rabbi Wise and the American Jewish Congress.[30]

Its general anti-Zionist ideology did not prevent the JLC from taking an interest in the Jewish population of Mandatory Palestine and socialist

11

experiments there. From its inception the Committee lent support to cooperatives, labour groups and Yiddish cultural institutions in Palestine, and embraced the principle that Jews wishing to emigrate there should be allowed to do so. When the British White Paper of 1939 virtually cut off Jewish immigration, the JLC protested vigorously and enlisted the help of its AFL and CIO allies in demanding that the gates be reopened for the desperate victims of Nazism.[31]

In its leadership the JLC had a uniquely rich resource to draw on in bringing American labour to an understanding of the European catastrophe. Both Vladeck and Dubinsky had travelled extensively in Europe in the mid-1930s. Dubinsky represented the AFL at a meeting of the governing body of the International Labour Organisation in Geneva in 1934, and took the opportunity to visit with French, Italian and Austrian trade unionists, completing the journey with a brief period in Warsaw and Lodz.[32] In the summer of 1935 Vladeck toured Europe, meeting with socialist and labour leaders, including Walter Citrine, IFTU President, and Walter Schevenels, IFTU Secretary, and pledging 'Labor Chest' funds to support anti-Nazi exiles.[33] Vladeck ended his journey in Poland, where he addressed mass meetings, visited Bundist institutions and conferred with trusted comrades. Many of the leaders of the Workmen's Circle and the Jewish unions made similar trips to their former homes in Eastern Europe. They followed the European Yiddish press closely and published reports of their own travels and foreign correspondence in the *Forward* and the labour press.

Vladeck's untimely death at age 52 in October 1938 was a heavy blow, but the JLC staff was steadily enriched by the arrival of new émigrés, each with a special expertise. Polish Bundists Jacob Pat and Benjamin Tabachinsky became, respectively, JLC executive secretary and national fund-raising director. Dr Joseph Kissman came to America in 1937 to plead for financial assistance for the Romanian Labor League; he stayed on to become JLC research director and to liaise with hundreds of Romanian Jewish refugees who were scattered from Casablanca to Buenos Aires. Lasar Epstein, who had served for 20 years before the war as a Bundist representative in Tientsin, China, coordinated aid to the swelling East European Jewish refugee population of Shanghai. Adolph Held, who succeeded Vladeck as JLC president, was Polish-born and had returned to Warsaw as European director of the Hebrew Sheltering and Immigrant Aid Society (HIAS) from 1920 to 1925. In general, the Jewish socialists had a direct and detailed knowledge of European conditions which, however ideologically conditioned, served them well both in their rescue efforts and in their attempts to support the anti-Nazi underground from afar. What they did not have was the power to avert the looming catastrophe of the Final Solution, or to substantially alter US government policy. When the need to approach President Roosevelt arose, they knew they would be best advised to do it in the company of more influential allies, that is, their friends at the AFL.

By the end of the decade the resources of the JLC were stretched to the limit. The normal work of publicity, mass meetings and demonstrations continued. In addition, the JLC was now being called upon to help thousands of Eastern Jews driven out of Germany and into makeshift camps in Poland; to support Mensheviks and displaced Jewish scholars in Paris, Polish socialists in the USA, Italian anti-fascists in Switzerland, the German 'Spartacus Group' in southern France, Spanish anarchists fleeing the Franco regime, and a host of others.[34]

After the Nazi invasion of Poland and the fall of France, the JLC concluded that immediate action was needed to save European socialist and labour leaders, who would be prime targets of the Gestapo. Many of these political refugees had gathered in Vichy-controlled southern France and in Vilna, Lithuania where they waited uneasily, poised between Nazi-occupied Poland and the Soviet Union. What the JLC envisioned was a plan whereby the US government would grant emergency visas to those who were deemed to be in the most immediate danger.[35] The JLC compiled several lists that included Jewish and non-Jewish trade unionists and socialists, as well as Yiddish writers and Jewish communal leaders; the lists were arranged by nationality, and cases were ranked according to perceived urgency. Each visa would cover a family; and travel expenses would be borne by the JLC – using the facilities of HIAS in Lisbon and other organisations licensed to arrange transport and accommodation. David Dubinsky presented the plan to William Green, who in turn approached President Roosevelt. Roosevelt agreed to have the State Department issue a number of emergency visitors' visas. Making use of its network of contacts in Europe, the JLC tried desperately to get the necessary money and documents to those on the list. The operation in Marseilles was directed first by Frank Bohn, a New York socialist probably recommended to the AFL by the JLC, and later by German socialist Fritz Heine, who worked in concert with Varian Fry's Emergency Rescue Committee. Not all could be located in time, but well over 1,000 people were brought to safety under this programme in 1940-41.[36] Among those assisted under this initiative were Mensheviks Theodore Dan, Raphael Abramovitch, Gregor Aronson, Iracli Tseretelli, David Dallin and Boris Nicolaevsky; German Socialists Erich Ollenhauer, Max Braun, Marie Juchasz, and Alexander Stein; Italian anti-fascists Count Carlo Sforza, Franco Venturi, Alberto Tarchiani, Giuseppe Modigliani and Giuseppe Saragat; and Polish Bundists Shlomo Mendelson, Franz Kurski, Noach Portnoy, Efroim Zelmanowicz, and Alexander and Victor Erlich, among many others.

It is intriguing to speculate as to why the AFL and the Roosevelt Administration were so accommodating to the special visa proposal at this time. The answer is most likely to be found in domestic politics. William Green's opposition to Nazism was sincere, but his chief concern, almost an obsession, during the late 1930s, was the threat of the fast-growing rival labour federation, the Congress of Industrial Organisations (CIO). David Dubinsky, who had been an early supporter of CIO organizing drives, had reluctantly broken with the

13

AFL in September 1936 and worked behind the scenes for reconciliation between the two federations. In June of 1940 Dubinsky brought his 200,000 ILGWU members back into the AFL fold; in July Green presented the visa proposal to the President. From Roosevelt's point of view the pressing need was to put together an unbeatable majority for the November 1940 presidential election. He was seeking an unprecedented third term, and both the Jewish vote and the labour vote had to be secured. In the longer term, he wanted to bolster a consensus on preparedness and aid to his soon-to-be allies in Europe. The allotment of emergency visas to the AFL was only one of many such private concessions, designed to garner electoral support without setting off public alarm bells on either the Democratic or the Republican right.

Over the years a complex system of mutual aid and division of labour had grown up between all the groups concerned with Jewish survival. The older philanthropic organisations, notably the American Jewish Joint Distribution Committee (JDC) and the venerable HIAS, had a longstanding network of contacts around the world and budgets many times greater than the JLC's. The JLC sent money and supplies through the JDC or HIAS to arrange transit visas in China, Latin America, France, and Spain or for shipping goods through Teheran to refugees in the Soviet Union, for example. By the same token the JDC and HIAS sometimes transferred aid destined for Eastern Europe to the JLC, relying on its Bundist and other underground contacts. Political relations with the major Jewish defence organisations were a more difficult matter.[37] In 1938 the JLC affiliated to the General Jewish Council, the latest of a number of futile attempts to provide some basis for concerted action.[38] The Council met for several years, but foundered in interminable disputes over 'autonomy', jurisdictional matters, finances, and ideological and tactical differences.[39]

When the outbreak of war closed off the possibility of direct contact with Nazi-occupied Europe, and as the nature of Hitler's Final Solution for the Jews became more apparent, the JLC turned its energy to support of underground movements (both Jewish and non-Jewish) in Europe. It published reports written by its Bundist comrades and smuggled out of the ghettos and death camps; it supplied money for arms, for false documents, and to pay for safe hiding-places on the 'Aryan side'. It supported couriers and guides who shepherded refugees into Sweden, to Switzerland, and across the Pyrenees into Spain and Portugal, and it helped sustain enclaves of Jewish émigrés wherever in the world they were stranded.

How did the JLC's response to the rise of Nazism and the crisis of European Jewry differ from that of other American groups, both Jewish and non-Jewish? First, unlike many others on the left, its supporters kept the question of Jewish persecution at the centre of their consciousness and the top of their agenda. More specifically, the Committee's attention was focused on Eastern Europe, and especially Poland, when much of American anti-fascist opinion still saw, and reacted to, Nazi persecution as a German domestic matter. The JLC

14

understood that the Jewish masses of Europe were in the East; it was there that they would have to be reached and helped. A few were rescued by their direct efforts, many others were sustained in hiding, or in places of refuge around the world. For the millions who perished, it was not enough; for those who were saved, the benefit was incalculable.

Both the ideology underlying JLC activity and the base of contacts which would sustain its anti-Nazi work were part of a specific cultural/political heritage with deep roots, going back to a time when Nazi power and Nazi genocide were undreamed of. In the Bundist tradition, the JLC recognised the need to build working alliances with non-Jewish forces, whether in the US labour movement or the European socialist parties and trade unions. Through the JLC and its associated institutions many immigrant Jews in the USA in the inter-war period were able to take advantage of a unique confluence of Bundist/socialist ideology and American opportunities. What New York offered was the possibility of building mass labour, fraternal and cultural organisations, which in turn generated unprecedented financial resources, in an atmosphere relatively free of legal constraints on Jewish life. This fragile mix of socialist internationalism and Jewish cultural particularism, uprooted from its native milieu, flourished for a time in the invigorating, but potentially transforming, environment of the New World. And it conditioned the JLC's response to the catastrophe of Nazism. What it did not and could not do was divert the tragic course of history.

Notes

1.   David S. Wyman (1968), *Paper Walls: America and the Refugee Crisis, 1938-1941*, Amherst: University of Massachusetts Press; and *idem* (1984), *The Abandonment of the Jews: America and the Holocaust, 1941-1945*, New York: Pantheon Books. See also, Rafael Medoff (1987), *The Deafening Silence*, New York: Shapolsky Publishers.

2.   William D. Rubinstein (1997), *The Myth of Rescue: Why the Democracies Could Not Have Saved More Jews from the Nazis*, London: Routledge. In a similar, but more moderate, vein, see, Henry Feingold (1970), *The Politics of Rescue: The Roosevelt Administration and the Jews*, New Brunswick, NJ: Rutgers University Press and Verne W. Newton, ed. (1996), *FDR and the Holocaust*, New York: St Martin's Press.

3.   Irving Howe (1976), *The World of Our Fathers: The Journey of the East European Jews to America and the Life They Found and Made*, New York: Simon and Schuster; see also, Gerald Sorin (1985), *The Prophetic Minority: American Jewish Immigrant Radicals, 1880-1920*,

Bloomington: Indiana University Press.

4.   C. Morris Horowitz and Lawrence J. Kaplan (1959), *Estimated Jewish Population of the New York Area, 1900-1955*, New York: Federation of Jewish Philanthropies, p. 15.

5.   Bernard K. Johnpoll (1967), *The Politics of Futility: The General Jewish Labor Bund of Poland, 1917-1943*, Ithaca: Cornell University Press; Henri Minczeles (1995), *Histoire Générale du Bund: Un Mouvement révolutionnaire juif*, Paris: Austral; Antony Polonsky (1988), 'The Bund in Polish Political Life, 1935-1939', in Ada Rapaport-Albert and Steven J. Zipperstein (eds), *Jewish History: Essays in Honour of Chimen Abramsky*, London: Peter Halban, pp. 547-77; Daniel Blatman (1996), 'The Bund in Poland, 1935-1939', *Polin: Studies in Polish Jewry*, (9), 58-82; and Zvi Gitelman (1997), 'A Centenary of Jewish Politics in Eastern Europe: The Legacy of the Bund and the Zionist Movements', *East European Politics and Societies*, **11**, (3), 543-59. There is little scholarly writing on the Bund in the USA; a useful introduction is provided by Catherine Collomp (1997), 'Influences bundistes sur le mouvement ouvrier des Etats-Unis: de l'action syndicale au soutien des victimes du fascisme', paper presented at the conference, 'Le Bund à Cent Ans', Paris, October (copy at Robert F. Wagner Labor Archives, New York University).

6.   On the Menshevik emigration and their connections in the USA, see André Liebich (1997), *From the Other Shore: Russian Social Democracy after 1921*, Cambridge, MA: Harvard University Press.

7.   Will Herberg (1952), 'Jewish Labor in the United States, *American Jewish Yearbook*, **53**; Melech Epstein (1950, 1953), *Jewish Labor in the United States, 1882-1952*, 2 vols, New York: Trade Union Sponsoring Committee; *YIVO Annual of Jewish Social Science*, (special issue on the Jewish labour movement) (1976), **16**.

8.   See, for example, Deborah E. Lipstadt (1986), *Beyond Belief: The American Press and the Coming of the Holocaust, 1933-1945*, New York: Free Press.

9.   On the Communist-socialist struggle in the largest of the garment unions, see David Gurowsky (1978), 'Factional Disputes within the ILGWU, 1919-1928', PhD dissertation, State University of New York at Binghamton; and Stanley Nadel (1985), 'Reds versus Pinks: A Civil War in the International Ladies Garment Workers Union', *New York History*, January, pp. 48-72.

10.   Harvey Klehr (1984), *The Heyday of American Communism: The Depression Decade*, New York: Basic Books, pp. 113-15.

11.   *New York Times*, 5 April 1934. On JLC history, Gail Malmgreen (1991), 'Labor and the Holocaust: The Jewish Labor Committee and the Anti-Nazi Struggle', *Labor's Heritage*, **3**, (4), 20-35; George

Berlin (1966), 'The Anti-Nazi Activities of the Jewish Labor Committee in the 1930s', MA thesis, Columbia University; David Kranzler (1984), 'The Role in Relief and Rescue during the Holocaust by the Jewish Labor Committee', in Seymour Maxwell Finger (ed.), *American Jewry during the Holocaust*, New York: Holmes and Meier, Appendix 4-2; Arieh Lebowitz and Gail Malmgreen (eds) (1993), *Archives of the Holocaust, Vol. 14: Robert F. Wagner Labor Archives, New York University – Records of the Jewish Labor Committee*, New York: Garland. On chief JLC officers, B. C. Vladeck and David Dubinsky: John Herling (1939), 'Baruch Charney Vladeck', *American Jewish Yearbook*, vol. 41, pp. 79-93; Franklin Jonas (1972), 'The Early Life and Career of B. Charney Vladeck, 1882-1921: The Emergence of an Immigrant Spokesman', PhD dissertation, New York University; Max D. Danish (1957), *The World of David Dubinsky*, Cleveland: World Publishing Co; David Dubinsky and A. H. Raskin (1977), *David Dubinsky: A Life with Labor*, New York: Simon and Schuster; and *Labor History*, vol. 9, (Spring 1968), Special Supplement on David Dubinsky and the ILGWU.

12.   *New York Times*, 5 April 1934.

13.   *American Federation of Labor, Report of Proceedings of the Fifty-fourth Annual Convention, 1934*. Dubinsky and Raskin, op. cit., pp. 247-8. Citrine recorded the details of this journey in a travel diary, preserved in typescript in the archives of the London School of Economics. For the background of William Green's relationship with Dubinsky and the Jewish unions, see Robert Asher (1976), 'Jewish Unions and the American Federation of Labor Power Structure, 1908-1935', *American Jewish Historical Quarterly*, **65**, pp. 215-27.

14.   Files relating to the JLC's participation in the Labor Chest can be found in Records of the Jewish Labor Committee, Robert F. Wagner Labor Archives, New York University (hereafter JLC Records), box 16.

15.   Woll, born in Luxemburg in 1880, served as an AFL fraternal delegate to TUC conferences in 1915 and 1916, and to meetings of the IFTU in 1937 and 1938. Although he was, like Green, deeply conservative in all matters of domestic policy and staunchly anti-Communist, he was also profoundly opposed to Nazism, as the enemy both of labour rights and religious freedom. Dubinsky wrote, 'Woll made me kosher in the AFL leadership, which had no great love for Jews'. Danish, op. cit., p. 243.

16.   See, for example, Conrad Woelfel, Metal Engravers Union, Detroit, to B. C. Vladeck, 17 March 1935, JLC Records, Box 16, folder 15.

17.   On the boycott in general, see Moshe R. Gottlieb (1982), *American Anti-Nazi Resistance, 1933-1941: An Historical Analysis*, New York:

17

Ktav, pp. 181-296.

18.   The records of the Joint Boycott Council are in the Manuscripts Division, New York Public Library. The JLC's files on the JBC are in JLC Records, box 9. Having served its purpose, the Joint Boycott Council was disbanded in 1941.

19.   Edward S. Shapiro (1985), 'The World Labor Athletic Carnival of 1936: An American Anti-Nazi Protest', *American Jewish History*, **74** (March), pp. 255-73; and Gottlieb, op. cit., pp. 231-5. See also, JLC Records, box 13, folder 6, and clippings scrapbooks, 'Labor Athletic Carnival, 1936', and 'Labor Athletic Carnival, 1937'.

20.   Information supplied by Mark Brown, who, as part of his research for a forthcoming book on US attitudes toward the 1936 Olympics, has conducted interviews with Jewish and African-American athletes who participated in the Berlin Olympics, or who decided on their own initiative not to participate.

21.   See, e.g., JLC Records, box 32, folder 6 and box 31, folder 20.

22.   See files on aid to Poland and to the Romanian Labor League in JLC Records, box 49, folders 35-40, box 11, folders 1-6 and box 51, folder 34.

23.   Wyman, op. cit.; Richard Breitman and Alan M. Kraut (1987), *American Refugee Policy and European Jewry, 1933-1945*, Bloomington: Indiana University Press; and Sheldon Morris Neuringer (1980), *American Jewry and United States Immigration Policy, 1881-1953*, New York: Arno Press.

24.   On the distinction between the Jewish labour movement and non-Jewish labour on immigration matters, see David Brody (1955/56), 'American Jewry, the Refugees and Immigration Restriction (1932-1942)', in *American Jewish Historical Society Publications*, (45), 232; Neuringer, op. cit, pp. 238 ff.; and, on ILGWU attitudes, Sidney Kelman (1990), 'The Limits of Consensus: Unions and the Holocaust', *American Jewish History*, **79**, 342-6. For a more critical assessment of the JLC's role, see Charles Berlin (1971), 'The Jewish Labor Committee and American Immigration Policy in the 1930s', in C. Berlin (ed.), *Studies in Jewish Bibliography, History and Literature in Honor of I. Edward Kiev*, New York: Ktav Publishing House, pp. 45-73.

25.   Wyman, op. cit., ch. 5. Breitman and Kraut, op. cit., pp. 73, 107.

26.   See Adolph Held to American Jewish Joint Distribution Committee, 12 July 1939 (opposing the Rublee Plan), in JLC Records, box 7, folder 24.

27.   See, e.g., Carlo Tresca to JLC, August 1939, JLC Records, box 6, folder 16. Tresca's request for funds was granted.

28.   Harry Fleischman (1964), *Norman Thomas: A Biography*, New York:

Norton and Co., pp. 174-8; and W. A. Swanberg (1976), *Norman Thomas: The Last Idealist*, New York: Charles Scribner's Sons, pp. 210-16.

29. See, e.g., Norman Thomas to Isaiah Minkoff, JLC, 6 January 1939, re: Sam Romer, in JLC Records, box 11, folder 21; Phil Heller, International Solidarity Committee, to Lasar Epstein, JLC, 15 January 1946, in JLC Records, box 9, folder 18; and financial records of aid to Spanish refugees in David Dubinsky Papers, box 8, ILGWU Collection, Cornell University.

30. Report of meeting of JLC with labour Zionist groups, 4 January 1939, in JLC Records, box 10, folder 40. This initiative failed, and the wartime years saw several sharp confrontations between the JLC and leading Zionists; see, e.g., Report of meeting with C. Weizmann and D. Ben-Gurion, 29 May 1942, in JLC Records, box 13, folder 27. See also, C. Berlin, op. cit., pp. 61-3.

31. JLC press release on White Paper, 1 August 1939, in JLC Records, box 20, folder 20.

32. *New York Times*, 14 April 1935; and *Justice*, 15 May 1935. The AFL joined the International Labor Organisation only in 1934; in 1937, at the urging of the ILGWU, it finally affiliated with the IFTU. On American labour's international role, and the 'Labor Chest', the Anti-Nazi Boycott and other foreign policy issues from the vantage point of the AFL, see John W. Roberts (1995), *Putting Foreign Policy to Work: The Role of Organized Labor in American Foreign Relations, 1932-1941*, New York: Garland Publishing.

33. Information from Geert Van Goethem, based on his research in the TUC records at the Modern Records Centre, University of Warwick and the Archives of the Friedrich Ebert Stiftung, Bonn. This was one of several European trips Vladeck made in the 1930s.

34. On JLC support to leftists from a variety of parties and tendencies, see Gail Malmgreen (1994), 'Rescue and Resistance: The Jewish Labor Committee Fights Fascism', in *Israel Horizons*, **42** (2), p. 14.

35. See Isaiah Minkoff to David Dubinsky, 26 June 1940, outlining the rescue plan, in JLC Records, box 12, folder 2.

36. Historians disagree as to exactly how many visas were issued and how many were successfully used. On the rescue effort in Marseilles, Jack Jacobs (1996), 'A Friend in Need: The Jewish Labor Committee and Refugees from the German-Speaking Lands, 1933-1945', *YIVO Annual*, **23**, 391-417; Anne Klein (1998), 'Conscience, Conflict and Politics: The Rescue of Political Refugees from Southern France to the United States, 1940-1942', in *Leo Baeck Institute: Yearbook XLIII*, pp. 287-311; and Albrecht Ragg (1977), 'The German Socialist Emigration in the United States, 1933-1945', PhD dissertation, Loyola

University of Chicago, ch. 5. Several versions of the lists compiled by the JLC, for both Marseilles and Vilna, as well as biographical sketches of the proposed rescuees and extensive files of related correspondence can be found in JLC Records, boxes 38 and 39.

37.   These were, in addition to the JLC, the American Jewish Committee, the American Jewish Congress, and B'nai B'rith.

38.   The JLC's involvement in the General Jewish Council is documented in JLC Records, boxes 8 and 9. On the contentious relations between the major Jewish organizations, see Edward David Pinsky (1980), 'Cooperation among American Jewish Organizations in Their Efforts to Rescue European Jewry during the Holocaust, 1939-1945', 2 vols, PhD dissertation, New York University. Pinsky's background chapters fill in the history from 1933.

39.   On the GJC's demise, see Louis Lipsky (1940), 'The Lost Cause of Unity', *Congress Weekly*, 29 November, pp. 7-9.

CHAPTER TWO

White-Collar and Labour: Clerks and the Histadrut in British-Ruled Palestine[1]

David De Vries

The pivotal position of clerks in the state and the economy makes them exemplars for deciphering the reciprocal relationships between the experiences of people at the social bases of politics and large-scale structural transformations. Recent historical questioning of class formation has exemplified the need to analyse the market and workplace experiences and strategies of clerks, characterised by status ambiguity and multifaceted social imagery. Informed by a variety of theories of the state and 'the new working class', as well as questions of gender, white-collar research has joined forces with studies of the lower-middle classes in shifting attention away from the more distinct and organised manual and industrial workers. The blurring of boundaries between the two sides of the divide between white- and blue-collar work persists as a major topic of interest but has been recontextualised in social and cultural frameworks. This brings national and social formations to be viewed and examined as mutually dependent phenomena.[2] This chapter addresses the relationship between white-collar workers and nationalism, by introducing a cultural-symbolic approach in order to examine how national discourse became an essential 'point of production' of white-collar identities, particularly those of clerks and clerical work. Based on an analysis of the imagery that clerks use to describe their work experience, this discussion attempts to document and explain how and why nationalism, as a cultural system with an internal logic and specific stylistic devices, was employed by the clerks 'from below' to construct their occupational identity.

The association between white-collar workers and nationalism, particularly in the context of state building, has long attracted the attention of sociologists and historians. First, the emergence of non-manual workers as the social basis of bureaucratic organisations was linked to state formation.[3] Second, the role of white-collar workers in the evolution of national-capitalist economies and urban consumer communities was regarded as essential in linking state building and economic change.[4] Third, political and social histories of the nationalist Right centred on bureaucrats and clerical employees as standard-bearers of conservative politics.[5] Despite many differences such interpretations share a common structural approach. They view the development of white-collar work and workers as an inevitable outcome of the growth of statist and capitalist bureaucracies and emphasise the functional roles assigned to civil servants and clerks in the evolving structures. Moreover, in viewing low-ranking white-collar workers from above, these interpretations concentrate on how these workers were shaped and regimented by various bureaucracies. Similarly, the problematic relations between white-collar workers and labour are viewed through the eyes of powerful unions and labour movements. By focusing exclusively on the agency of élites, the crucial role of other agents in social and state formations is underplayed.[6]

Under the influence of social history and, more recently, of cultural history, these assumptions are now challenged. Scholars keen on connecting social and political histories and on substantiating cultural representations of material developments are beginning to approach the problems of white-collar workers from their perspective.[7] Following this emphasis on the relationship between the social and political languages of clerical workers, as well as on the contexts within which they have developed, a further analysis is made here of the cultural ways in which the clerks themselves formed their occupational identity. This is highlighted by the fact that the clerks' social make-up was culturally 'emplotted' not only in terms specific to low-ranking white-collar workers but also in those borrowed from the blue-collar sector and from society's cultural resources at large.[8]

As one of these resources, national discourse has been a social and a cultural formative factor in the lives of the working and middle classes. In restraining social conflict and obfuscating demarcations based on class and status, nationalism served as a powerful social and cultural force in structuring and restructuring social identities and relations.[9] As the following analysis attempts to show, this power can be better understood by focusing on the symbolic use that clerks made of national discourse as part of their larger struggle for recognition and social advancement. This self-interested utilization of a political language is demonstrated in the case of the Jewish clerks of pre-state Palestine. The case is presented first, followed by a three-fold view of the loci where the construction of occupational identity took place: the search for clerical work, work itself, and collective action.[10]

The Case

The issue of why and how clerks used national discourse to construct their identity was particularly relevant to Jewish society and settlement in British-ruled Palestine (the Yishuv). It was during this period between the early 1920s and late 1940s that the practice of Zionism reached maturity. The Arab-Jewish demographic balance changed as the result of Jewish immigration and armed conflict. Jewish colonisation and settlement brought a radical transformation of the human and geographical landscape of Palestine. Significantly, the import of Jewish capital and the construction of a segregated Jewish economy greatly enhanced the economic development that was so crucial to the realisation of Zionism in conflict-ridden Palestine.[11]

The institutionalisation of Zionism, Palestine's economic development and the way in which Zionism handled the Arab-Jewish conflict, brought about enormous growth in the number of clerks assigned the tasks of control and administration. The importation of Jewish capital and immigration intensified the growth of services in the economy which reached 47.9 per cent of the total Jewish workforce in 1948 when the state of Israel was established. Clerks, the largest sector of the new service class, emerged as the major force in the Yishuv's social structure and in 1946 constituted 13.4 per cent of all adult Jewish workers (22,000 clerks out of approximately 164,000 workers). This was accompanied by a radical improvement in clerks' salaries and working conditions and by a strengthened presence in the labour movement. By 1946, 14,000 clerks, two-thirds of all Jewish clerks and 12.3 per cent of the membership of the General Federation of Labour (Ha-Histadrut Ha-Klalit, 114,000 members) joined the Union of Clerks (Histadrut Ha-Pekidim), making it one of the most powerful unions of the labour movement.[12]

Such developments appeared, however, in sharp contrast to society's attitude towards clerks and their low social prestige. This can be primarily explained by the dominant role played by the Jewish labour movement in Palestine, particularly after the mid-1930s. Through the control of the Histadrut and Zionist institutions, Mapai, the leading party in the labour movement, made organised labour the focus of politics, economics, and culture. The centrality of the labour movement in the Zionist project, reflected in the evolving political language and the veneration of physical and agricultural work, determined many of the patterns of the politics of status in the Yishuv.[13] A second factor, Zionist ideology, played an essential role in social and national formation, which provided the basic consensus around which a variety of social forces realigned. In its labourist and constructivist version this ideology came to dominate the Yishuv's ideological field, becoming an essential yardstick against which almost all the activities of interest groups were measured. Key concepts in this consensus included the realisation of Jewish sovereignty in Palestine through the conquest of land and labour, the creation of a Jewish working class through the inversion of the traditional Jewish social pyramid and productivisation and the idealisation of the pioneer in agriculture and construction.[14]

In this consensual language of social change and national utility, white-collar work and workers, and clerks in particular, were either neglected or marginalized altogether. Tension ensued, giving rise to a variety of incongruities in the Yishuv's system of social symbols between the clerks' sense of being in demand, as well as their gradually improving material status on the one hand, and their low cultural prestige on the other; between the dominant discourse of agrarian and labour constructivism, which downgraded clerical workers on the one hand, and the fact that labour constructivism gave way to institutionalisation on the other. Strained by the

23

clash between a relatively advantageous status and social scorn and disoriented by the sense of the unfair cultural and moral fate to which Jewish society and the labour community in particular consigned them, the clerks set to work on a cultural strategy.[15]

This strategy, the focus of the discussion below, has hardly been dealt with by earlier scholarly treatment of the growth of the service stratum in the Yishuv. Since the late 1950s an ideological-élite approach chose to explain the association between the Jewish clerical stratum and nation-building in terms of the prominent role that high-ranking clerks and bureaucrats played in cultivating Zionist ideology and praxis. As functionaries of Zionist institutions, the dominant party of Mapai, and the labour unions, the clerks' interests went hand in hand with the needs of Zionism and turned these workers into trustworthy servants who had a vital political and ideological function. Thus Zionism, as an élite-made ideology, emerged as the chief determinant of the clerks' occupational identity as well.[16] An alternative explanation using a power-élite approach was introduced in the 1970s. It argued that the social attitudes of bureaucrats should be viewed as a part of a strategic bargain that they had arranged with politicians. In this exchange, the clerks were active agents of political change who should be guaranteed mobility and material well-being, and the politicians were then to receive the loyalty and electoral support of this service class. The identity-formation of this growing stratum was thus linked to the Yishuv's manipulative political culture and to the illegal practices of the dominant labour party, which needed bureaucrats.[17]

Both explanations stressed the need of many social groups to integrate in a cultural system that revered pioneering and the values of nation-building. Moreover, maintaining that the politics of Palestine and the Yishuv were conflictual justified the second approach because it diverted attention to sectorial interests and power politics. The focus on the alliances that the labour movement struck with opposing political groups allowed this approach to reveal how ideological pragmatism and the reformism of Yishuv (and later Israeli) social democracy were conjoined. However, because they share the élitist approach to traditional white-collar research, both explanations consider all facets of the clerical experience to be predetermined by state-building; and their emphasis on high-ranking party and union bureaucrats uncritically assumes the cohesion of the Zionist and collectivist orientation of Jewish clerks. Even the concession that within Zionism there were conflicting ideologies does not help these explanations from continuing to neglect the rank and file who fought out these contestations, which were culturally and symbolically constructed. Although a political consciousness among most ordinary clerks, as well as their full-fledged participation in a power scheme organised by the dominant party, was assumed, the reproduction and cultural dynamics of politics in society as a whole were ignored. In reducing the workings of politics to institutions and the places of decision-making, the extent of the politicisation of work and the self-interested activity reflected by the imbuing of work experience with national images were underplayed.[18]

The following discussion applies categories of social and cultural history to assert that a social-symbolic analysis is essential to an explanation of the production and reproduction of the clerks' social identities, for it then takes account of the actual material and cultural locations where these took place. When observed from the level of the labour market, the workplace, and everyday labour politics, as well as from an analysis of the archival sources of the clerks themselves, it is possible to see how the clerks expressed their grievances against elements of Zionist political language.[19] By focusing on the political nature of the clerks' occupational discourse and on the role that Zionist discourse played in organising their perceptions, a meaningful encounter can be shown to have unfolded between interrelated languages. In this encounter the clerks culturally shaped their occupational identity by making use of, manipulating, and mobilising dominant ideologies.[20]

The Search for Clerical Work

Nowhere did clerks invest so much rhetorical effort to counter the status-prestige incongruity as in the depiction of their positions and interests in the labour market, where the search for work and the struggle to maintain their positions were conducted. This was not surprising because it was in the labour market that Zionism acted as a political platform of colonisation, Jewish autonomy, and actualised segregation. It was in the labour market that the language of building, ascetic pioneering, conquest of land and labour, productive work, and constructivism had been dominant from the first two decades of the century; and, despite the managerial responsibility and administrative knowledge inherent in the clerical occupation, it was in the labour market that clerical work was first given less functional significance.[21]

As can be gauged from their publications during the 1920s and 1930s, the clerks' dual discourse was founded on the notion that each individual's search for employment bore collective, national and, certainly, more than sectional significance. Finding a job, for example, meant not only a material change for the individual immigrant or unemployed clerk but was described as a moment of joining the mass of Jewish immigrants and workers already integrated in the new economic environment. The absorption of Jews, a highly political issued in British Mandatory Palestine, in which a national Arab-Jewish conflict was evolving, was viewed as a criterion for the country's economic capacity. By the same token, the Jew becoming a clerk in Palestine could be, at least symbolically, considered part of the social and economic foundations of the nation in the making, a worthy member of a community of colonisers.[22]

This logic applied to all vacancies for clerks; hence, a clerical position in one of the Jewish national institutions (the Zionist Executive, the Jewish

25

Agency) meant participating in state-building and in creating a new bureaucracy. A portrayal of some of these Zionist institutions is cited in one of the early publications of a small Jewish Clerical union in Jaffa in 1921:

> Could we possibly envision the Anglo-Palestine Bank with all its branches in Palestine and Syria, the Palestine Office with all its departments (technical, agricultural, educational, etc.), the Committee of Delegates [Va'ad Ha-Tsirim] with its branches, towns and plantations committees, schools and the like, existing without clerks?

The answer was clear:

> When, in the near future, we come to build the Jewish settlement on new foundations and on a large scale we will need a large number of expert and experienced clerks, who know how to navigate our ship in the course desired and befitting the great destination.[23]

National Hebrew clerking [*Pekidut Ivrit Le-Umit*] was set in contrast to Jewish clerical work in the Diaspora and to the Baron Rothschild bureaucracy, brought to Palestine at the end of the nineteenth century to administer privately owned settlements [*Moshavot*]. The first, the public administration of religious and charitable institutions, demonstrated the non-constructive and non-productive nature of clerks in the Diaspora; the second reflected the self-interested, bourgeois, and nationally indifferent tradition of Jewish clerks working for philanthropists. Both were removed from the collective memory. If clerks in national institutions had any legacy at all, they pointed out, it should have been Arthur Ruppin's Palestine Office, one of the main precursors, in the first two decades of the century, of the colonisation infrastructure of the Zionist movement. It was argued that a position in one of the Zionist institutions was a contribution to the perpetuation of the Palestine Office tradition. The notion of a national clerk was seen to embody the interests of these institutions by moulding their nationalism, and his image was an indispensable force without which Zionist fulfilment would not have been possible. Statist identification was cultivated from very early on.[24]

The images of clerical employment were further elaborated in the struggle to maintain them. The intentions of Zionist leaders, particularly in the early 1920s, to re-select professional clerks for immigration and give them precedence in job allocations over clerks already in Palestine, were vehemently opposed as anti-national policy. At the end of the 1920s and the early 1930s, attempts to cut expenses in Zionist institutions by dismissing large numbers of administrators, accountants, bookkeepers, and steno-graphers were fiercely resisted on the same grounds. While portraying themselves as enthusiastic supporters of Jewish immigration, the clerks also brought enormous pressure to bear on their employers to enable them to participate in and influence the employment process, specifically the economic absorption and selection of immigrants. Their claim for preference rested, among other things, on their roles as town-dwellers during heightened military tension and as rearguard defenders of the Yishuv in confronting the Arab threat. As such, non-combatant clerks were entitled to control their work environment, to dedicate themselves to seeking employment during hostilities, and to preserve their preferential status. After all, any neglect of the Yishuv's economic tenacity could entail an enormous national and collective cost.[25]

The language of job-seeking in the private Jewish sector (banks, insurance companies, shops, and commercial businesses) was structured in similar terms. As a sector considered prone to the workings of individual interest and rationalised calculation, this sector had to be staffed, the clerks' argued, by 'educational forces' like themselves, who were nationally and collectively oriented. To get a clerical job in the private sector was seen as a step on the road to fulfilling the national goals of beating Arab clerks in the contest over positions in banking; disseminating Hebrew where previously Yiddish, Russian, German and Polish had been spoken; and persuading employers to recognise the nationally oriented Union of Clerks. The private employers, suspected of masking capitalist interests by showing a superficial loyalty to Zionism, had to be influenced no less than the market or the national bureaucracy. Moreover, since the private economy was largely urban, the clerk was also responsible for educating this employer on the need to purchase Jewish products produced in Palestine [*Totseret Ha-Aretz*]. A regular contributor to the bulletin of the clerks' union, signing himself Office-man [*Misradai*], wrote in October 1938:

> You bought some clothing woven or knit in a Jewish [*Ivri*] factory – you thereby employed your brother or your sister and you kept them alive together with yourself, just as you share in the building of our village when you make a point of eating the crop and produce of Jewish [*Ivrim*] farmers.

He went on to list iron safes, cupboards, elevators, steel furniture, ledgers, shelves, typewriters, copying paper and other stationery that a clerk could buy or make his employer buy, concluding:

> Office workers can in fact abstain from foreign produce. There are things which are not yet produced in the country, but they can be, and only when an assertive demand is heard will they be produced here ... Office utensils do not float in the air by themselves. People buy them ... There is no closer redeemer of the office utensils industry than office workers and their union.[26]

As important as their exemplary struggle to improve working conditions and to create an office environment in which Hebrew was spoken and Hebrew-rendered typewriters (nationalised by the name, Ivriia) were used, the clerks' self-assigned national mission was to develop the private economy. The clerks were not supposed to overturn the employers' natural economic preferences in favour of national goals and considerations; rather, by means of their common urban setting and consumer habits, clerks were to turn the hierarchical and authoritative relationship between themselves and their employers into joint membership in a nationally oriented collective.[27]

In both the public and private Jewish sectors and in the semi-public organisations employing clerical workers (such as neighbourhood associations and hospitals), clerks ceased to be individual job seekers. Instead, they saw themselves emerging as a collective force contriving to limit those employers suspected of non-national practices, such as employing Arab workers or hampering the absorption of Jewish immigrants. This was, however, an imaginary force, since the Union of Clerks, affiliated to the Histadrut, succeeded in organising only a fraction of the clerks in the private sector. In addition, the labour exchanges of the Histadrut, operated by town Labour Councils and destined to enforce the limitations on employers, were unable to gain control over the market and exert their influence over the unorganised clerical rank and file. This was why, argued the clerks, the Histadrut was in great need of them: a nationally organised labour movement needed many office workers to fulfil efficiently the movement's national goals in the labour market. Since the Histadrut was widely regarded as the main force in the realisation of Zionism, getting a clerical position in Histadrut institutions was depicted and encouraged not as instrumental collectivism but as participation in the constructive effort of the Zionist movement in general. The socialism of the Pekid Ha-Histadrut (a Histadrut functionary) was expressed not so much by upholding equality or by collectively organising clerks in the labour movement but by serving the institutions of this chief executor of the Zionist project. Unionised clerks working in the private sector were assigned similar roles. The Union of Clerks and the Histadrut were portrayed as training grounds for educators, both of Zionist institutions needing guidance in national bureaucracy and of those of Jewish private capital whose loyalty to Zionism, argued the clerks, had to be taught. A labour movement, representing 'a working-class with a national destiny' (a phrase coined by David Ben-Gurion), had to absorb as many 'pioneering' clerks as its operations required.[28]

To be counted among the clerks of the British Mandatory Government (government offices, the railway works, and so forth), the joint Arab-Jewish municipalities in Haifa and Jerusalem and the international oil companies operating in Palestine, was described as being part of a national mission. Clerks established a Jewish foothold in Arab-dominated sectors and contributed to the larger Zionist project by decreasing Jewish unemployment through the use of imperial and imperial-associated economic forces. Although the number of Jewish clerks who attained employment in this sector was small (they comprised only some 23 per cent of all government clerks during the 1920s), they became standard-bearers of collective protest against anti-Jewish discrimination in the labour market. In these campaigns, which aimed for a larger share of Jewish workers in British economic ventures and local government, the clerks meant to mobilise larger political forces – Zionist and Yishuv institutions – to serve their own interests. This

28

was clearly reflected in the words of one of the chief Histadrut functionaries in March 1930 when, following the eruption of Arab-Jewish violence a year earlier, the Passfield White Paper shook Jewish-British relations:

> The question of governmental clerking has – besides its Zionist-Jewish-settlement value – particular importance for the Clerks' Union ... It is time to start ongoing action in this field. Conquering work in the government sector for the Jewish clerk must be one of the chief items on the agenda of our union in the coming period. This is not an easy task ... Possibly for clerking the fight is particularly difficult because the roads are not paved, but we are not free to shirk action in this direction. The Histadrut institutions, the Jewish Assembly and the Zionist Executive will not withhold their support, for the consequences of this matter are important not only for the Jewish clerk seeking work, but for the Jewish settlement and the Zionist movement.[29]

Moreover, the clerks were mobilised by the same forces and described themselves as willing soldiers in Zionist campaigns. The national-oriented rhetoric that accompanied the clerks' struggle to find employment thus combined with the larger political battles of the labour movement. In this mutual mobilisation Zionism proved to be an effective force in blurring the 'collar line'.

This had further implications. In the eyes of Jewish labour (clerks included) the main culprit obstructing the Jewish 'conquest of work' was the Jewish capitalist. These capitalists, the clerks claimed, preferred to employ cheap Arab labourers to serve the interests of business, rather than hire Jewish workers who would serve the collective struggle of nation-building. The clerks supported the domination of the Jewish labour market by Jewish workers [*Avoda Ivrit*], a thorny issue in the Yishuv. Their bulletins and periodic publications allowed for the possibility, albeit limited and restrained, of organisational and material cooperation between Jews and Arabs in both the Jewish and non-Jewish economic sectors. Joint Jewish-Arab labour action was in principle acceptable to them for material ends without altering the clerks' belief in the segregation of the market along national lines. This was manifested dramatically in 1926 during a joint Arab-Jewish strike of clerks in the privately owned Singer Company in Tel-Aviv during the devastating economic crisis and again in 1946 during another joint strike among government clerks on the eve of the 1948 war. In both of these unique cases, organised and non-organised clerks were involved, and the Union of Clerks approved action only after the action had already begun. In the clerks' discourse, as in the Zionist discourse in general, material supra-national cooperation was often taken to serve Zionist colonising principles. Once ambiguity was legitimised as a strategy, occupational sectionalism, instrumental collectivism, and national loyalties could go hand in hand. In the Histadrut and the union-led collective search for work originally defined by manual groups of workers as the construction of a segregated and autonomous Jewish economy, and which non-unionised low-ranking clerical workers were called to join, the clerks could claim to hold a key position.[30]

The Office

While clerks depicted their market experiences as being located in this new occupational stratum in collectivist and national contexts, how could the scorn towards clerks in the general be accommodated in Zionist discourse? How could clerks enter an ideological field largely dominated by occupational and political groups that espoused values and contents that were seemingly diametrically opposed to their own? How was it possible to create the labourist-national community of sentiment and identity of interests, noted in the Council of the Clerks' Union meeting of December 1931 as 'enhancing the sense of solidarity between the clerical community and the general community of workers'? In confronting the new redundancy policy of Zionist institutions, the meeting went on to decide that

> The Council sadly notes that with each crisis that besets the Yishuv, the Hebrew clerk is swept by waves of scorn, occasionally bordering on hatred, in spite of the fact that his work is an inseparable part of the general Jewish-settlement endeavour. A misconception persists that the clerk is not affected by the difficulties of the Zionist movement and Jewish settlement, either as a worker or as a Zionist, and there are those who tend to say that the clerk is responsible for these difficulties.[31]

Such solidarity was defined, as we shall see later, as one of the aims of the affiliation of the Union of Clerks to the labour movement. But it was in the cultural handling of workplace experiences and of the evolution of the clerical occupation that the construction of the clerical workers' occupational identity began. While the discussion of the search for work was worded in terms of the general Zionist language of colonisation, building and autonomy, descriptions of the clerical labour process and office work [*Avoda Misradit*] appropriated the language of collective pioneering and labour constructivism. Likened to the farmer's field, the mason's construction site and the industrial worker's production line, the office [*Misrad*] became the stage upon which the drama of the 'national clerk' unfolded.[32]

The most blatant strategy was to turn everything clerical into labour, to ascribe labourist traits to their work. As a symbolic practice this was carried out first by differentiating between the mass of low-ranking clerks and executive and managerial clerks. Differences in working conditions, income, lifestyle, and role orientations were emphasised, thus distancing the clerks from the negative connotations of authority and control. The clerks' bulletins, characteristically name *Pinkas* [*Notebook*] and *Shurot* [*Lines*], repeatedly argued that the salaries of managerial clerks were determined by prestige and status, while those of the ordinary clerks were calculated by actual performance. In times of necessary cuts and layoffs, therefore, sums should be subtracted from the high salaries of managerial clerks and

30

reallocated to those among the lower ranks. The cash-nexus of the clerk should not have to compete with the responsibility attributed to the trustworthy managerial clerk. In contradistinction to the latter, ordinary clerks, it was argued, did not aspire to rise above the public which they served. They were closer to the Zionist collective than to their superiors. The low-ranking clerk was free, active and independent because of his national aspirations. He was not a slave to order or discipline as required by the professional work culture of the high-ranking clerks.[33] The argument linking youth and freedom with Zionism was reflected, for instance, in a letter to the clerks' bulletin, *Pinkas*, in 1935:

> For we [the low-ranking clerks] know. The manager is sure to see to it that the bookkeeping in his office is in order, but will he mind whether or not the Hebrew written and spoken at the office is Hebrew indeed? Will he care if his correspondence with the government is in Hebrew or not? And is it not common among some of our managers to respect the English speaker and scorn the clerk who knows 'only' Hebrew, be it the most perfect?[34]

Furthermore, clerks conceived of occupational mobility not only in terms of attaining executive or administrative clerical ranks but also in terms of further contribution to service, an enhanced national loyalty, and a vigorous effort to educate the public. These were idealised, especially by the Union of Clerks, as desired aspirations. The descriptive language served to conceal the fact that proximity to authority, and better conditions, were leading the clerks towards embourgeoisement. When, in 1930, the secretary of the Haifa Labour council, Abba Khushi, accused Haifa's Jewish clerks of becoming 'labour-aristocrats' and of not joining the local branch of the Clerks' Union for that reason, he was answered aggressively. However, his accusation, founded as it was on solid facts, such as differences in income and lifestyle between ordinary workers and high-ranking clerks, was a sore point with union activists among the mass of ordinary clerks. After all, they had evolved an elaborate technique to imply not only that clerks were associated with labour but that there also existed a distinct class of owners, employers and managers to which only the executive clerks belonged. This symbolic practice of imagining the existence of opposing social groupings emerged among Jewish workers in general, but with the clerks it took on a somewhat hyperbolic dimension. Their need to construct a community sharing labour-class sentiments was stronger than their recognition of the actual relative peace that characterised Jewish society despite its inner diversity.[35]

Another way to associate clerking with the labour movement used every available device to appropriate the world of the Zionist labourer. Here national, medical and eugenic images were closely linked. The clerk was not only compared to the farmer but also to industrial construction workers. He was represented as being productive, non-parasitic, a standard-bearer of moral values, physical and healthy. In a society whose intellectual élites inculcated social contrasts based not on class difference but on social utility, these associations and allusions were well placed. The qualifications perceived as necessary for becoming a clerk included the willingness to work hard, readiness to sacrifice comfort and family, even the ascetic appreciation of sweat work. The clerks were not just employed in offices – they were the offices because 'they do all the main work in these institutions, it is they who [were] the wheels that turn the great administrative machine'.[36] Stenographers were described as sweating over their pads; the work of the scribes and the typists as consuming enormous energy and demanding great power. The bookkeeper's preparation of the balance sheet was compared to construction workers being exposed to the glaring Palestinian sun. Office work was as demanding as any fieldwork. Long working hours, especially in private and government offices, caused suffering and a sense of sacrifice resembling that of the road builders in the Galilee, of builders shaping the infrastructure of Tel-Aviv and of agricultural labourers in the Jezreel Valley. The hyperbolic exaggeration of the physical was applied to every aspect of office experience. The clerk was a mind worker (*poel-ruach*) and a member of collective 'labour clerking' (*ha-pekidut ha-ovedet*). National images were blended with creativity and production: the heat and stifling atmosphere at the office were described as more difficult to bear than the conditions of the manual worker. A mid-1930s publication dedicated to the physical well-being of the clerk argued that the preservation of the body of the working man was a public matter, that physical and mental work were closely linked. The clerk way belong to the category of those who work with their minds, but 'mental work requires immense concentration and demands strenuous activity of the nervous system'. Working in the office, like any other sort of labour, was meant to teach clerks that 'the labourer's health guarantees his victory', that Herzl's call to 'train not only your minds but also your muscles: be strong and upright' was imperative, that walking to the office was preferable to a car ride that robs one of his money, and, finally, that 'muscles and mind are the foundations of might'.[37] Another clerical booklet, devoted to the value of vacations, claimed:

> A clerk needs some rest from work no less than any other toiling man. And greatly mistaken are those who say that because the clerk's work does not require him to strain his muscle as does the manual labourer it follows that his fatigue is also less great ... His fatigue is not of course the outcome of 'muscular work' because the clerk does not employ his muscles so much, but it is a product of 'exerting muscular energy' ... even if he does not do any visible physical work.[38]

Work was not just clerical but the realisation of the functional and social significance of clerking. (The work *Pakid*, clerk, became in the words of one of the Histadrut leaders, *Tafkid*, meaning role or function.) The clerk was attributed constructive qualities, and clerical work was revered. Many clerks, both in the public and private sectors, were formerly labourers; and their short labourist past, particularly as union members, was essential for this wording. Office work fed on the legacy of the Palestine Office, no ordinary

32

office, formal and alienated, but an active Zionist agent the functionaries of which adored the Hebrew labourer and advocated siding with the labour movement.[39]

In times of intensified national conflict, the clerks strove to highlight the labourer who left his job to join in the battle. The clerk also relinquished his desk and pen to take up arms. Thus, the clerk-as-pioneer could easily turn into the clerk-as-soldier. The supreme expression of this facet of their self-portrayal was to found in the clerks' request that their participation in the 1948 war effort should not be forgotten. A summary of the activities of the Clerk's Union during 1945-48 included clerks in the secular Labour-Zionist version of the original remembrance [*Yiskor*] prayer.

> Let the People of Israel remember their sons and their daughters who, forsaking the plough and the desk, the workshop and the building top, exchanged spade for mortar, ruler for machine-gun and the weaver's loom for the artillery battery; and few against many set out to defend the state of Israel and the entire people of Israel, and by their lives and deaths sanctified the name of Israel upon its land.

No other occupational group exerted such an effort to be included in the imagery of the soldier and the culture of the fallen. Later in the publication there was a further elaboration:

> Under the spell of the great tidings of the state of the News emerging before our eyes and with the zeal of the good old tradition of Jewish Defence, thousands of clerks are leaving their offices and taking up arms to rebut the bloody offensive of the enemy that has attacked us from every direction. From the office seat the clerk goes to the trench, and the fountain-pen is replaced by the machine-gun. In this way masses of clerks come out to join the heroic war of Israel to set up the state of Israel and to defend it from all its foes.[40]

For an occupational group so dependent on the clerical-bureaucratic market, the next phase was quite natural. The clerks perceived the establishment of the state in 1948 as an economic buffer against instability and potential decline. The latter were the consequences of the deterioration in the living standards of the Jewish lower-middle class in Palestine during the 1940s, the shock wave felt by private capital institutions following the Second World War, and the undermining of British bureaucracy in 1946-47. The state served as a panacea for the clerk's anxious images of economic downturn because it appeared not only as a stable supplier of clerical jobs but also as a source for a variety of cushioning devices which had been achieved and refined over the long Mandate period. These devices included savings, securities, pensions, loan funds and various benefits that had accrued from the bureaucratic economy.

Regarding the state as an economic asset, the clerks were assured that it was possible to confront proletarianisation and that their income and living conditions could serve as the yardstick for other social groups. They found in service a sense of proximity to economic and political power, of participation in decision-making and in the practical business of state-making. They saw no better source for their prestige, since the state bestowed cultural capital and social dividends and served to integrate the clerk with the pioneer. The notion of service was now transferred from the informal, pre-sovereignty bureaucracy to the state and served to legitimise the clerks' quest for social status and value. No wonder, therefore, that with the initial formation of statist culture in the early 1950s, the state and service came to dominate the clerk's life. Working hours were followed by leisure time spent with one's fellow clerks; the office was a main topic of conversation at home; and service to the state, not simply the civil service, was the arena in which nationalist aspirations were fulfilled. What began as personal and group dedication to office work between 8 a.m. and 3 p.m. continued with the glorification of the state and the Israeli flag at home and in the songs and lyrics sung at outings. The state became a major component of the social identity of this large stratum of urban cultural consumers and an essential factor in the social and cultural construction of their lives.[41]

In the symbolic turning of the clerk's work experience into labour, a further transformation took place. The language of labour, usually a terrain dominated by one-dimensional terminology, was forced to encompass images of ideal clerical work itself. What was considered constructive and productive was enlarged to include things clerical: the usage of Hebrew typewriters, spoken Hebrew, polite service, precision, orderliness, and cleanliness.[42] These were included in what one clerk activist unabashedly entitled, 'The Ten Commandments of the Clerical Mount Sinai'. The office performance of the clerk was presented as a worthy model for other workers because of the responsibility that their work demanded; their tidiness and industriousness made clerking an exemplary profession.[43]

Promoting and improving Hebrew stenography was likened to any other nation-building activity, for it disseminated the language (especially the usage of vocalised Hebrew for immigrants), gave it a role in economic and professional activities, and aimed to contribute to efficiency and to the building of a better technical future. The educational role of the clerks in the labour market was thus applied here as well. Administrative efficiency was meant to have a national value (Taylorism was revered by leaders of the union as early as the end of the 1920s); clerical productivity was linked to constructivism; and loyalty to the workplace carried a universal meaning, especially in times of national strife. Concern with the professionalisation of clerking and the demand for expertise, which emerged in the early 1930s, served to limit the pressure of immigrants and the unemployed on working clerks, but they also aimed to have an educational impact on other occupations. In the national conflict and in state-building, all these qualities (professionalism, trustworthiness, efficiency) came to dominate the language of labour no less than the fact that the latter came to dominate the world of clerical work.[44]

Collective Action

The permeation of labour market and workplace experiences with collectivist and nationalist imagery served to mask sectorial interests and to smooth away potential areas of conflict between clerks and manual labourers. At the same time however, it left enough leeway to legitimise the relative material advantages of the clerks over other types of workers. These advantages became a focus of very intense symbolic activity, located mainly at the level of labour relations. The search for clerical positions and office experiences were nationalised and blurred the clerks' autonomy and distinction. However, using the same discursive devices for labour relations and struggles for improvement did the opposite.

Once clerical work was defined as labour, it followed that the office, like the factory and the construction site, was an arena where the commodification of the clerk had to be opposed. Treated by employers as machines, alienated from the product, make to work for hours on end and paid low wages, clerks were endowed with a role in labour's general struggle for decommodification. In the eyes of private employers, argued one union activist,

> The clerk is nothing but a machine that has to be worked to the maximum and with minimal expenditure. There is no concern with wear and tear, they are not bound by any national-public creed and are not accountable to anyone.[45]

This self-image was clearly reflected in the demand of clerks in Jewish national institutions for fair treatment during the expenditure cuts of the early 1930s and, later, in numerous campaigns for humane working conditions in small commercial businesses. As on many other occasions, straightforward demands were presented in the typical and familiar language of the morally angered worker. Directing their anger in particular against Zionist national institutions organised clerks demanded to annul the notion that economising in Zionist expenses could be achieved by making clerks redundant. This struggle, spreading also to municipalities and to the labour movement, was one of the fiercest labour disputes of the early 1930s. It reached the debating halls of the Zionist congresses, and threatened to paralyse the workings of the Jewish Agency and its executive departments. It was following this struggle that the clerks could boast of their powerful union position and of the value of their struggles to labour in general, and also in the wider recognition of their major role in the Zionist project. As in other sectors, the image of workers' powers was closely connected to social standing and national worth. After all, the sweat of labour, like moral wrath, was not exclusive to one type of worker. Furthermore, when actually expressing protest the clerks felt they had something to teach other organised workers.[46]

The clerks directed their collective action on two fronts – the employer and other workers, including the labour movement – that exemplified their symbolic technique. Employers were continually approached with a mixture of bold demands for the improvement of working conditions and conversely with apologetic, self-righteous exclamations that it was all for the national good. The clerks' struggle to improve working conditions, though a sectorial affair, was made to appear to other workers as endowed with collectivist and unionist values. Raising wages, institutionalising free time and various fringe benefits, and establishing the norm of an eight-hour work day were advocated and advanced as a potential contribution to raising the level of working conditions of Palestinian labourers in general. This was particularly evident in the portrayal of the social and political role of collective bargaining. Clerks argued that, far beyond serving their interests in national and semi-public institutions, the attainment and general enforcement of collective agreement had an educational impact on the labour market as a whole, a point discussed in the clerk's bulletin in 1929:

> The collective agreement brings not only better material conditions but also elevates the clerk's human self-consciousness and liberates him from spiritual enslavement.[47]

Similar to the search for work, the agreement epitomised the collective nature of the clerical labour process and organisation, and demonstrated the clerks' success in contriving to limit the power of the employer. It also meant that the large numbers of non-unionised clerks working in the private sector, who were bound by personal contracts or by none at all, were stigmatised either as being likely to side with employers against organisation or as a bad influence on organised clerks. Limiting the employer and educating the unorganised rank and file were two aspects of the same collectivist mission.[48]

While the arguments against employers were restrained by ordinary clerks who sought to distance themselves from those of higher rank who enjoyed superior standards of income and living, the plans put forward for the benefit of fellow workers entailed more problematic notions. For example, the clerks took pains to legitimise economic cushioning devices such as loan funds savings, pension schemes and insurance benefits that preserved their standards of living. These, they claimed, were not material expressions of advantageous positions but constituted a cultural goal that created an image of normal well-being for the rest of the workforce, both the basis for aspiration and proof of Jewish progress in Palestine. The clerks equipped the Zionist collective not only with orderliness, precision and politeness, and not only with a process of collective bargaining that quelled industrial strife, but also with normalisation and modernisation. What began as an ideological endeavour in the labour market and the workplace, purported to create an identity of interest with labour in general, continued here with a discursive scheme to mask sectorial advantages.[49]

Thus, the clerks managed to legitimise their superior working conditions and material status without excluding themselves from the ranks of labour and the mass of ordinary town-workers. However, the dual language, presenting sectorial interests as being valuable for labour and the nation overall, reflected the ambiguous positions of the clerks in the labour movement. Suspicion grew in the Histadrut regarding the clerks' split loyalties between the labour movements and the political forces opposing it. This ambiguity became the focus of an ongoing debate among the clerks, in which some called for dissociation from the Histadrut.[50]

The clerks primarily sought to rebuff the allegation, levelled at them by other labour groups and some Histadrut leaders, that they were a 'labour aristocracy'. It was here that the clerks perceived the symbolic joining of the working class as most essential and took steps to blur the demarcation lines between office and manual work and between the urban and the agricultural environment of labour. Their employment and achievements in the workplace were presented as beneficial to labour in general. Since the early 1920s clerical discourse determined the starting-point of professionalisation by appealing to all clerks to become knowledgeable in accountancy, to acquire many languages and specialise in stenography and typewriting. Professionalism meant to set the clerks apart from the rest of labour, but at the same time to serve as its model. Through professional clerking, so it was argued, labour at large could be presented as executing a scientific work. The harnessing of professional work to the national cause, and the regimentation of obedient bureaucrats and technical experts to the authority of the politicians, were integrated, and made to appear as carrying political significance. The issue of professional qualifications was made ambiguous: on the one hand, they described these as necessary to protect the clerks from competition; on the other, they propounded the idea that clerking should remain 'open' to all who accepted its norms, as determined by the union.[51] In the conditions of pre-state Palestine, specialisation meant closing the ranks of the clerical profession to immigrants, the unemployed and other workers.

Within these limits, the depiction of the clerks' union as an umbrella organisation for a variety of clerical workers and professionals accurately reflected the universal character of the Histadrut itself. The clerks were given, they claimed, a central role in the organisation and bureaucratic operation of the socialist economy propounded by the Histradut. Clerks, office employees and service workers in general were integrated into the Community of Workers (*Tsibur Ha-Ovdim*), thus creating a unified political force, the internal stratification of which did not weaken its standing and power in society. This was made evident by the clerks' workplace representational power (see Table 2.1).

Table 2.1

Membership Structure of the Union of Clerks,* January 1949

Type of Work and Work Places	Clerk	%	Labour Committees	%
Histadrut Institutions	4,800	23.5	57	13.5
National and Public Institutions	3,500	17.2	95	22.5
Industry	2,500	12.2	70	16.6
Private Companies and Offices	2,200	10.8	53	12.6
Nurses	1,300	6.4	-	-
Cooperatives	1,200	5.9	27	6.4
Municipalities and Local Councils	1,100	5.4	29	6.9
Commercial Establishments	1,000	4.9	30	7.1
Military and Governmental Offices	1,000	4.9	-	-
Banks	800	3.9	36	8.5
Other	400	2.0	25	5.9
Unemployed	600	2.9	-	-
TOTAL	20,400	100.0	422	100.0

*Does not include 9,000 state employees (*Ovdei Medina*): 5,000 clerks and 4,000 in the police, public works and transport.

Source: Be-Mivchan Ha-Ma'aseh.

By proving themselves a national asset and an influential unionising factor, the clerks advanced a consistent claim to join the 'labouring class' (*Ha-Ma'amad Ha-Oved*). In September 1941, when the initial information on the destruction of European Jewry reached the Yishuv, the clerks' union was portrayed as 'the great cohesive link in the great chain of labour, the labour of the hands and that of the mind of the expelled and dwindling Jewish people'.[52] A typical notion was that of 'organisational conquest'. This denoted the spread of organisation to non-unionised clerks in the private and public-government sectors while alluding to a collective-national struggle and the Zionist flag's conquest of land, as had been shown in the 1926 comments of a clerk in the 'Zionist Army':

> The worker ... either urban or agricultural, is at the front: he is the one who fights and creates the [labouring] class, ... who bears most of the suffering entailed by life at the front. And the institutional worker [the clerk] is the rearguard, so to speak. No doubt his role is also important ...

[and] his role is not easy, [for] he too does not often enjoy many comforts. But his very existence and labour fulfil the needs of the army at the front.[53]

And, in the same vein, a decade later:

The one doomed to remain in the rear must know that he is part of the front and has to work for it. Without the ordered life in the rear, the front cannot endure. The workers at the cashier's box, the writing-desk, the typewriter, the auditing book, and at the shop shelf, will prove during these tumultuous times that they are willing to bear the yoke when required to do so.[54]

The association of clerks with the labour movement was portrayed as worthwhile because the movement needed an urban social base and Jewish spearhead in the British Mandatory government. The movement's purpose was to advance Jewish claims for legislating labour laws, to demand that Jews receive preference in work allocation, and to supply political information. More effectively, the clerks proclaimed their singularity in that they were the only sector in the labour movement able to bridge the tensions and conflicts between labour and liberal-bourgeois Zionism. The latter dominated the Zionist movement until the 1930s and remained as a pool of Zionist resources for a long period. After all, clerks were the labour force of the national institutions, the workers closest to the British administration, and representatives of the Histadrut in the private Jewish sector. The total dependence of the labour movement on Zionist political centres, in matters of finance, immigration, settlement and political pressures, as well as on the private economy in matters of employment, lent force to these images of mediation. It also gave the symbolic tactic a new dimension, for it turned the clerks' ambiguous social position as a sort of lower middle-class labour into a level which bettered their political standing and enhanced their status.[55]

The clerks' union, dominated as it was by clerical employees of Zionist and Histadrut institutions and organised as a national union, demanded, however, power and autonomy *vis-à-vis* the local Labour Councils and the central Histadrut institutions in order to promote their specific interests. This duality was reflected in the title of the clerks' organisation, which was not called a union but a Histadrut, the title given to the larger General Federation of Labour. The union's headquarters were called a *Merkaz* (a centre), as would be the case with a political party or major Histadrut organ. These titles carried a political meaning that became obvious in the fierce conflict in the late 1940s between two large groups of clerks: one in the Jewish economy and organised in the Union of Clerks; the other in British governmental offices and organised with the Union of Railway, Post, and Telegraph Workers. Both were general national unions, or union federations (*Histadruiot Artsiot*); their membership and centres spread throughout the country and, after Israel was established, claimed to be the only union representing the clerks. The terminology used in this representation conflict, which later perpetuated the split between ordinary clerks and civil servants (state workers, or *Ovdei Medina*), described the relative distance of each group from the labour movement and the clear association of the former with labour throughout the Mandate.[56]

Such an association was significant. Though well-organised and strongly represented in the Histadrut, the clerks did not demand a change in the principles of the existing prestige system or the power structure of the union in the Histadrut. They neither challenged the Zionist or socialist discourse nor wrested prestige from pioneers and manual workers. All the clerks wanted was to improve their situation by becoming integrated in practical ways with the existing occupational-prestige hierarchy, even though the latter had been founded on collectivist, Labour-Zionist, nation-building terminologies. Later on this served the clerk's movement. Clerks accumulated cultural capital by appropriating part of the Zionist perception of the social order and its system of cultural preferences without altering the mode that determined the system of prestige in the first place. This even alleviated some of the hardships of the post-1948 period, such as the threat of proletarianisation and social decline.[57]

When state-making reached a crucial stage after 1945, service to the labour community and to the nation, setting up labour and statist institutions, educating the public in bureaucratic manners, and creating a public propriety for modern society became essential catchphrases. The notion of service was appropriate for this occupational group both in conceptual and practical ways. It related to a series of abstract ideas concerning the social order and justified the need for workers' organisation. It illustrated the order that prevailed over the chaotic environment (immigrants' absorption, intra-labour tensions, national conflict), and it legitimised the national practices or urban society.[58]

The culture of service, applied both to the community of labour and to the national community, enabled the Zionist Jew to stay in town, work at the office, and enjoy better standards of living while feeling that he belonged among pioneering labour and agricultural workers – an important tool in making a new Jewish society and serving as a soldier in the Arab-Jewish conflict. Similar to the national role in the labour market, and to the educational mission of office work, the culture of service was essential in the creation of images of attachment to the symbolic discourse of Zionism. Thus, the cultural handling of the clerks' occupational identify not only reproduced the meaning that Labour-Zionism had for ordinary people but also proved to be a powerful force in its persistence. Endorsing Zionism was enhanced by a self-interested association with the state, which the clerks perceived as their rightful guardian. The diversity of this social imagery was crucial in strengthening the links between clerical workers and the labour movement which had earlier provided the clerks with a community and now dominated the state-building process. Its significance, however, also lay in its construction of the clerks' support of the segregative orientation of Labour-

Zionism, their criticism of the private employers' half-hearted Zionism, and their active participation in establishing the national bureaucracy. It should be added that the clerks' union was male dominated. The clerical appropriation of the physical dimensions of the work of the agrarian, construction and industrial pioneers determined the masculine style of the terminology of the clerk's body, despite the invigorating feminisation of clerking since the end of the 1930s, and particularly after the establishment of the state of Israel. Furthermore, special reference was made to the importance of space. In order to be productive the woman typist needed a room of her own so as not to be disturbed by the noises around her. 'In this room', explained an expert writer

> Needs be lots of air and light (and when necessary also suitable shadow). In winter the room should be heated and fixed temperature needs to be assured (the cold makes it difficult to sit in one place and influences first and foremost the fingers, hands and the legs). It is worthwhile also to see to isolation in order to decrease the noises of the machines ... It is very important that the room is aesthetically and suitably organised and tidied. It affects the mood and the will to work.

And another writer referring in 1950 to productive abilities added,

> Everybody admits that working as a telephonist wrathes the nerves and requires more stamina than any other work. It requires better nutrition and suitable salary. Moreover: working as a telephonist is not so simple that it can be assigned to anyone. It requires intelligence, quick grasping and understanding of the other.[59]

These indirect references indicate sensitivity of the clerks' union to a potential diminution of the status of the profession as more women were employed.

Conclusion

The clerks' cultural strategy can now be redrawn. They 'spoke' the Zionist language that revered pioneering, agricultural work and manual productive labour; moreover, they adopted essential aspects of the Zionist national and labourist languages which were most relevant to this society, its status image and its perceptions of prestige. They created a terminology parallel to that of the pioneer in discussing Zionist agrarianism and Jewish self-defence. They focused their quest for prestige on concepts which legitimised service, collective trust and dedicated bureaucracy. At the same time, they appropriated these concepts in a variety of ways to suit their own occupational experiences. They sought to undo the symbolic incongruity between their material status in Yishuv society and the low social prestige accorded them by using the same aspects of Zionist ideology that derogated them in the first place. In portraying themselves both as autonomous and as part of the collective, by veiling material differences between their work and manual labour, and by legitimising their sectorial advantages as being nationally imperative, they combined occupational boundary work and demarcated their professional autonomy with efforts to receive social recognition and gain influence.[60]

The dual strategy of working within the context of the Zionist discourse while manipulating it for sectorial interests was a routine procedure for many social groups in inter-war Palestine. However, no stratum other than the clerks developed such a subtle and collusive verbal symbolism, employing, for their own purposes, basic tenets of Zionism as a tool box from which some aspects were selected and imbued with 'clerical contents'.[61] Imbuing clerical work with national and statist orientations and narrating it in terms of clerks' relations with the labour community and society in general gave the occupation its form. At the same time this perpetuated the Zionist state-building ideology among the clerks and reproduced the symbols of statism which characterised the Jewish labour movement and on which the Zionist undertaking depended. Occupational self-definition of clerks and of many other social groups was as much a part of Zionist ideology as was constructing a Jewish national community in Palestine; both were served by common cultural images and symbols. The two were so closely connected at one point that professional definitions and images teemed with national terminology and, in turn, played a role in the persistence of Zionism.[62]

Hence, the case of Palestine's Jewish clerks has wider implications than it first appears. As a varied and a dynamically changing occupational stratum, the clerks appeared to utilise any means that would clarify their social location and promote their collective interests. In state-building movements of the kind that intertwine nationalism with social restructuring, they used an ideological mixture as a reservoir of terms to appropriate and manipulate for their own purposes. In clinging to an encompassing national vision that maintained society as a communal or a movement-like entity, the clerks could both legitimise advancement of their interests and take pride in their social and non-isolationist behaviour. They played a major role in the construction of statist and capitalist bureaucracies and thus took part in social and political transformation. However, as mediators between these bureau-cracies and community, the clerks also maintained traditional patterns, assuring that community and bureaucracy were not antithetical and enabling bureaucracies to use collectivist and national discourse, and not only technocratic ideologies, to legitimise their expansion and authority.[63] That white-collar workers should be located in such a pivotal position does much to explain their multifaceted status and consciousness.[64]

As this analysis shows, clerical work was historically and culturally constructed not only by material and social developments but also by an active cultural utilisation of national discourse and practices. The changing circumstances and nature of white-collar work should be thus contextualised in a socio-political perspective. The politics of status, authority relations, and

42

union politics have an enormous impact on occupational and professional identities – even more so when these elements are culturally interpreted and reinterpreted as part of a group experience. The fact that these socialist and national movements revered physical and materially productive work and derogated clerical work while themselves undergoing institutionalisation and bureaucratisation, emphasises the political and cultural nature of occupational identity making. On the other hand the fact that shaping this occupational identity is imbued with national imagery shows the variety of cultural strategies available to confront economic and social change. When the blurring of the divide between white- and blue-collar work is perceived not only as an outcome of material and organisational processes but also as a symbolic strategy, then the impact of that imagery can be better understood.[65]

The clerks' cultural strategy sheds light on the workings of social bases of nationalism and on the way that ordinary people experience state formation. The clerks' experiences in the labour market, at the office, and in their collective action have shown a cultural dimension that has to be taken into consideration when examining the social history of national movements. The clerks particularly demonstrated how state-building societies confer privileged status not only by formal means, but also by their cultural and symbolic roles in the formation of a given prestige system.[66] Moreover, when national discourse is perceived not as an abstract ideology – to be either worshipped or rejected – but as a negotiable symbolic system susceptible to manipulation, its power in ordering and explaining chaotic reality becomes better understood.[67] Since it can be constructed and reinterpreted in a variety of circumstances and by various social forces, the dynamic and non-linear nature of national discourse is exposed. In this sense the changing face of nationalism and the persistence of its symbolic power may be proved by future research to depend also on social groups whose collective practices are often perceived as mainly specific to themselves.

Notes

1. This chapter was originally published as De Vries, D. (1997), 'National Construction of Occupational Identity: Jewish Clerks in British-Ruled Palestine', *Comparative Studies in Society and History*, vol. 39, no. 2, (April). It has been substantially amended for this book.
2. Adams, C. E. (1984), 'Germany's Women Clerks: Class and Gender Conflict, 1890-1914', PhD thesis, Harvard University; Braverman, H. (1974), *Labour and Monopoly Capital: The Degradation of Work in the Twentieth Century*, ch. 15, London: Monthly Review Press; Lockwood, D. (1989), *The Blackcoated Worker: A Study in Class Consciousness*, Oxford: Clarendon Press; Sobel, R. (1989), *The White-Collar Working Class: From Structure to Politics*, New

York: Praeger; Strom, S. H. (1992), *Beyond the Typewriter: Gender, Class and the Origins of Modern American Office Work, 1900-1930*, Urbana: Illinois University Press.

3.   Crozier, M. (1984), *The Bureaucratic Phenomenon*, Chicago: University of Chicago Press; Dahrendorf, R. (1987), *Society and Democracy in Germany*, New York: Doubleday; Lampert, N. (1979), *The Technical Intelligentsia and the Soviet State: A Study of Soviet Managers and Technicians, 1928-1935*, London: Macmillan. Hyman, R. and Price, R. (eds) (1983), *The New Working Class? White-Collar Workers and their Organziations*, London: Macmillan; Kaelble, H. (1986), *Industrialization and Social Inequality in Nineteenth-Century Europe*, Leamington Spa: Berg; Armstrong P. et al. (eds) (1986), *White-Collar Workers, Trade Unions and Class*, London: Croom Helm.

4.   Galbraith, J. K. (1989), *The New Industrial State*, London: Pelican; Mandel, E. (1975), *Late Capitalism*, London: New Left Books.

5.   Speier, H. (1932, 1988), *German White-Collar Workers and the Rise of Hitler*, New Haven: Yale University Press; Peukert, D. J. K. (1991), *The Weimar Republic: The Crisis of Classical Modernity*. London: Allen Lane, pp. 151-8. Kocka, J. (1980), *White-Collar Workers in America, 1890-1940: A Social-Political History in International Perspective*, ch. 4, London: Sage Publications.

6.   Koshar, R. (ed.) (1990), *Splintered Classes: Politics and the Lower Middle Classes in Interwar Europe*, New York: Holmes and Meier.

7.   Aron, C. S. (1987), *Ladies and Gentlemen of the Civil Service: Middle Class Workers in Victorian America*, New York: Oxford University Press; Blumin, S. R. (1989), *The Emergence of the Middle Class: Social Experience in the American City, 1760-1900*, Cambridge: Cambridge University Press; Wishnia, J. (1990), *The Proletarianising of the Fonctionnaires: Civil Workers and the Labour Movement under the Third Republic*, Baton Rouge: Louisiana State University Press; Zunz, O. (1990), *Making America Corporate, 1870-1920*, Chicago: University of Chicago Press; Berlanstein, L. (1991), *Big Business and Industrial Conflict in Nineteenth-Century France: A Social History of the Parisian Gas Company*, Berkeley: University of California Press.

8.   Davis, H. H. (1979), *Beyond Class Images: Explorations in the Structure of Social Consciousness*, London: Croom Helm; Wilson, C. P. (1992), *White-Collar Fictions: Class and Social Represen-tation in American Literature, 1885-1925*, Athens: The University of Georgia Press.

9.   Eley, G. (1981) 'Nationalism and Social History: Review Essay', *Social History*, **6** (1), 83-107; Hroch, M. (1985), *Social Preconditions of National Revival in Europe: A Comparative Analysis of the Social Composition of Patriotic Groups among the*

Smaller European Nations, Cambridge: Cambridge University Press; Patterson, H. (1988), 'Neo-Nationalism and Class', *Social History*, **13** (3), 343-9. Howe, S. (1989), 'Labour Patriotism, 1939-1983', in Samuel, R. (ed.), *Patriotism: The Making and Unmaking of British National Identity*, vol. 1, pp. 127-39, London: Routledge; Anderson, B. (1990), *Imagined Communities: Reflections on the Origin and Spread of Nationalism*, London: Verso; Coakley, J. (ed.) (1992), *The Social Origins of Nationalist Movements: The Contemporary West European Experience*, London: Sage.

10.   Bleicher, J. (1989), 'The Cultural Construction of Social Identities: The Case of Scotland', in H. Haberkampf (ed.), *Social Structure and Culture*, pp. 229-41, Berlin: Walter de Gruyter: Burke, P. (1992), 'The Language of Orders in Early Modern Europe', in M. L. Bush (ed.), *Social Orders and Social Classes in Europe since 1500: Studies in Social Stratification*, pp. 1-12, London: Longman; Morris, J. (1993), 'Towards a European History of the Petite Bourgeoisie', in M. Fulbrook (ed.), *National Histories and European History*, pp. 182-203, Boulder: Westview Press; Gillis, J. R. (1994), 'Memory and Identity: History of a Relationship', in J. R. Gillis (ed.), *Commemorations: The Politics of National Identity*, pp. 3-24, Princeton, NJ: Princeton University Press; Joyce, P. (1994), *Democratic Subjects: The Self and the Social in Nineteenth-Century England*, pt 3, Cambridge: Cambridge University Press.

11.   Horowitz, D. and Lissak, M. (1978), *The Origins of the Israeli Polity: The Political System of the Jewish Community in Palestine under the Mandate*, Chicago: University of Chicago Press.

12.   Nemirovsky, M. (1929), *Jewish Clerks in Palestine: A Statistical Survey with Nineteen Tables*, Tel Aviv: Mischar Ve-Ta'asia; *Be-Shnot Ha-Shloshim* [*In the Thirtieth Anniversary*], Tel Aviv: Histadrut, 1951; Ha-Machlaka Le-Statistika Shel Ha-Histadrut Ha-Klalit, *Sikumim* [*Summations*], 18 August 1946; *Be-Mivchan Ha-Ma'ase: Histadrut Ha-Pekidim, 1945-1948* [*In Test of Practice, The Union of Clerks, 1945-1948*], Tel Aviv: Histadrut Ha-Pedidim, 1949; Ofer, G. (1987), *The Service Industries in a Developing Economy: The Case of Israel*, New York: Praeger, pp. 87-8.

13.   Rosenfeld, H. and Carmi S., (1976), 'The Privatization of Public Means, The State-Made Middle Class, and the Realization of Family Values in Israel', in J. G. Peristiany (ed.), *Kinship and Modernization in Mediterranean Society*, pp. 131-59, Rome: The Centre of Mediterranean Studies; Don-Yehiya E. and Liebman, C. S. (1981), 'The Symbolic System of Zionist Socialism: An Aspect of Israeli Civil Religion', *Modern Judaism*, **1**, 123-48; Shapiro, Y. (1984), *Ilit Lelo Mamshichim* [*An Elite with no Successors*], Tel Aviv: Sifriat Poalim, ch. 2, and pp. 132-3; Shafir, G. (1989), *Land, Labour and the Origins of the Israeli-Palestinian*

Conflict, 1882-1914, Cambridge: Cambridge University Press, chs 1, 6, 8; Lissak, M. (1994), 'Mivneh Ta'asukati, Naya'ut Ta'asukatit Ve-Simlei Status Ba-Yeshuv Ha-Yehudi He-Chdash, 1918-1948' ['Occupational Structure, Occupational Mobility and Status Symbols in the New Jewish Settlement'], *Iunim Be-Tekumat Israel*, **4**, 345-77. For a regional perspective, see E. Burke III (1994), 'The History of the Working Classes in the Middle East: Some Methodological Considerations', in Z. Lockman (ed.), *Workers and Working Classes in the Middle East: Struggles, Histories, Historiographies*, pp. 303-19, New York: State University of New York Press.

14.   Weinryb, Dov B. (1938), 'Me-Ba'aiot Ha-Pekidut Ha-Yehudit' ['Among the Problems of Jewish Clerking'], *Shurot*, **4** (December), 3; Shapiro, Y. (1975), *Achdut Ha-Avoda Ha-Historit* [*The Formative Years of the Israeli Labour Party: The Organisation of Power*], Tel Aviv: Am Oved, chs 3, 5, 7; Metzer, J. (1976), '"Hon Leumi" Ke-Musag Yesod Ba-Tsionut: Hashkafat Ha-Olam Ha-Kalkalit Ba-Machshava Ha-Tsionit, 1918-1921' ['"National Capital" as a Basic Concept in Zionism: The Economic World View in Zionist Thought, 1918-1921'], *Falk Discussion Papers*, no. 763, Jerusalem: Falk; Almog, S. (1993), 'Chalutsiut Ke-Tarbut Chilufit' ['Pioneering as an Alternative Culture'], *Zion*, **58** (3), 329-46.

15.   Weinryb, 'Me-Ba'aiot Ha-Pekidut Ha-Yehudit'; for an earlier treatment of prestige, see Mills, C. W. (1951, 1970), *White Collar: The American Middle Classes*, pp. 240-49, Oxford: Oxford University Press.

16.   Arian, D. (1958), 'The First Five Years of the Israeli Civil Service', in R. Bachi (ed.), *Scripta Hierosolymitana*, vol. 3, 340-77; Eisenstadt, S. N. (1987) *Israeli Society*, London: Weidenfeld and Nicolson, pt I; Lockman, Z. (1993), 'Railway Workers and Relational History: Arabs and Jews in British-Ruled Palestine', *Comparative Studies in Society and History*, **35** (3), 601-27.

17.   Shapiro, Y. (1977), *Ha-Deomkratia Be-Israel* [*Democracy in Israel*], Ramat-Gan: Massada, chs 5-6; for a critique, see Ram, U. (1995), *The Changing Agenda of Israeli Sociology: Theory, Ideology, and Identity*, New York: State University of New York Press, ch. 5.

18.   Shalev, M. (1992), *Labour and the Political Economy in Israel*, Oxford: Oxford University Press.

19.   Data on these aspects are found in primary sources of the clerks themselves: minutes of meetings, correspondence and reports of the Union of Clerks, its bulletins, and also in archival sources relating to non-unionised clerks. Indirect sources include primary and secondary material of the Histadrut and of public and private establishments where clerks were employed. The archival material

46

of the clerks' union is found in the labour movement archives in the Lavon Institute in Tel Aviv [hereafter LA]. For meeting minutes and correspondence of the clerks' union, see LA/IV-236. Relevant British material is found in the Israel State Archives in Jerusalem. The files of Zionist institutions are found in the Central Zionist Archive in Jerusalem.

20. Geertz, C. (1973), *The Interpretation of Cultures*, New York: Basic Books, chs 1, 5, 8; Sewell, W. H. Jr (1979), 'Property, Labour, and the Emergence of Socialism in France, 1789-1848', in J. Merriman, (ed.), *Consciousness and Class Experience in Nineteenth-Century Europe*, pp. 45-63, New York: Holmes and Meier; Walters, R. G. (1980), 'Signs of the Times: Clifford Geertz and Historians', *Social Research*, **47**, 537-56; Burke, P. (1990), 'Historians, Anthropologists, and Symbols', in E. Ohnuki-Tierney (ed.), *Culture Through Time: Anthropological Approaches*, pp. 268-83, Stanford: Stanford University Press; Steinberg, M. W. (1994), 'The Dialogue of Struggle: The Contest over Ideological Boundaries in the Case of London Silk Weavers in the Early Nineteenth Century', *Social Science History*, **18** (4), 505-41.

21. Barber, B. (1993), 'Inequality and Occupational Prestige: Theory, Research, and Social Policy', in B. Barber (ed.), *Constructing the Social System*, pp. 165-91, New Brunswick: Transaction Publishers.

22. *Din Ve-Cheshbon Shel Histadrut Ha-Pekidim* [*Report by the Union of Clerks*], 1925-27; and *Divrei Ha-Kinus Ha-Artsi Ha-Rishon Shel Pekidei Batei Mischar* [*Minutes of The First National Assembly of Commercial Clerks*], Tel Aviv, May 1938.

23. A.Y.S.H., 'Ha-Pakid Ve-Ha-Yeshuv' ['The Clerk and the Jewish Settlement'], in *Michtave Chozer*, Agudat Ha- Pekidim, Yafo (1922), 3, LA/IV-43-25; see also the notion of the clerks' constructive role in the Zionist undertaking, in Histadrut Ha-Pekidim, *Alon Ha-Va'ad Ha- Merkazi*, **3**, (May 1933), 3; in 1931, membership of the clerks' union reached 1,522, mostly male clerks. Some 635 were employed in public Zionist institutions; 188, in public and private banks; 469, in private trading houses and offices; 86, in industry; 125 unemployed; and 19 were unclassified. None worked in the government because association was not allowed. In 1937 there were in Palestine 12,486 Jewish clerks (12 per cent of all Jewish workers): 1,475 worked for Zionist and Histadrut institutions; 1,054, in private and public banks; and only 305 in government. See *Din Ve-Cheshbon Shel Histadrut Ha-Pekidim* (August 1929-November 1931); Preuss, W. (1938), 'Tsibur Ha-Pekidim Be-Eretz Israel' ['The Clerks' Community in Palestine'], *Pinkas*, **1** (June), 4-7.

24. R., 'Matsav Ha-Pekidim Be-Eretz Israel' ['The Condition of the Clerks in Palestine'], *Michtave Chozer*, Aguadt Ha-Pekidim, Yafo,

1922, 3-6, LA/IV-143-25; Preuss, W. (1928), 'Pekidim Yehudim Be-Eretz Israel, Matsavam U-Tenaei Avodatam Be-5688' ['Jewish Clerks in Palestine, Their State and Working Conditions in 1928'], *Choveret Le-Inianei Ha-Pekidim* (Tishrei 5689) [September], p. 13; Roland, A. (1938), 'Im Hofa'at "Sifri'at Ha-Pakid"' ['With the Emergence of "The Clerk's Library"'], *Pinkas*, **9-10** (October), 8; 'Devar Ha-Va'ad Ha-Merkazi Shel Histadrut Ha-Pekidim' ['Leader of the Central Committee of the Union of Clerks'], *Shurot*, **5** (March 1939), 1.

25. *Tazkir Histadru Ha-Pekidim Be-Eretz Israel La-Va'ad Ha-Tsirim Ue-La-Va'ad Ha-Poel Shel Ha-Va'ad Ha-Yehudi Ha-Zemani* [*Memorandum of the Clerks' Union of Palestine to the Jewish Delegates' Committee and the Executive of the Jewish Temporary Committee*], February 1919, LA/IV-143-1; A. Globman, 'Ovdei Tenua o' Avdei Misrad' ['Movement Workers or Office Slaves'], *Pinkas* (1 March 1930), 3-6; Histadrut Ha-Pekidim, Senif Cheifa, *Bulletin*, **2** (January 1931), 1-4; Histadru Ha-Pekidim, *Din Ve-Cheshbon La-Ve'ida Ha-Revi'it Shel Ha-Histadrut Ha-Klalit* [*Union of Clerks Report to the Fourth General Convention of the Histadrut*] (1932); Baki, M. (1938), 'Lekach Echad Mini Rabim' ['One Lesson of Many'], *Pinkas*, **9-10** (October 1936), 4-7; 'Be-Ikvot Ha-Yamim' ['Following the Days'], *Shurot*, **2** (August), 1.

26. Misradai, D. (1938), 'Ovdei Misradim – Eich Itmechu Ba-Ta'asia?' ['Office Workers – How Would They Support Industry?'], *Shurot*, **3** (October), 11-12.

27. On national roles, see correspondence in 1931: LA/IV-236-1-115, and LA/IV-236-1-116; Histadrut Ha-Pekidim, *Alon Ha-Va'ad Ha-Merkazi*, **8** (July 1934); for Hebrew typewriters, see advertisement in Ivri'ia, *Pinkas*, **11-12** (February 1937).

28. For organisation see LA/IV-250-72-1-633; Histadrut Ha-Pekidim, *Din Ve-Cheshbon La-Ve'ida Ha-Chamishit Shel Histradru Ha-Pekidim* [*Union of Clerks' Report on the Its Fifth Convention*] (1933-41); Y. Ayalon, 'Ha-Hitstarfut Le-Histadrut Ha-Ovdim' ['The Joining of the Workers' Federation'], *Shurot*, **9-10** (December 1939), 5-6; for clerks in the private sector, see the minutes of *Ha-Kinus Ha-Artsi Ha-Rishon Sehl Pekidei Ha-Mischar* [*First National Convention of Commercial Clerks*], Tel Aviv, (May 1938); Ben-Gurion, D. (1925), 'Ha-Yi'ud Ha-Leumi Shel Ma'amad Ha-Poalim' ['The National Destiny of the Working Class'], *Kuntres*, **210** (24 Adar 5685) [20 March].

29. Nemirovsky, M. (1930), 'Matsaveinu Be-Pekidut Ha-Memshala' ['Our Condition in Government Clerking'], *Pinkas*, **1** (March), 11; note also the data on pp. 7-9 offered to support the argument that between 1921 and 1929 the share of the Jews in Palestine's population rose from 11.6 to 18.9 per cent but that of Jewish clerks

in government positions decreased from 26.2 to 22.5 per cent.

30. For the Singer affair, see *Din Ve-Cheshbon La-Ve'ida Ha-Shlishit Shel Ha-Histdrut Ha-Klalit* [*Report to the Third Histadrut Convention*] (1927), 59-60; for the 1946 strike, see *Shurot*, February-November, 1946; and *Be-Mivchan Ha-Ma'aseh*.

31. *Hachlatot Mo'etset Histadrut Ha-Pekidim* [*Resolutions of the Council of the Clerks' Union*] (17-19 December 1931), in Din Ve-Cheshbon. *Shel Histarut Ha-Pekidim La-Ve'ida Ha'Revi'it Shel Ha-Histadrut Ha-Klalit* [*Union of Clerks' Report to the Histadrut Fourth General Convention*] (1933), 26-9. The term 'Public [Mass or Community] of workers' was the labour movement's common substitute for class and was based on communal self-descriptions of the Jewish community in the Diaspora.

32. *Pekidut* referred to clerking and *avoda misradit* to office work. One writer of *Shurot*, the bulletin of the clerks' union and one of the best guides to clerks' discourse, gave himself the pen name of Misradai, thus creating an identity between the clerk and his workplace. This was quite common: construction union activists named themselves *banai*, builder; and industrial workers signed their names as *poal-charoshet* (industrial worker). Pseudonyms also protected individuals from the reaction of the authorities.

33. For differentiation between clerks, see Ger, 'Ha-Pekidut Ha-Tsiburit' ['Public Clerking'], *Ha-Poel Ha-Tsair*, **15-16** (15 Nissan 5679) [15 April 1919]; *Alon Chaverim* (2 Tishrei 5687) [10 September 1926], 8; W. Preuss, 'Pekidim Yehudim Be-Eretz Israel, Matsavam U-Tenaei Avodatam Be-5688' ['Jewish Clerks in Palestine, their State and Working Conditions in 1928'], in *Choveret Le-Inianei Ha-Pekidim* (Tishrei 5688) [September 1928], 13; for the trustworthy employee, see Walley, P. (1991), 'Negotiating the Boundaries of Engineering: Professionals, Managers and Manual Work', *Research in the Sociology of Organisations*, **8**, 191-215.

34. Argov, A. (1935), 'Al Chilufei Pekidim' ['On Exchanging Clerks'], *Pinkas*, **3** (October), 24.

35. Mo'etset Poalei Cheifa, *Din Ve-Cheshbon Shel Ha-Va'ad Ha-Poel Lishnat 5689-5690* [*Report of the Haifa Labour Council Executive for the Year 5689-5690*], Haifa (January 1931), 9; idem, *Din Ve-Cheshbon Al Pe'ulut Ha-Mo'atsa Be-5691* [*Report on the Activities of the Haifa Labour Council in 1931*], Haifa (January 1932), 18-19.

36. R. 'Matsav Ha-Pekidim Be-Eretz Israel' ['The Condition of the Clerks in Palestine'], in *Michtave Chozer*, Agudat Ha-Pekidim, Yafo (1922), 6, LA/IV-143-25; see also D. Weinryb, 'Me-Ha-Ba'aiot Ha-Sotsiologiot Ba-Arets' ['Among the Sociological Problems of the Country'], *Mozna'aim*, **5** (29), (Sivan 5697) [May-June 1937], 539-40.

37. For the building image, see Ben-Tovim, Y. L. (1930), 'Pekidim.

Aleph: Ha-Pinkasan' ['Clerks, A: The Bookkeeper'], *Pinkas* (March), 28; for the climate aspect, see Chaiut, B. (1938), 'Shmirat Ha-Bri'ut' ['Health Keeping'], *Pinkas* (October), 26; for the health aspect, see *Keitsad Ishmor Ha-Pakid Gufo? [How Shall the Clerk Maintain his Body?]*, Tel Aviv: Histadrut Ha-Pekidim Ve-Hapoel, 1938; for the 'mind-worker', see A, Khoushi, 'Havai Ha-Chaim Ve-Harama Ha-Tarbutit Shel Tsibur Ha-Ovdim' ['Way of Life and Cultural Level of the Public of Workers'], *Draft*, Abba Khousi Collection, Abba Khoushi Archives, Haifa University, File 19; for productivity, see Ger, 'Ha-Pekidut Ha-Tsiburit' ['Public Clerking'].

38.   Kaplan, U. (1937), *Keitsad Yemaleh Ha-Pakid Et Yemei Chufshato? [How Shall the Clerk Spend his Vacation Days?]*, Tel Aviv: Histadrut Ha-Pekidim. See also De Vries, David (1997), 'Productive Clerks: White Collar Productivism and State Building in Palestine's Jewish Community, 1920-1950', *International Review of Social History*, **42** (2).

39.   For Pakid and Tafkid, see Remez, D. (1936), 'Efod Bad' ['Cloth Efod'], *Pinkas*, **8-9** (April), 3-5; for the clerks' labourist past, see Nemirovsky, M. (1932), *Matsavam Shel Pekidei Batei Ha-Mischar [The Condition of Commercial Clerks]*, Tel Aviv: Histadrut Ha-Pekidim, 9, 11, 19; for the legacy of the Palestine Office, see Ha-Ma'arechet (1939) 'Devar Ha-Va'ad Ha-Merkazi Shel Histadrut Ha-Pekidim' ['Leader of the Central Committee of the Union of Clerks'], *Shurot*, **5** (March), 2.

40.   *Be-Mivchan Ha-Ma'aseh*, 4 and 7.

41.   'Be-Ikvot Ha-Yamim' ['Following the Days'], *Shirot 2* (August 1938), 1; Zvi Greenberg, 'Ha-Tafkid Ve-Ha-Ma'ase Shel Histadrut Ha-Pekidim Be-Medinat Israel' ['The Role and Practice of the Union of Clerks in the State of Israel'], *Shurot*, **91**, (2) (July-August 1949), 8-13. Between 1945 and 1949, the number of unionised clerks working in Jewish national institutions rose from 1,800 to 3,500 and those working in Histadrut institutions rose from 1,800 to 4,800, according to *Be-Mivchan Ha-Ma'ase*, 32; for data on the decline of clerking in the 1950s, see Rolbant, S. (1961), *Ha-Mivneh Ha-Demographi, Ha-Kalkali Ve-Ha-Chevrati Shel Tsibur Ha-Pekidim Be-Israel [The Demographic, Economic and Social Structure of the Clerks in Israel]*, Tel Aviv: Histadrut Ha-Pekidim, 55-6.

42.   For the national qualities of commercial clerking, see *Ha-Kinus Ha-Artsi Shel pekidei Ha-Mischar [The First National Assembly of Commercial Clerks]*, Tel Aviv, May 1948, 3.

43.   On the Mount Sinai image, see Ben-Tovim, Y. L. (1938), 'Pekidim' (Tsilumei Rega) ['Clerks' (Still Photographs)], *Shurot*, **4** (December), 6-7; on qualities, see Ben-Tovim, Y. L. (1930), 'Pekidim. Aleph: Ha-Pinkasan' ['Clerks. A: The Book-Keeper'],

Pinkas (March), 28; Histadrut Ha-Pekidim, *Alon Ha-Va'ad Ha-Merkazi Shel Histadrut Ha-Pekidim* [*Bulletin of the Central Committee of the Union of Clerks*] (June 1934), 18-19; Flanberg, D. (1935), 'Mitsvot Aseh Le-Pekidei Ha-Mischar' ['Positive Precepts to Commercial Clerks'], *Pinkas*, **4-5** (December), 22-3.

44. For stenography, see Mimon, Y. (1928), 'Al Ha-Stinographia Ve-Atidoteha' ['On Stenography and its Future'], *Choveret Le-Inianei Ha-Pekidim* (Tishrei 5689) [September], 28-30; for professionalization, see 'Be-Ikvot Ha-Yamim' ['Following the Days'], *Shurot*, 4 (December 1938), 1; and Lubetkin, M. (1935), 'Be-Oto Inian' ['On the Same Issue'], *Pinkas*, **4-5** (December), 18-19; for support of Taylorism, see Bernstein, Y. (1930), 'Ha-Irgun Ha-Mada'I Ba-Avoda Ha-Misradit' ['The Scientific Organisation of Office Work'] *Pinkas*, **2** (September), 6-12; for clerks as national builders, see Haft, Y. (1939), 'Boker Tov Haya' ['Good Morning that Was'], *Shurot*, **5** (March), 2; for the educational aspects, see Zavol, G. A. (1938), 'Ha-She'elot Shel Pe'ilut Tarbutit Bein Pekidei Ha-Mischar' ['The Questions of Cultural Activity Among Commercial Clerks'], *Ha-Kinus Ha-Artsi Ha-Rishon Shel Pekidei Ha-Mischar* [*The First National Assembly of Commercial Clerks*], Tel Aviv, May, 18-21.

45. Ch. Ben-Ze'ev (1930), 'Pekidei Misradim U-Batei Mischar' ['Office Clerks and Commercial Establishments'], Pinkas, **2** (September), 32. The writer also alludes to the European notion of the contrast between appearance and income: 'La misère en habit-noir'.

46. For the struggle against cuts in Zionist national institutions, see for example LA/IV-236-2-227. Histadrut Ha-Pekidim, *Din Ve-Chesbon* [*Report of the Clerks' Union*] (August 1929-November 1931); Argov, A. (1935), 'Al Chilufei Pekidim' ['On Exchanging Clerks'], *Pinkas*, **2** (October), 23-5. See also the clerks' union correspondence with the Jewish Agency in Histadrut Ha-Pekidim, *Din Ve-Cheshbon La-Ve'ida Ha-Revi'it Shel Ha-Histadrut Ha-Klalit* [*Union of Clerks' Report to the Histadrut Fourth General Convention*] (1933); Meltser, N. (1958), 'Me-Saviv Le-Ba'aiat Ha-Ye'ul Ba-Pekidut' ['On the Problem of Making Clerical Work More Efficient'], *Shurot*, **169** (January), 6.

47. Ch. Gavrielli, 'Ha-Politika Ha-Ta'arifit Shel Histradut Ha-Pekidim' ['The Tariff Politics of the Clerks' Union'], Choveret, *Le-Inianei Ha-Pekidim* (Tishrei 5689) [September 1928], 14.

48. For images of collective bargaining, see LA/IV-250-36-1-1895-a and LA/IV-250-36-1-1896; Bendix, L. (1938), 'Chozeh Ha-Avoda Ve-Erko La-Oved Ha-Ivri' ['The Work Contract and its Value for the Jewish Worker'], *Shurot*, **3** (October), 8; for non-unionised clerks, see LA/IV-250-27-1-61-B.

49. On 'cushion devices', see for example LA/IV-250-72-1-3215 and

LA/IV-236-1-104.

50. This ambiguity is reflected in the relations between the Haifa Labour Council and the local branch of the clerks' union. See LA/IV-236-1-118 and 119. For the dual loyalty, see Repetor, B. (1937), 'Ha-Pakid Be-Tenu'at Ha-Avoda' ['The Clerk in the Labour Movement'], *Pinkas*, **11-12** (February), 9; and LA/IV-236-1-84.

51. For qualifications, see LA/IV-250-36-1-1898-a; Weinryb, D. (1938), 'Me-Ba'aiot Ha-Pekidut Ha-Yehudit' ['Among the Problem of Jewish Clerking'], *Shurot*, **4** (December), 3-4; Immanuel D. (1951), 'Rationalizasia Be-Avodat Ha-Misrad' ['Rationalisation in Office Work'], *Shurot*, **113** (May), 7.

52. For clerks' union as an umbrella organisation, see Histadrut Ha-Pekidim, *Din Ve-Cheshbon a-Ve'ida Ha-Chamishitm* for the great chain image, see the short introduction by the editor of *Shurot*, **23-4** (September 1941), 1; see also the national language of urban labour in De Vries, D. (1994), 'Proletarianisation and National Segregation: Haifa in the 1920s', *Middle Eastern Studies*, **30** (4), 860-82. In 1922, only 6 per cent, or 500, of 8,500 Histadrut members were also members of the clerks' union. In January 1949, the share of unionised clerks among Histadrut members had risen to 21.7 per cent (20,400 in the clerks' union out of 94,000. These numbers did not include spouses nor 9,000 state employees, including 5,000 clerks and 4,000 in the police, public works and transport). In 1949, the clerks' union membership in Jerusalem constituted 29.8 per cent of the town's Histadrut membership; in Haifa, 20.7 per cent; and in Tel Aviv, 22.2 per cent. See *Be-Mivachn Ha-Ma'aseh,* and *Beshnot Ha Shloshim*, **3-5**, 335.

53. M. Krupnik, 'Histadrut Ha-Pekidim' ['The Union of Clerks'], *Kuntres*, **258** (2 Iyar 5686) [16 April 1926].

54. Ha-Ma'arechet, 'Be-Ikvot Ha-Yamim' ['After These Days'], *Shurot*, **2** (August 1938), 1.

55. Repetor, B. (1937), 'Ha-Pakid Be-Tenu'at Ha-Avoda' ['The Clerk in the Labour Movement'], *Pinkas*, **11-12** (February), 8-9; for the role of clerks in a socialist economy, see Meltser, N. (1938), 'Ha-Matsav Ha-Kalali Shel Pekidei Ha-Mischar' ['The General Condition of Commercial Clerks'], *Ha-Kinus Ha-Artsi Ha-Rishon Shelo Pekidei Ha-Mischar [The First National Assembly of Commercial Clerks]*, Tel Aviv (May), 3; see also the poem by Shalom, Sh. (1951), 'Pekid Medinat Israel' ['The State of Israel's Clerk'], *Shurot*, **109** (January), 1.

56. For autonomy, see for instance the case of Haifa in Mo'etset Poalei Cheifa, *Din Ve-Cheshbon*, 1931, 9; for the alter conflict, see *Be-Mivchan Ha-Ma'aseh;* on unionising state clerks see LA/IV-72-1-2368-c. In 1956, 25 per cent of Histadrut membership were clerks (including state employees). Clerks in industry and manufacture

constituted only 20.2 per cent; see Har-Paz, C. (1960), 'Shinu'im Demographi'im Ve-Chevrati'im Be-Uchlusi'at Ha-Histadrut' ['Demographic and Social Changes in the Population of the Histadrut'], *Mo'ed: Yovel Ha-Arabai'im Shel Ha-Histadrut* [*Fortieth Anniversary of the Histadrut*], Tel Aviv: Histadrut, 605.

57. Histadrut Ha-Pekidim, *Din Ve-Cheshbon Shel Histadrut Ha-Pekidim La-Tekufa Yanuar 1950-Mertz 1952* [*Union of Clerks Report for the Period January 1950-March 1952*], Tel Aviv: Histadrut Ha-Pekidim, 1952; Amir, I. (1959), *Histadrut Ha-Pekidim Be-Yerushala'im Ba-Asor Ha-Rishon La-Medina* [*The Union of Clerks in Jerusalem during the State's First Decade*], Jerusalem: Histadrut Ha-Pekidim.

58. On the notion of service, see S. N. Eisenstadt (1967), *Israeli Society*, London: Weidenfeld and Nicolson, ch. 1; for a local example see S. Kodesh (ed.) (1953), *Ma'asim: Ha-Histadrut Be-Cheifa Ba-Shanim 1945-1953* [*Deeds: The Histadrut in Haifa in the Years 1945-1953*], Haifa: Mo'etset Poalei Cheifa, pp. 14-16, 27-53.

59. Ben-Moshe, (1948) 'Mangenon Ha-Medina Ha-Ivrit Ve-Tsibur Ha-Pekidim' ['The Jewish State Apparatus and the Community of Clerks'], *Shurot*, **76** (January), 5-6; Cohen, Tsvi (1948), 'Histadrut Ha-Pekidim Be-Shnat Tav-Shin-Chet' ['The Union of Clerks in 5708'], *Shurot*, **84** (October), 2-5; *Be-Mivchan Ha-Ma'aseh;* Greenburg, Z. (1950), 'Tarbut Ivrit Ve-Chinuch Pekidim' ['Hebrew Culture and Education of Clerks'], *Shurot*, **108** (December), 4-7. Telephonistit (1950), 'Ha-Telphonist'iot' ['The Women-Telephonists'], *Shurot*, **104** (August), 17. Feminisation is reflected in the fact that between 1931 and 1961 the share of Jewish women in the Jewish labour force employed in governmental and public services increased from approximately 11.7 per cent to 20.8 per cent, and their share in the Jewish labour force employed in the private sector of commerce, banking and insurance increased from 10.4 per cent to 27.4 per cent. See Mills, E. (1961), *The Census of Palestine, 1931* (Alexandria), vol. 2, and (1961), *Population and Housing Census 1961* (Jerusalem), vol. 21, pp. 18-23.

60. Gieryn, T. F. (1983), 'Boundary-Work and the Demarcation of Science from Non-Science: Strains and Interests in Professional Ideologies of Scientists', *American Sociological Review*, **48** (6), 781-95; Giddens, A. (1979), *Central Problems in Social Theory* (Berkeley: University of California Press), ch. 5. See also De Vries, D. (1997), 'Productive Clerks: White-Collar Productivism and State-Building in Palestine's Jewish Community, 1920-1950', *International Review of Social History*, **42**.2 (August), 202-18.

61. Swidler, A. (1986), 'Culture in Action: Symbols and Strategies', *American Sociological Review*, **51** (2), 273-86.

62. Chazan, H. (1994), 'Talking Community: The Rhetorical Construc-

tion of a Social Concept', *Israel Social Science Research*, **9** (1-2), 49-50; and Tilly, C. (1995), 'Citizenship, Identity and Social History', *International Review of Social History*, **40**; Supplement, 5-8.

63. Calhoun, C. (1980), 'Community: Toward a Variable Conceptualisation for Comparative Research', *Social History*, **5**, 107-27; Littler, C. R. (1982), *The Development of the Labour Process in Capitalist Societies*, London: Heinemann, pp. 38-42; Herf, J. (1984), *Reactionary Modernism: Technology, Culture and Politics in Weimar and the Third Reich*, p. 16, Cambridge: Cambridge University Press.

64. Compare with Lockwood, *The Blackcoated Worker*, pp. 125-33.

65. See also Kocka, J. (1981), 'Class Formation, Interest, Articulation and Public Policy: The Origins of the German White-Collar Class in the Late Nineteenth and Early Twentieth Centuries', in S. Berger (ed.), *Organising Interests in Western Europe*, pp. 63-81, Cambridge: Cambridge University Press.

66. Kocka, *White Collar Workers in America*, pp. 267-84.

67. See Somers, M. (1992), 'Narrativity, Narrative Identity, and Social Action: Rethinking English Working Class Formation', *Social Science History*, **16** (4), 607-9.

CHAPTER THREE

British Jewry and Labour Politics, 1918-39

Deborah Osmond

This chapter aims to examine British Labour politics in relation to issues of 'Jewishness' in public and political life. The concept of 'Jewishness' is discussed in the light of the impact of the First World War, and with regard to the role played by gender and sexuality in defining the Jewish image. The chapter then turns to the world of Labour.

The Impact of the First World War

David Feldman and others have suggested that in London, the Anglo-Jewish élite was always notable for its affiliations with the institutions of the propertied classes.[1] The First World War, however, altered perceptions of Jewish integration in public life. While it was not the sole reason for shifts or changes in political and social acculturation, the war did expand the grounds for new and often contradictory expressions of citizenship and Britishness. Organs of the London press, such as the *East London Observer* (*ELO*) praised Jews for their 'response to the call' and noted the Jewish presence in the war effort as a display of patriotic duty. Both the 'sons of alien parents' and 'the great Jewish families of England' contributed their quota.[2] By the end of the war, there were no less than 5,000 entries into His Majesty's forces of Yiddish-speaking reserve constables from the East End, and Jewish soldiers in the services.[3] Newspapers such as the *ELO* emphasised the unification of British Jews with their 'Russian brethren' fighting for the Tsar in the Russian-British allied forces.[4] Participation in the war on both sides bestowed a greater sense of approval on these Jewish efforts to display a new public spiritedness, albeit one celebrated mostly for its elements of difference. Later, however, the *ELO* aroused suspicion about unnaturalised Jews who refused to cooperate under the Military Service Agreement between Britain and Russia in 1917. The act made conscription into the British forces mandatory for Jewish males, or else they were liable for deportation.[5] As Geoffrey Alderman explains, within the East End ghetto attitudes towards the perceived legitimacy of Britain's fight with Germany and Jewish conscription were mixed, because Jews on either side might potentially kill each other, an act of profanity for all religious Jews.[6] Before the Military Service Agreement in 1916, the *ELO* expressed disgust for the Jewish immigrant who expressed any reluctance to being a soldier:

> If the Government show weakness in their determination and allow themselves to become victims of the 'political refugee' trick, we fear the consequences will be serious. The misbehaviour of any offensive foreign bounder, or the impertinence of a Whitechapel Jew boy, may light the smouldering fires of native feeling.[7]

The contradictory impressions of Anglo-Jewish patriotism especially as it was observed in the East End districts, was not diminished after 1918. Alderman argues that although the war had ended, and no Jew could be classified as an enemy alien, there was still a great deal of popular and media pressure which branded Jews as potential traitors and untrustworthy citizens.[8]

This period reflects the conflicting attitudes towards Anglo-Jewry in the public world, but also Jewish communities' internal contradictions about their own representation. Celebrated author of Anglo-Jewish cultural and political life, Israel Zangwill, declared at the beginning of the War that '[t]here is, indeed, no country so beloved by the Jews as England'.[9] That Zionism had placed its legalised centre in London under the auspices of the World Zionist Organisation (WZO) also contributed to the conception of England as a safe haven, not only for Jewish patriotism; the presence of Zionism in London endorsed an image of a pluralistic nation, tolerant of other forms of Jewish political expression. Furthermore, the declaration of the British Mandate in Palestine after 1917 injected a new legitimacy into popular attitudes towards Jewish identity during the post-war era.[10] Calling themselves 'Englishmen of the Jewish persuasion', the League of British Jews was formed a week after Balfour fomented opposition to the idea of a political homeland.[11] Founded by Conservative MP Lionel de Rothschild, and Sir Philip Magnus, the League of British Jews also demonstrated the fragmented consensus and the vacillating notions of Britishness and Jewish nationhood. That it was possible to display different political and religious fealties – to be a Jew and not a Zionist – gave greater purchase to Anglo-Jewry in public life during the period. It did, however, create some confusion.

In the period following the First World War, popular slogans such as the 'rights of small nations' and a more pluralistic notion of Britishness imbued Labour politics, providing a new forum for addressing Anglo-Jewish identity within Labour's understanding of socialist Zionism and Palestine.[12] Mapping the inter-war period in Anglo-Jewish political culture affords an opportunity to discuss at least some of the tensions which existed in representations of 'Jewishness', as well as the factors which created new attitudes towards the social and cultural integration of Jewish Britons.

To suggest that the inter-war period was one of complete transformation for Jewish Britons is, however, a simplification. Rather, Jewish life experienced small but significant changes in local strains of political culture. As Julia Frances Bush and others have suggested, in 1918 'Jews began, for the first time, to enter the foreground of East London politics'.[13] The cause of this had less to do with demographic expansion than with the halt to immigration which made integration – both political and social – more of a likelihood. Furthermore, as Bush argues, integration was also caused by the fact that the 'foreignness of the ghetto' could not outlive the original generation of immigrants. Assimilatory habits, however, were varied, as the international nature of Jewish immigration was still a factor and 'living reality', especially in East London.[14] Still, the patriotism brought by the War and the gradual divestment of the area's 'foreignness' reflected radical shifts in the way 'Jewishness' was portrayed in public life. The alien features of the Jewish East End, once seen as a 'Hebrew colony'[15] did not completely disappear after 1918, but the war and generational differences became a new barometer through which public apprehensions about Jewish life could be measured differently.

Integration 'habits' in political culture also changed. Anglo-Jewish oscillation between the political left and right began to merit the nation's attention. In 1926, for instance, commentary in the *ELO* suggested that acculturation commanded a more direct influence upon the political geography of London. Even a suspected shift in voting loyalties to the Conservative Party – however slight – expanded the grounds for understanding the cultural and political readjustments within communities. Whether immigrants posed a 'foreign threat' in the wake of the war, Jews came to be seen as Britons rather than immigrants, voters rather than aliens. In 1926, the *ELO* reported that the change in political orientation amongst Jews vanquished the fringe socialist element seen as part of the alien menace:

> Sooner or later, we suppose someone will come forward to claim the Jewish vote, which, formally Liberal, has now gone over entirely to modern conservatism, which can hardly be distinguished today from the moderate Liberalists of the middle and late Victorian era. The Jewish 'Reds', despite their noisy harangues and dirty looks, do not really count in this journey.[16]

The need for separateness, whether it be through Yiddish-speaking trade unions, political parties and newspapers such as *Polishe Yidel* (*Little Polish Jew*) and *Arbeiter Friend* (*Workers' Friend*) may have dwindled by the end of 1918. The indefatigable presence of 'Jewishness' in public life, beleaguered with a complex number of political associations, did not. This was especially apparent in the world of labour. Discussion about the 'Jewishness' of labour by groups such as the Fabian socialists, and the wider movement in general, articulated a prescriptive definition of the Jewish working class.

The Role of Gender and Sexuality

Although it is not linked so closely to the exterior components of labour's relationship with Zionism and Jewish political culture, acknowledging the role of gender and sexuality within this discussion helps to illustrate the images associated with 'Jewishness' which penetrated labour politics during the period. Using gender analysis as an introduction to the history of Anglo-Jewish identity in the Labour movement is a useful way of understanding more generally the public perceptions of 'Jewishness' as they came to be formed in the twentieth century. Underlying most representations of ethnic identities exists the complex role played by women as the intrinsic possessors, or, biological carriers 'of the race'.[17] Within the context of modern Jewish history, recent work by Paula E. Hyman has argued that in Western societies, Jewishness and femininity have frequently been conflated, often resulting in Judaism's burdensome association with cultural and political abnormalities.[18]

Gender analysis in the history of Jewish political culture shows that the weaknesses commonly attributed to women have been placed categorically upon Jewish communities as a whole. This has been reinforced by the rigid norms dictating the modern Western understanding of the separate spheres, the realms traditionally occupied by men and women. In the post-emancipation societies of Western Europe and North America, the limited role of women in public life was often challenged by the economic realities facing Jewish immigrants. In the late nineteenth and twentieth centuries, for instance, Eastern European immigrants and their children contested the boundaries between domestic and public life that characterised middle-class gender norms.[19] Furthermore, as Hyman suggests, the role of the mother as the upholder of religious ritual and values became increasingly important during the process of assimilation by which immigrant families integrated into middle-class culture. In 1875, for instance, the London *Jewish Chronicle* commented with apprehension that 'there is no feature of the age more dangerous or more distressing than the growing irreligion of women'.[20]

This particular fear was by no means unique to the English or British milieu; concerns such as these were articulated in all societies of the West where Jewish communities had experienced civic emancipation and subsequent assimilation. German-Jewish newspapers at the turn of the century also commented upon the role of women 'who carry the world on their shoulders by caring for the home ... If the religion of the home falls, so does the world of religion'.[21]

The bourgeois ideal of femininity often impeded women's access to the public sphere and also saw religiosity as an appendage of feminine behaviour; and so, women retained greater 'markers' for Jewishness than did men. There were exceptions, albeit only a few, who received any attention

58

and much greater notoriety for their public exhibition. The 'salon Jewesses' of the nineteenth century, the most well-known of which included Rahel Varnhagen, Dorothea Mendelssohn and Henrietta Herz, found temporary sanctuary in the company of Berlin's intellectual élite. Still, the tide of anxiety amongst community and religious elders who inculcated women's strict preservation of the 'sacred realm' – religious education, dietary habits, such as the keeping of a kosher kitchen, and especially philanthropy – also determined that the outward landscape of class identity in public life remained vastly encoded with the culture of Jewish masculinity. In Britain in the twentieth century, Sally Alexander's recent work on women in the interwar years provides a glimpse of this in the world of labour. In her study 'Memory, Generation and History', Alexander describes one historical actor as distinguishing between her feminine self, and her own personal history, and the masculinity of a political culture to which she became associated because of her Jewish background.[22] Within the British context, Alexander's exploration of the connection between gender and Jewish identity in Labour politics has made an invaluable contribution, and helped to establish historical interpretation in an area where it is obviously needed. As Gareth Stedman Jones has suggested, the language of class in England has developed without the force of pre-existing notions of citizenship and, in contrast to the French and American models, state republicanism.[23] It has, however, faced competing forms of discourse from within existing class structure, and the elusive languages of class have often exhibited imprints of the tension between ethnicity and gender.[24] As Alexander has shown, masculinity played a potentially important role in perceptions of Anglo-Jewish class politics. Although it is outside the realm of this chapter, tracing the construction of a masculine class language during the inter-war period reveals what has always been on the surface of Jewish relations to class and labour in Britain. The writing of Israel Zangwill at the turn of the century exhibits this tension most saliently. Many of his stories express the repulsive complementarity of Jewishness and femininity in public life. Illustrated most flagrantly in his novel *Ghetto Tragedies* (1892), the depiction of the synagogue and Jewish women are turned into a burlesque, where wives are brought to sit 'in their wigs and earrings behind a curtain which cut them off from the view of the men. The general ungainliness of their figures and the unattractiveness of their low-browed, high cheekboned and heavy jawed faces would have made this pious precaution appear somewhat superfluous to an outsider'.[25] Anglo-Jewish life, in both fictional accounts and political culture, reflected the lack of concord between religiousness and gender, as well as the tension this created in occupation and class structure.

Just as gender and the role of women is inextricably linked to any comprehensive study of Judaism, and has often been undervalued as a useful category for analysis in the modern Jewish historical context, the realm of this outward and predominantly male Jewish culture within 'class' needs to be investigated in greater detail. Indeed, the history of Eastern European Jewish migration can be seen as an aperture through which to view the ways prescribed notions of class often reset the parameters of its own boundaries.[26] These include how gender roles were redefined and reordered, and also the political and national concerns offset by the various permutations and changes in class identification over time.

It follows that in twentieth century Jewish life, masculinity became a dominant, if not all-encompassing feature in the discursive realm of political culture.[27] The position of women as the upholders of 'domestic Judaism' did not entirely seal off their visibility from public view. Rather, the features to Jewish political culture in Britain – and perhaps all of the West – were earmarked by masculine 'versions' of 'Jewishness' removed from the cultural or religious rituals within the structure of the domestic and private sphere. Of course, there remain many exceptions, especially in North America as scholars of Jewish and feminist history have shown in recent years.[28]

The fissure between the religiosity of the domestic and public realms meant that Jewish public life accommodated, or at least allowed itself in varying degrees to be permeated with, notions of Britishness, citizenship and 'respectability'. And yet, as Stedman Jones and others have suggested, in England more than any other country, the word 'class' 'has acted as a congested point of intersection between many competing, overlapping or simply differing forms of discourse – political, economic, religious and cultural – right across the political spectrum'.[29] One point of similarity in accounts of Jewish labour is that the articulation of difference, and what Hyman and others have called 'Otherness' traditionally used in the nineteenth century to describe the Gentile, was used with its own internal logic demarcating 'Jewishness' and its qualities. This imaging of difference between the Jew and Gentile can be seen most clearly in the *Chronicle*'s depiction of British Prime Minister Benjamin Disraeli:

> ... the chief interest in this unparalleled career does not lie for the Jewish community in the Jewish descent of the Earl ... but rather in his having throughout his life glorified the race from which he sprang, identified himself with its history, and thus reflected ray of his own lustre upon the community in which he was born and from which he was estranged apparently by a mere accident. Unlike some other men of Jewish descent who achieved greatness, and who denied the rock whence they were hewn, BD (Benjamin Disraeli) prided himself upon his extraction. BD belongs to the Jewish people, despite his baptismal certificate. His talents, his virtues and shortcomings alike, are purely of Jewish cast.[30]

Praised and admired by the Anglo-Jewish press, Jewish working men at the turn of the twentieth century were described in much the same way as during the Chartist campaign. Although, like the *Chronicle*'s depiction of Disraeli, they could not 'escape' their Jewishness. In his lecture on behalf of the Jewish Working Men's Lecture Association, the Revd A. L. Green[31] gave the following address, describing Jewish working men as filled with aspirations to be amongst the highest order of English aristocrats, with the honourability and integrity of the proverbial working Englishman:

> ... from the lowest they rapidly mount, when they will, to the highest steps of the ladder of social and political life; and two generations enables them, and sometimes one generation alone sufficeth, to exchange Cox's Square for Grosvenor Square; Petticoat Lane for Park Lane; and Booker's Gardens for Clarendon Gardens. The poor have done this – as you know to our national credit – and will do it again; they are made of the finest ringing metal, and if they but screw their courage to the sticking post, there is no reason why at no very distant day many who are now among what is termed toilers, and to whom the word toil has a painful significance – there is no reason ... why they should not be among the Brasseys, the Morleys, the Morrisons, and the Peabodys of the age, and take rank among our own eminent and successful men, and induced by the same leverage, unflagging industry, commanding intelligence, and unsullied integrity.[32]

Similarly, in a report on the Jews of Middlesborough in Yorkshire, Jews are described as poor but 'really hard-working men, striving by dint of toil to obtain a livelihood'.[33] Far from being strictly the view of the intellectual élite, the possibilities for such Jewish social and cultural integration into the working classes meant that assimilation at the turn of the century became a possibility through labour. Still, the realm of possibility determined later by the war, and integration as a natural by-product of generational differences, did not impart unqualified Britishness within labour's realm.

The World of Labour

If London's *Jewish Chronicle* is any indication, the subject of 'Jewish' labour aroused significant attention. Moreover, precisely the elements which perpetuated the dichotomy between the 'separate spheres' of religiosity and secularism – whether seen in the context of gender or in terms of class politics – infused discussions of Jewish labour. In March 1921, the *Chronicle* issued a supplement to their regular edition newspaper called 'The Labour Problem in Rabbinic Literature' by Revd A. Cohen. Cohen's article carried a tone of lament for what he regarded as the loss of spirituality in contemporary labour:

> One of the most urgent problems of our day is the state of ferment in the world of labour. This unrest not only causes serious disturbances in

61

business intercourse, thus checking the even flow of trade, but it hinders the establishment of peaceful conditions within the State which is an essential pre-requisite to the task of reconstruction after the ravages of war ... If we penetrate deep enough, shall we not discover that fundamentally there exists a psychological obstruction to the path of peace and contentment? Is there something in the mentality of the working class which tends to breed strife, and, until its elimination has been successfully accomplished, will continue to hinder the possibility of a final settlement?[34]

The conclusion Cohen made in terms of finding this 'final settlement' is that work, and more specifically, ideas about manual labour, should be viewed by British Jews precisely as the ancient rabbis did: as a divine gift 'ordained by God for the welfare of man'. According to Cohen, the troubled condition of trade unionism and socialism in Britain had been caused by the labourer, who was 'too self-centred'. The labourer debased the intellect to the point where it 'belittles the part which is played by brain, and hence exaggerates his own importance'.[35]

Cohen believed that the relationship between employer and the employed should be interdependent, where both accepted mutual responsibility for the other. He scorned the notion that both parties had entitlement to articulating their exclusive interests. The consequences for neglecting such a responsibility were that the 'labour world becomes an explosive magazine where at any moment a spark may cause an upheaval and widespread disturbance'.[36] The rabbi also made implicit references to a specifically Anglo-Jewish audience. His choice of writing in the *Jewish Chronicle* about the unwieldy power of British trade unions against the 'divine gift' of labour suggested that he had a specifically Jewish audience in mind.

Despite his description of a universally self-absorbed labour mentality, Cohen's article prompted much negative response from readers of the paper. 'If Mr. Cohen does not desire to confine his remarks ... to Jews' wrote a Mr Gunter from Stepney, 'but directs his attacks against Labour, irrespective of creed or race, why write to the Jewish Chronicle?'[37] Letters to the editor also called into question Cohen's pejorative view of Soviet Russia. For many British Jews, the new Soviet republic came to be regarded as the safest haven against political anti-Semitism, and the decline of persecution and pogroms seen as the result of Jewish absorption into the Soviet proletariat masses. The novels of Simon Blumenfeld, such as *Jew Boy* (1931) and *Phineas Kahn: Portrait of an Immigrant* (1937) depict the anglicised second generation of East London's Jewish families in the 1920s and 1930s 'looking to the East' and to the great 'Soviet Experiment' as a refuge and sanctuary cleansed of anti-Semitism and capitalist exploitation. Blumenfeld's work provides an accurate although fictional telescope into an aspect of Anglo-Jewish life, reflecting the central place of class in community structure. In this respect,

Cohen's article echoed serious concerns about the political and cultural associations made between class and Jewish identity during the period.

Another response, in the *Jewish Chronicle*'s letters to the editor from a Mr Isidore Warstki, demanded that Labour deserved sympathy and respect, instead of posing more incendiary attacks at a time when unemployment in Britain had reached unprecedented heights.[38] Mr Gunter's letter in the following passage, however, is more direct:

> Today, even as in the time of Moses, the worship of the golden calf flourishes amazingly, and not least in the synagogue. To bring up the new generation with a better and more humane conception, we also need a Moses, who will lead us into a land flowing with the milk of human kindness, where bouquets are not handed out to the rich and scorn and hatred to the workers.[39]

The metaphysical connotations attached to Labour and the repercussions for its 'secularisation' were not uncommon issues discussed in both political and religious circles in Britain.

What informed Jewish attitudes to Labour practice, such as concern over the upholding of a peaceful state, also traversed political and particularly socialist circles. Moreover, the *Jewish Chronicle*, the 'mouthpiece of progressive upper-middle-class Jewry' made inferences about distinctly Jewish attitudes to Labour which found expression in the rhetoric of the wider labour movement and Labour Party.[40] Labour leader and Prime Minister Ramsay MacDonald's *A Socialist in Palestine* (1922), for instance, credited 'Jewishness' and Labour as the twinned elements to 'good socialism' in his portrayal of the co-operatives and farming achievements of Jewish settlers in Palestine. MacDonald, as Paul Kelemen points out, referred to other considerations which argued that Jewish Labour practice in Palestine deprived the Arab claim to self-determination of 'complete validity'.[41] MacDonald believed that the Arab populations 'did not and cannot use or develop the resources of Palestine' and, more importantly, that 'Palestine and the Jews can never be separated'.[42] Furthermore, the 'New Jew', the labourer in Palestine, intuitively turned the Middle Eastern landscape into a British oasis. For MacDonald, the Jewish presence made the East more palatable, and the British element to the appearance of settlements and cities provided a familiar point of cultural reference:

> When one walks through Tel-Aviv and sees its trim fresh houses, its shops, its little factories, its printing establishments, the illusion of Palestine vanishes. One feels as though this place were across no sea, as though it were a short railway journey from London or any other Western town. It might be an English watering-place with a Continental touch about it. But when one has done the sights and sits down in the bright sun-bathed room in the hotel whither I was brought, and asks from the interested ones the meaning and purpose of it, the material conditions

fade and the idealism behind it comes out. Then one begins to understand the nature of the Return; and this mingling of work and faith, of materialist energy and idealist spirit, meets one throughout Palestine.[43]

It is precisely the 'almost English' element which made Jewish Zionist labour so remarkable and justifiable as a political cause. The ideal of a Jewish national homeland was actually a Palestine in dissolution, a place where labourers carried the markings of the English and mimicked its civility. It is arguable that, as Feldman and others have suggested, the discourse on the Jews of Palestine was not strictly about Jews alone.[44] Rather, in this case it reflected Labour leader Ramsay MacDonald's conception of an embryonic national identity and its utopian possibilities with constructive British elements.

Later in the 1930s, Susan Pethick Lawrence, a member of the Labour Party NEC remarked that the Jewish settlements in Palestine were 'utopian', and that 'Jews had introduced elementary Labour legislation, recognised the principles of trade union organisation and established co-operative settlement'.[45] Lawrence thought the co-operatives in Palestine were reminiscent of William Morris' utopian novel *News from Nowhere* (1896), and in general an inspiration to Western socialists.

These aspects of understanding Jewish Labour, and the advocacy of a political and religious homeland for the Jews, affords an opportunity to evaluate more closely the relationship between ethnicity and Labour's idea of nation and the working classes. Post-colonial theory and the work of Homi K. Bhabha, Anne McClintock, Reina Lewis and others is useful for providing analyses of race, imperialism and its relationship to conceptions of statehood and class consciousness in the nineteenth and twentieth centuries. It also helps to decipher the ambiguity of British political and social attitudes toward Jewish communities in both Britain and Palestine. In *The Location of Culture* (1994), for instance, Bhabha emphasises that the 'global link between colony and metropolis' aided in part the formation of new identities which developed out of the relationship between coloniser and colonised. Taken from the perspective of Bhabha, MacDonald's contribution to the discourse on 'Jewish' issues helped to redefine the relationship between Jews of the 'colony', or mandated territory, with their Jewish metropolitan counterpart in London.[46] The Labour Party never planned to treat Palestine, and for that matter Britain's only other mandated territory, Transjordania, as a colony. Labour's colonial policy, however, emphasised the primacy of socialisation and self-government, and carried the same sentiments as those observed by MacDonald in Palestine in the early 1920s created by Jewish settlers.[47]

Jewish labourers and workers created idyllic working class communities with British characteristics, and consequently perpetuated a juxtaposition between British Jews and those who had fled Europe to the settlements of

64

Palestine.[48] The contrast tended to demonstrate the superiority of Jews in the East. As Theodor Herzl, founder of the modern political Zionist movement in Europe had promulgated at the turn of the century, '[I]t is under the sign of Labour that the Jewish people is going to Palestine … when the Jewish peasant again holds the plough firmly in his hands, the Jewish question will be solved'.[49] In keeping with Herzl's proposed solution, the political and spiritual cartography of Judaism could be settled in Palestine. However, for MacDonald, this could be mediated by a British element. Similarly, *Poale Zion* declared at the outbreak of the Second World War to the 39th Annual Conference of the Labour Party at Bournemouth that only in a Jewish national home 'the puzzle of the world, will find rest. The Jews will become once more a normal people'.[50] For Labour, the inter-war years were an era of reflection and ideas of Jewish identity became inextricably linked to these images of a socialist Palestine.

Finally, from MacDonald's accounts, the nexus between the spiritual and physical components of Jewish labour in Palestine rendered the combination of both 'Jewishness' and Labour an unfinished social and religious product in the Diaspora. This incongruity between Labour and 'Jewishness' outside Palestine became the central rallying point from which MacDonald and pro-Zionist labourites, such as London Labour Party leader Herbert Morrison in the 1930s, argued for Jewish rights to a national homeland. While Labour's political concerns and personal understanding of Jewish identity should not be conflated, MacDonald's version of Jewishness became seminal in the formation of Labourist discourse on Palestine. For MacDonald – and for Labour during the 1920s – the socialist Jew in the Diaspora was near to a cultural and political oxymoron. Labour's conception of the Jew had spiritual and political qualities which could only be rejuvenated effectively through a return to a Jewish homeland. As shown in MacDonald's recollections, the socialist definition of Labour relied upon a spiritual essence in which in any other environment rendered the Jew bereft of political vitality and authentic religious feeling:

> Nothing is stranger for the blasé materialist and man of the world to see how in recent years, from every nation under the sun, Jews – the proletariat from whom has been crushed almost the last remnant of national tradition and religious belief, equally with the bourgeoisie whose prosperity has brought upon them a similar fate – have listened to this alluring call, and their hearts have gone back to Palestine.[51]

Conclusion

When viewed in relation to the historiography of modern Jewry, the labour left's articles and impressions about Palestine and Jewish settlements taciturnly express the complex and ambiguous nature of what might be called the Jewish turn[52] in twentieth-century Anglo-Jewish history. Similar to Patrick Joyce's use of the 'linguistic turn', this episode in labour's discourse on Jewish identity calls into question the place of culture in class in the 'social imaginary' of British historians; during the inter-war period ideas about Jewish identity continually reinserted themselves into discussions of labour. For labour 'Jewishness' was more elusive a trait than could be explained with exclusively political or religious definitions.

Some historians have attempted to show that regardless of material conditions, labour has meant something fundamentally different in each national context.[53] Given this assessment, there is reason to believe that within the same national setting, labour lodged an abundance of separate and disparate meanings of 'Jewishness' often discussed by opposing political and communal forces. The reasons can be explained in a number of ways: first, the labour movement and the party's conception of Jewish labour during the inter-war years was intrinsically Zionist. It was not, however, intrinsically philo-Semitic or concerned explicitly with 'Jewish issues'. Yet on another level it is arguable that labour's commitment to the idea of a rightful Jewish homeland was founded upon the hopes of seeking out the external successes of English labour ideology in its embryonic of nationhood.[54] There is little evidence later on to support any notion that the labour movement or the party supported other immigration schemes besides that of Palestine. In regards to labour's socialist and Zionist stance, it is unlikely that labour would have chosen to support the Soviet plan to form a 'Jewish State' in Biro-Bidjan in 1928, for example.[55] Perhaps, as Alderman and others have suggested, *Poale Zion's* affilitation with Labour in the 1920s was the main reason why the party absorbed the precepts of labour Zionism which called for all socialists to 'couple their Zionism with the aspiration of toiling humanity for a social order of free labour, equality among the nations and universal peace'.[56]

Acknowledgements

The author would like to thank Dr Stephen Brooke, David Bronstein and the Faculty of Graduate Studies at Dalhousie University.

Notes

1.   Feldman, David (1989), 'The Importance of Being English: Jewish Immigration and the Decay of Liberal England', in David Feldman and Gareth Stedman Jones (eds), *Metropolis London: Histories and Representations Since 1800*, pp. 56-84, London: Routledge.

2.   *East London Observer*, 'Jews and the War: East London's Part', 12 December 1914; 'Anglo-Jewish Uprising: Jews at the Front', September 1914. 'East London and the War', 5 September 1914.

3.   *East London Observer*, 'Jews and the War: East London's Part', 12 December 1914.

4.   *East London Observer*, 'Anglo-Jewish Uprising: Jews at the Front', 12 September 1914.

5.   For a detailed discussion of this see Alderman, Geoffrey (1989), *London Jewry and London Politics, 1889-1986*, pp. 61-5, London: Routledge.

6.   Alderman, *London Jewry*, p. 62.

7.   *East London Observer*, 5 August 1914, p. 4. Cited in Alderman, *London Jewry and London Politics*, p. 62.

8.   Alderman, *London Jewry*, p. 65.

9.   *East London Observer*, 'East London and the War', 5 September 1914.

10.   Sir Alfred Bar, R. Hon., MP (1923) 'The Palestinian Problem', in Leon Simon and Leon Stein (eds), 'Awakening Palestine', p. 1, London: John Murray Hyperion Press.

11.   Alderman, *London Jewry*, p. 65.

12.   Ellis, John S. (1998), '"The Methods of Barbarism" and the "Rights of Small Nations" War Propaganda and British Pluralism', *Albion*, **30**, 1, 49-75. Ellis looks at the Boer War, the First World War and the associations made between ideas about Britishness and the United Kingdom as a multinational state at the centre of a multinational empire.

13.   Bush, Julia Frances (1978), 'Labour Politics and Society in East London During the First World War', PhD thesis, Queen Mary College, University of London, p. 300.

14.   Bush, Julia Frances, 'Labour Politics', pp. 263-300. On this point regarding the 'international reality' of East End Jewish life see also, Kahan, Arcadius (1986), 'The Urbanisation Process of the Jews in Nineteenth-Century Europe', in Roger Weiss (ed.), *Essays in Jewish Social and Economic History*, Chicago: University of Chicago Press.

15.   In 1903, William Evans Gordon declared the East End 'a Hebrew Colony, unlike any other alien colony in the land', which formed 'a solid and permanently disinct block – a race apart ... in an enduring island of extraneous thought and custom', Gordon W. E. (1903), *The Alien Immigrant*, London: William Heinemann, p. 7. In 1907 the *Illustrated Evening News* made incendiary attacks against immigrants, declaring Jews 'a litiginous foreign colony' which disrupted 'everything ... especially wages', 'The Aliens in England:

the Immigrant Problem', *Illustrated London News*, **30** (April), 1904, p. 657.

16. *East London Observer*, 'Political Sheep-Trotting in East London', 19 October 1926.

17. Williams, Patrick and Chrisman, Laura (eds) (1993), 'Introduction', *Colonial Discourse and Post-Colonial Theory: A Reader*, New York: Harvester Wheatsheaf, p. 17.

18. See 'Introduction' and 'The Sexual Politics of Jewish Identity', in Hyman, Paula E. (1995), *Gender and Assimilation in Modern Jewish History: The Roles and Representations of Women*, Seattle: University of Washington Press.

19. Ibid.

20. *Jewish Chronicle*, 12 March 1875, p. 801, in Hyman, Paula E., *Gender and Assimilation*, p. 46.

21. See Hyman's discussion of Marion Kaplan's 'Priestess and Hausfrau: Women and Tradition in the German-Jewish Family', in Steven M. Chohen and Paula E. Hyman (eds) (1986) *The Jewish Family*, pp. 62-8, New York: Holmes and Meier; 'Paradoxes of Assimilation', in P. E. Hyman, *Gender and Assimilation in Modern Jewish History*, pp. 46, 48-9; Hannah Arendt's post-Second World War biography of the German Salon Jewess and founder of the cult of Goethe, Rahel Varnhagen, particularly ch. 13, 'One Does Not Escape Jewishness', in *Rahel Varnhagen: The Life of a Jewish Woman* (1974), revised edition, New York: Harcourt Brace Jovanovich, pp. 216-25.

22. Alexander, Sally (1994), 'Memory, Generation and History: Two Women's Lives in the Inter-War Years', in her *Becoming a Woman and Other Essays in 19th and 20th Century Feminist History*, London: Virago Press.

23. Jones, Gareth Stedman (1982), 'Introduction', *Languages of Class: Studies in English Working Class History 1832-1982*, Cambridge: Cambridge University Press, p. 2.

24. See Todd Endleman (1979), *The Jews of Georgian England, 1714-1830*, Philadelphia: Jewish Publication Society of America. Anna Clark (1995), *The Struggle for the Breeches: Gender and the Making of the British Working Class*, Berkeley: University of California Press, p. 26.

25. Zangwill, Israel (1893), *Ghetto Tragedies*, London: McClure and Co., p. 5.

26. See the work of Friedman-Kasaba, Kathie (1996), *Memories of Migration: Gender, Ethnicity, and Work in the Lives of Jewish and Italian Women in New York, 1870-1924*, New York: State University of New York Press.

27. See also the historical continuity on this point expressed in the work of Hilene Flanzbaum whose work on Jewish-American identity in post-war American literature also includes these predominantly masculine traits. Hilene Flanzbaum, 'The Imaginary Jew and the American Poet', *English Literary History*, **65** (1998) John Hopkins University Press, pp. 259-75.

28. See the work of Gerald Tulchinsky, who discusses the formation of Jewish unions in Montreal, Canada, including the International Ladies Garment Workers' Union (ILGWU), in 'The Third Solitude: A. M. Klein's Jewish Montreal, 1910-1950', *Journal of Canadian Studies*, **19**, (2), Summer 1984, 96-112.

29. See note 23.

30. 'Earl Beaconsfield', *Jewish Chronicle*, 18 August 1876, p. 312.

31. The title of rabbi was often 'Anglo-Judaised' to reverend. See Lloyd Gartner's discussion of this in 'The Religion of the Immigrant', *The Jewish Immigrant in England, 1870-1914*, London: George Allen and Unwin, 1960, p. 190.

32. *Jewish Chronicle*, 3 January 1873, p. 555.

33. 'The Jews of Middlesborough and Jewish Labour', *Jewish Chronicle*, 3 January 1873, p. 559.

34. Revd A. Cohen, 'The Labour Problem in Rabbinic Literature', *Jewish Chronicle Supplement*, March 1921.

35. Ibid.

36. Ibid.

37. *Jewish Chronicle*, 'The Rabbis and Labour', a reply to the Revd A. Cohen, from Mr A. Gunter, 15 April 1921, p. 25.

38. *Jewish Chronicle*, 'A Word for Labour', by Mr Isidore Wartski, 15 April 1921, p. 24.

39. *Jewish Chronicle*, 'The Rabbis and Labour', Mr A. Gunter, p. 24.

40. Endelman, Todd (1987), 'The Englishness of Jewish Modernity', in Katz, Jacob (ed.), *Toward Modernity: The European Jewish Model*, Oxford: Transaction Books, The Leo Baeck Institute, p. 235.

41. Kelemen, P. (1996), 'Zionism and the British Labour Party: 1927-1939', *Social History*, **21**, (1), 73.

42. MacDonald, J. Ramsay (1923), 'In Palestine Now', in Leon Simon and Leonard Stein (eds), *Awakening Palestine*, London: John Murray, Hyperion Press, p. 18.

43. MacDonald, 'In Palestine Now', pp. 12-13.

44. Feldman, David (1994), *Englishmen and Jews: Social Relations and Political Culture 1840-1914*, New Haven: Yale University Press, p. 11.

45. *Jewish Chronicle*, 'Labour Party and the Disorders: Co-operation in Interests of Jew and Arab', 16 October 1936, p. 20.

46. Bhabha, Homi K. (1994), '*The Location of Culture*', New York: Routledge, p. 212.

47. Archives of the British Labour Party, 'The Colonial Empire' 1933/6, p. 5, 6.

48. A list of these settlements during the period and their location in Palestine can be found in S. Levenberg's (1945), *The Jews and Palestine: A Study in Labour History*, 2nd edn, Westport: Hyperion Press.

49. Herzl, Theodor, quoted in 'The War and the Jewish People: Memorandum submitted to the 39th Annual Conference of the Labour Party at Bournemouth by the Jewish Socialist Labour Party (Poale Zion) of Great Britain, 1940', point 6, Archives of the British Labour Party, 1940/27 329 (LAB). A4.

50. Ibid., pt 12, p. 5, Archives of the British Labour Party, 1940/27 329 (LAB). A4.

51. MacDonald, Ramsay (1922), *A Socialist in Palestine*, London: Jewish Socialist Labour Confederation, Poale Zion London Bureau, p. 17.

52. Gershom Scholem uses this term to explain the way in which many young German Jews, the sons of middle-class bourgeois Jews arrived on the threshold of Zionism despite their position in a post-assimilatory generation void of strong religious stricture of secular lifestyles and education. His use of this turn of phrase is very different than its usage here, although there are points of similarity. See 'With Gerhom Scholem: An Interview', p. 5. From *Shdemot: Literary Digest of the Kibbutz Movement*, No. III, Spring, 1975, pp. 4-43. Interview conducted by Muki Tsur and Abraham Shapira. Translated from Hebrew by Moshe Kohn.

53. See Joyce, Patrick (1997), and his 'Refabricating Labour History; or, from Labour History to the History of Labour', *Labour History Review*, **62** (2), 147-52.

54. See Kelemen 'Zionism and the British Labour Party', on this point. The idea that it was a working class experiment of Soviet Russia.

55. Levenburg, S. (1945), *The Jews and Palestine: A Study in Labour Zionism*, 2nd edn, Westport: Hyperion Press, pp. 26-7.

56. Ben-Gurion, David, 'Socialist Zionism', in *What is Socialist Zionism? Aims and Principles of the United Socialist Zionist Party*, Poale Zion Zeire Zion American, n.d., p. 7, Levenberg Papers, Section 1/1.

CHAPTER FOUR

'Le soleil du socialisme commence à se lever sur le monde': The Utopian Visions of Labour Zionism, British Labour and the Labour and Socialist International in the 1930s

Christine Collette

The international socialist Emile Vandervelde, speaking to 5,000 people in Tel Aviv, was moved by his 1928 Palestinian visit to express the high hope that: *'Le soleil du socialisme commence à se lever sur le monde'* (the sun of socialism is beginning to rise on the world).[1] While, in his opinion, each of the major European parties had contributed something special to the development of socialism, in the case of the British their long history of trades unionism, Zionism was an exciting new departure. Its strength came 'from the soil'; the agricultural base of its socialist experience, the collective ownership of land and the fact that each carried out his own labour, without exploiting another. Its inspiration was a vision, a *'grand idéal'* in Vandervelde's words, at once nationalist and socialist. Condemning European nationalism as a force of capitalist imperialism, Vandervelde perceived Zionism as a new type of nationalism, of international importance because it did not rest on class division: rather than oppress Arabs, Zionists offered new economic life to the region for all to share.

It was remarkable that a nationalist vision should act so powerfully upon an internationalist, and Vandervelde's analysis of Zionism was controversial within the international Labour Movement. The controversy points both to the difficulty of understanding others' visions and to the complexities of the terms nationalism and internationalism when used by socialists. An appreciation of the way Zionist, international Labour and British Labour visions impacted on each other helps clarify these respective *grands idéals*. Retaining considerable powers of attraction through the 1930s, each was obscured by the compromises demanded by the international situation. Springing, in each case, from a broad movement that required a vision of sufficient scope to appeal to a disparate membership and to achieve internal cohesion, the *grands idéals* were necessarily multifaceted. They are described in this chapter as utopian, following Lucy Sargisson's definition of Utopia as an imaginary space that our thoughts inhabit, allowing us to critique our present time and place.[2] This imagined space is not necessarily perfect, an ending place, because it may yet include struggle for something better; nor is it a definitive blueprint for a future society, because it contains room for the unknown. It is a site from which we empower our political thinking and refresh ourselves through consideration of our *grand idéal*. Each of the utopian visions in set in its political context below and their relationship to each other is then discussed.

The British Labour Movement

The British Labour Movement was formed of the Labour Party and its affiliated organisations, including Poale Zion, and the trade unions. The National Executive committee coordinated party and trade unions. The Communist Party of Great Britain (CPGB) had been denied affiliation to the Labour Party and was thus removed from the mainstream. It is the mainstream which this chapter considers. In the 1930s, the British Labour Movement's critique of Conservative/National governments was articulated through contrast with a society, to be gradually achieved through reformist socialism, wherein workers' rights and needs would be privileged. Part of these utopian imaginings was the British Labour Movement's sense of internationalism, of workers' solidarity and sense of common identity transcending national class consciousness.[3] Informed by a real knowledge of the sufferings of people under dictatorship, provided by British Labour's international contacts, this international philosophy led to a commitment to fight fascism, in contrast to the National government policy of appeasement. British Labour's internationalism was not anti-nationalistic, because workers' acknowledgements of class imperatives sprang from understanding their position in their own society and from their struggle for citizenship. Rather, having achieved citizenship, workers would be able to reach out to other states' labouring classs. James Middleton, Labour Party secretary, expressed it thus: 'The socialist does not substitute internationalism for nationalism, but building on a genuine nationalism, stretches out to socialists in other lands and seeks to build up a wider policy of internationalism'.[4]

Middleton's position was not free from ambiguity; but it is a good example of utopian imaginings, including struggle and being open to outcomes. His was not the only vision of internationalism; for instance, his predecessor, Arthur Henderson, who was important in the reconstruction of the Labour and Socialist International, had a richer view of workers' international solidarity. The official expression of British Labour's kaleidoscopic international vision lay in the hands of William Gillies, Labour Party International Secretary. Gillies was at the heart of Party international policy, making contacts, informing, advising, servicing the Party International Subcommittee which advised the National Executive and thereby the

Parliamentary Party and trades unions. As a sounding board for a wider body of opinion, Gillies made use of the Imperial Advisory Committee, chaired by Leonard Woolf, with its Palestine subcommittee. This was not a party committee and, having no direct access to the parliamentary party, was less influential than the Party's own International Subcommittee.

One of the major areas which Gillies, and the British Labour Movement in general, failed to address was the way in which nationalism, citizenship and 'the wider policy of internationalism' were gendered issues. While much of the Labour Movement's development had been inspired by the fight to win full civil, political and industrial rights for men, it had been slow to identify fully with women's campaign for enfranchisement. It has been argued that political participation based upon Western ideas of citizenship within militarised territorial boundaries is problematic for women, being based on patriarchal assumptions of gender identity which identify women as subordinate homekeepers.[5] Moreover, the British Labour Movement reflected the gendered labour market; while women accounted for half the Labour Party membership, they were underrepresented in the trades unions, because men preponderated in full-time, long-term jobs.[6] Similarly, British Labour's imaginings were ethnically limited due, in part, to its development as a national party and in part to the operation of a racist labour market.[7]

The Labour and Socialist International

The Labour and Socialist International embodied the imaginings of its various member parties: international solidarity and eventual victory over capitalism. Its secretary Friedrich Adler, himself of Jewish descent, described this outcome as 'the final triumph of the fighting proletariat'.[8] Past accounts of the International have tended to describe its separate parties, rather than its collective identity[9] and it was, in practice, difficult to get its members to work together. In its early years, the search for peace and disarmament was the International's main priority, and its achievement was to include both former allies and belligerents. There was then a real sense of the construction of a vigorous international body: multilingual, its members well-travelled, its activities confined not merely to the political sphere but spread into its relationships with the International Federation of Trades Unions and such diverse bodies as the Sports International, Arbeiter Radio International, the Education International, the International of Socialist Lawyers and the Union of Local Authorities. After 1933, fighting fascism of necessity became the prime focus and the International was damaged by the loss of strong parties, such as the German, Austrian and Czech parties, in fascist and non-democratic countries.

Throughout, the International was largely Eurocentric, despite efforts to broaden its scope, and it thus represented the countries which Zionists hoped to leave. The American Socialist Party stayed aloof and Arab people, those in Africa and Asia, were not represented. The predecessor of the Labour and Socialist International, the Second International, because it comprised member states, had refused affiliation to Poale Zion. Dr S. Levenberg, a member of the Second International Bureau of was of the opinion that: 'there was an indifference to the national problem and unfriendly attitude to Zionism'.[10] The Poale Zion request for a separate Jewish section of the Second International was also refused. However, British Labour, which recognised Jewish claims for a national home, played a large part in the reformation of the Labour and Socialist International after the First World War and Levenberg reported that British interest meant that: 'The Poale Zion confederation was enabled to take an active part in the various socialist consultations dealing with the peace settlement and the reconstitution of the International.'[11] It was therefore decided that Poale Zion be included through the device of recognising its Palestinian party as a nationality. Poale Zion groups in other countries would be recognised through the Palestinian party, which was allowed two votes. In 1930 the Palestine Labour Party (Miflegeth Poale Erezisrael) was formed of Poale Zion and the Zionist Labour Party, and this was then recognised as the Palestinian section of the International.[12]

Reflecting its member parties, the International also failed to fully include women. There was a Women's Advisory Committee and Adelheid Pop had a seat on the executive as women's representative, but women as a group had no power within the International. In many of the European states from which its participants were drawn women had no voting rights. Socialist and trade union women were consulted by the League of Nations when the latter debated the status and nationality of women in 1936. The Hague Convention of the International Labour Office in 1930, followed by the Montevideo Convention of 1933, recommended complete gender equality but fears about family stability and protection of women workers contributed to the general failure to ratify these conventions. International trade union women had demanded that women should have the choice of taking their husbands' nationality or retaining their own on marriage and keeping the husbands' or reverting to their own if the marriage ended.[13]

In addition, the International suffered from the rivalry of the Communist International and the split between Socialist and Communist parties in member states. Communists shared much of the socialist international vision but imagined its achievement by revolutionary means. From 1918 some parties, such as the Independent Labour Party and the Polish Bund, tried to build bridges between socialist and communist wings, but apart from participation in united and popular front politics in some member states, unity was never achieved. The left-wing parties of Poale Zion had considered affiliating to the Communist International.[14] A second split, as the Second

World War approached, was between neutral Central and Eastern European states and belligerent opponents of fascism, such as the British Labour Party.

Labour Zionism

Jewish people were involved in and shared the imaginings of both national and international Labour Movements and were not, necessarily Zionist, struggling instead for an accommodation within their country of residence. The Polish Labour Bund, the most notable of the inter-war Bund groups that had originated in Tsarist Russia, is a good example and was affiliated to the Labour and Socialist International as one of the national, Polish parties.[15] Labour Zionism, however, refracted socialism through a search for a territorialised national identity. Zionism was a function of Western nationalism, which, in consolidating the idea of an indigenous, ethnic population, excluded Jewish people: Zionist utopianism was both a critique of this exclusion and its corollary. It was informed by Western socialism. Prof. Gorni is of the opinion that Zionism is inherently revolutionary, not only in its future hopes, but in its present activity.[16] He points to the ambivalence of Zionist thought; utopianism was sometimes seen as an evil because it evaded present realities. Early twentieth-century Palestine is seen by Gorni as second stage Zionist utopianism, socialistic, class oriented, related to a socialist world view, where workers were both the objects and the implementers of the ideal.[17] Poale Zion developed as a meeting point of Zionist and socialist thought. The numbers in membership in Palestine were by far the minority; for the 1928 Labour and Socialist International Congress, Poale Zion estimated 4,000 members in Palestine and 25,000 worldwide, of whom 5,000 were women.[18] However, the Histadruth, the General Federation of Jewish Labour, had 26,700 members in Palestine. The Histadruth was affiliated to the International Federation of Trades Unions.

The Histadruth and Poale Zion/Palestine Labour Party formed the mainstream of Labour Zionism with which this chapter is concerned. It should be noted, however, that there were other left Zionist visions. Paole Zion notified the International of the existence of the very small 'Paole-Zion Communists'. The left wing of Hapoel Hatzair [*sic*] (*le parti ouvrier socialiste*) issued '*feuilles socialistes*' (socialist pages) which critiqued the predominance of bourgeois leaders and held that the balance of Zionism/socialism was weighted in favour of the former; they were promptly expelled from the party. Writing to protest their expulsion, the left group claimed it had been misunderstood; the reason cited had been a negative attitude to immigration and to Jewish right to work in Palestine.[19] The group maintained that it sought rather a change in emphasis, a concentration on the socialism of Poale Zion, a democracy rather than nationalist politics.

Creation of a trades union representing Arabs and Jews plus agrarian reform were the left goals and their corollary was the formation of an independent workers' party and class war within Palestine. Numbering the large majority of Jews in the Diaspora as members of Palestinian Poale Zion, '*La théorie et la practice du "parti ouvrier Palestine*"' was seen as an unhelpful device by the leftists, a false solution to the Jewish problem. More useful would be alliances with the socialist movements in the countries where Jews lived and worked; '*nous déclarons contre le palestine-centralisme*' (we declare against Palestinian centrism). However, the leftists also condemned the Bund for '*la position négative aveugle du bund vis à vis l'oeuvre palestine*' (the Bund's negative and blind position against the Palestinian oeuvre).

As the leftists alleged and reflecting contemporary Western politics, Zionist utopianism, including that of Labour Zionists, was imperialist. Arthur Koestler justly wrote:

> They (Zionists) did not come, as other Europeans had come to dark continents before them, with shotguns, glass beads and fire water, nor with missionaries either ... They came pushed by persecution and by hunger for a land of their own.[20]

There was, however, a consciously imperialist sense of bringing light to a dark continent; David Plavskin, of the Palestinian Hebrew executive of the Workers' Movement of Tel Aviv used the lighthouse metaphor. Claiming that: 'Palestine must be the place where the Jews will become a real people', Plavskin wrote that Japan and the Mohammedan nations of India and Egypt would fight Europe, but that the Jewish state would be:

> a new Belgium in the wild Near East ... a new state for Europe in its pilgrimage ... a new civilisation for all Arabistan ... a useful staging post for British going to India ... a new lighthouse for civilisation in the Near East.

He valued Jewish immigrant culture, because of its Zionism, as superior to that of 'Arab tribes that wander like gypsies' and needed to be 'gathered and civilised'.[21] By the 1930s such utopian imaginings interacted with Jewish settlement in Palestine. As Rachel Elboim-Dror has written:

> Zion, as a promised land, is a universal symbol ... Zionism was also a utopian movement which produced a society ... dealt with a very well known and concrete place, which served as a symbol of visions while being transformed into the reality of the Jewish state.[22]

The Western orientation of the vision problematised Arab settlement so that the promised land was the site of continued struggle, over the immigration quotas fixed by the British according to their estimate of economic capacity, over coexistence with Arab people and over labour relations.

This Zionist utopia was also gendered. Rachel Elboim-Dror is of the

76

opinion that while there were diverse Zionist imaginings, all held a similar view of women. Gender equality was proclaimed but dealt with in a romantic way, so that traditional prejudice remained. She claims that Jewish women immigrants were often better educated than their male counterparts and some, of course, were from a socialist revolutionary background.[23] These women were faced by British Mandate regulations, which denied women the vote in municipal elections, with the sole exception of Tel Aviv. On the pretext of following the example of the Ottoman Empire, British Mandate laws punished the adultery of a wife and her lover more harshly than that of her husband, unless the husband brought his mistress into the home. Palestinian Labour Movement women protested strongly against these measures. Women workers were half the membership of the General Federation of Jewish Labour in Erez-Israel. The General Council of Women Workers of that body wrote to the British Labour Party and the Labour and Socialist International to protest these measures, in addition to lobbying the government of Palestine, the Colonial Office, the League of Nations and women members of the British House of Commons. Their case was that the excuse that many Arab women were illiterate did not stand up, as Arab men were similarly illiterate:

> It is ... evident that the limitation is placed by the law upon the women solely because they are women ... The cultural level of a country cannot be raised by means of denying the people elementary civil rights.

The women's council stated that women had frequently been elected to municipal office in Tel Aviv and that Jewish women participated actively in politics, the professions, agriculture, construction and industry.[24] In fact, on the evidence of women's biographies and diaries, Dror writes that many women accepted gender stereotypes even while campaigning for the franchise; it was socialist women who tried to live out their imaginings by working alongside men and who felt betrayed, abused and humiliated when frustrated in their search for full equality.[25] The British Labour Party received protests about the adultery laws also from the Howard League for Penal Reform; Cicely Craven wrote both as secretary of the Howard League and in a personal capacity.[26] William Gillies sent these letters and the Jewish women's protest to J. L. Cohen of the Zionist Committee, but there is no record of a reply.[27]

There are special difficulties in comprehending how a 1930s Labour Zionist perceived her/his nationality. Work on narrative methodology has revealed that people who have experienced several cultures have options about their sense of national/cultural belonging and this is especially true of Israeli Jews who escaped persecution. Gabrielle Rosenthal has written that the idea of 'belonging' to a nation, as a lifetime identity, is inappropriate for this group of people. She gives an example of two women, Jewish under

Jewish law, who both grew up in multilingual Czechoslovakia before 1938. Both identified as Jewish people; one felt close to German culture and to French and Czech culture, and had experienced shock when, in Rosenthal's words: 'her persecution as a Jew illustrated to her in the cruelest way possible that she was regarded as "only" a Jew'. The other, whose family was from the Austro-Hungarian part of Slovakia, identified as Hungarian although she had never lived in Hungary – and thus never experienced Hungarian anti-Semitism.[28]

The three types of utopian imaginings, Labour Zionist, British Labour and International Labour, emanating from broad based movements, were each loose collections of thought rather than a single body of opinion. Sargisson's work is important for understanding the way in which utopianism can allow the exploration of difference without fracturing relations between disputants.[29] Nevertheless, there are remarkable similarities between the three philosophies. Each was deeply patriarchal and problematised women's position behind good intentions and semi-Romantic ambiguity; all were Western oriented and problematised ethnic relations. Ideas of national ethnic identity, past, present and future, were present in each; yet socialism, privileging class over national identity, underpinned the domestic and International Labour utopias. An international perspective was the corollary. The second part of this chapter considers how the three utopianisms impacted and reflected each other when, in the 1930s, the need for a Jewish national home was so urgently felt and the British and International Labour Movements were struggling for the expression of international and national resistance to fascism.

Labour Zionists and British Labour

First, relations between the utopianism of British Labour and Labour Zionists. The details of Labour Party political support for Zionism have been recently described by Paul Kelemen and will not be repeated. Kelemen's statement that: 'The party's pro-Zionism became firmly entrenched in the inter-war years' is broadly endorsed. A handwritten 1920 memorandum indicating transmission of this position to Prime Minister Lloyd George is an example.[30] Apart from the MacDonald government 1931 proposal of a balanced response, recognising Arab interests, the Labour Party championed Jewish rights to settlement in Palestine from its first position statement in the 1917 Labour Party and Trades Union Congress war aims memorandum until 1939, support being more warmly given as the 1930s progressed.[31] Indeed, the Labour Party files rarely record so consistent a pursuit of policy.

Indicative of British Labour relations with Labour Zionists, and of Gillies's influence and attitude was his response to the present of a case of Jaffa oranges from the Palestine Joint Cooperative Society in 1933. Gillies, often irascible, was unusually gracious and friendly, hoping that his habit of drinking the juice of three oranges a day would become universal.[32] Gillies relied on Berl Locker of the Zionist Central Office for his information and on J. L. Cohen. He invariably forwarded information from Labour Zionists to his International Committee. In 1933, Gillies was reluctant to endorse unrestricted immigration to Palestine; he represented British Labour policy of supporting a Jewish homeland but did not share Zionist imaginings of this as a fixed locality.[33] As relations between Jewish settlers and the Arab population in Palestine grew more tense and the British Mandatory Authorities limited immigration, Labour Zionists proposed three reasons why British Labour should support the lifting of restrictions. The first, as noted by Kelemen, was shared utopian imaginings of intra-state workers' solidarity; this was what had appealed to Vandervelde, Jewish and Arab solidarity along with nationalisation of the land and the absence of hired labour. The second reason was Western imperialist utopianism; the third, International Labour inter-state solidarity and resistance to fascism and anti-Semitism.

Echoing the gift of a box of oranges, the strike in the Kfar-Sabah orange groves in 1934 exemplified the imaginings of workers' solidarity and demonstrated the difficulties in practice. David Plavskin was suspected of paranoia when he first wrote about Arab attacks on Jewish settlers as a result of the strikes. Gillies forwarded the letter to Cohen as usual, writing: 'I always like to have a Jew on my side when I am at cross purposes with another Jew.' Cohen suggested questions be asked in Parliament.[34] Plavskin then broadened the grounds of his appeal for support, citing both workers' solidarity and Western imperialist arguments. He claimed that the anti-strike ordinances of the mandatory authorities were affecting labour rights in the building and agricultural sectors and that Arab workers were undercutting strikers at Kfar-Sabah. Following peaceful demonstrations, the leaders had been sentenced to hard labour. Arab workers were exploited 'in hunger and sweat' and child labour was used; Jewish civilisation was the necessary remedy. Plavskin made a final appeal to reformist socialism, reminding the Labour Party that communists were excluded from Palestinian Labour unions.[35] Here he was disingenuous, because an earlier (1930) letter Plavskin had sent to the Communist International and copied to the British Labour Party had asked for 'unity of the socialist organisations', stating that this unity had been achieved in Palestine.[36] From this time on, Jewish workers' organisations were perceived by British Labour as representative of Palestinian workers; Arab membership and participation was problematised and seen as part of the continual struggle; utopian imaginings grounded in workers' intra-state solidarity were shared with Jewish people.

Appeals on grounds of resistance to fascism and anti-Semitism also began in 1934. Locker wrote to Gillies of the 'violent growth' of anti-Semitism in

Europe: 'The situation of the great bulk of the Jewish people was never so deplorable and so full of danger for Europe.'[37] Both British Labour and Labour Zionists shared the sense of ultimate threat to their utopias. Locker protested that immigration had been restricted just at the point of danger, despite an increase in economic capacity in Palestine. Complaining of a shortage of labour, destroying the balance of wage levels and causing a loss of agricultural labour in towns, he warned of the resultant friction between Jewish owners of land and Arab workers. Wage levels were determining a division of primary – Jewish – and secondary – Arab – labour market sectors. The Jewish Labour Federation was attempting to organise Arabs, with some small success.

As the British Mandatory Authority proposed setting up a legislative council and the British government proposed partition, Jewish protest grew. Amending Gillies' 1933 position Attlee, Labour Party leader, made a House of Commons statement of support for a Jewish national home.[38] In turn, Poale Zion supported utopian Labour Party imaginings by giving support in the 1935 British election, holding public meetings for Labour candidates and issuing an appeal to Jewish people to vote Labour.[39] Poale Zion reiterated the argument that Jewish colonisation benefited Arab workers and protested that the legislative council would ensure a Jewish minority in Palestine.[40] The Imperial Advisory Committee cautioned against the legislative council and the restriction on immigration. The International Subcommittee forwarded the warning to the parliamentary Labour Party and Lord Snell, leader of the Labour opposition in the House of Lords, duly asked the government for postponement.[41] The legislative council was, however, announced, causing growing tension in Palestine. Locker wrote to Gillies of Arab attacks on Jews and of the patchy success of the Arab general strike.[42]

Some fracture in British and Zionist Labour views were heralded by ANTIFO, the organisation for the struggle against fascism and anti-Semitism in Palestine, whose platform echoed that of the *'feuilles socialistes'*. The ANTIFO asked in 1936 for help: 'to effect the solidarity of Jewish and Arab workers' and claimed that agents of Hitler and Mussolini were agitating in Palestine. Suggesting a workers' press in different languages, Jewish and Arab workers' clubs and common organisation, ANTIFO privileged intra-state workers' solidarity over Zionism.[43] Some support within the British Labour Movement for Arab workers became evident following the 1936 unrest, but the policy of the National Executive and of the Parliamentary Labour Party did not change. In 1937, for instance, the Imperial Advisory Committee began to consider measures of reconciliation, which implied recognition of Arab interests. These included the unthinkable, adhesion to economic criteria for immigration and regulation of immigration for a decade, so that Arabs were ensured of majority status in Palestine.[44] Arthur Creech Jones, of the Workers' Travel Association, wrote to Gillies forwarding a report from Mary Pumphrey, a trades unionist traveller: 'Her point of view is pro-Arab, but none the less the report is worth reading.' Pumphrey wrote that there was much immigration, some of it illegal; that Arabs were emerging from centuries of Turkish rule and resented Jewish purchase of fertile lands; and that Jewish trading ventures were suspect because they relied on outside support for success.[45]

The Advisory Committee continued these themes, considering memoranda from George Mansur, secretary of the Arab Labour Federation, who wrote that Arabs had experienced true democracy and would now be slaves. His opinion was that Jewish collective farms were: 'nothing more than expensive model farms or plantations'.[46] Mansur also complained of police brutality and Jewish attacks on Arab villages.[47] There is no record of answers to any of Mansur's protests. Illustrating the lack of commitment to gender issues amongst both British Labour and Labour Zionists, no action was taken to investigate Mansur's report of the British army rape of a 12-year-old child, Sophie Ibrahim Hamond.[48] In 1939, the Palestine Arab Workers' Society wrote to the chair of the British Labour Party protesting British 'unreserved support' for Zionism 'which is but a capitalist and imperialist movement' and threatened that this would cause Arabs to embrace national socialism. Gillies forwarded the letter to Locker, who advised that the Arab workers' party was under the control of Arab landlords, while Jewish workers were making strenuous efforts to involve Arabs.[49]

Meanwhile, as Plavskin had done in 1934, Cohen again reminded Gillies that his utopianism was reformist, rather than revolutionary and showed knowledge of Gillies' anti-Communist stance. Gillies was deeply opposed to the Communist Party of Great Britain (CPGB) on the grounds of its hostility to the Labour Party. He believed that the division of workers into Communist and Socialist wings allowed the growth of fascism and used the term 'communazis' to denote his disapprobation. The CPGB was small, but international communism was a force with which to reckon. Gillies was to the forefront in resisting united and popular front activity internationally, perceiving such cooperation to be merely a ruse to win Communist recruits. He was deeply suspicious of communist 'front' organisations that sought to attract members through mounting seemingly neutral bodies; he had published *The Communist Solar System* about these 'front' groups. Cohen wrote: 'I know you have frequently accused (communists) of bedeviling the situation in some of the countries of Europe; certainly, this has been their object in Palestine.'[50] This was written 11 months after the Cable Street battle when Jewish people, CPGB and Independent Labour Party members amongst many in the broad British Labour Movement had resisted Mosley's British fascists. However, there could be no surer way of convincing Gillies of the justice of the Zionist cause than to demonstrate its antipathy to communism. In 1939, the Independent Labour Party, which had not reaffiliated to the Labour Party in 1932 and explored united and popular front collaboration, appealed for working-class unity in the Jewish cause. Gillies told Middleton that this was merely a slogan, as the Independent Labour Party had previously denounced the call for a Jewish national home as an expression of British imperialism.[51]

When the government Royal Commission recommended the partition of Palestine in 1937, the Labour Party remained a staunch supporter of Jewish resistance to this policy. David Ben-Gurion was amongst those whom Gillies termed 'representatives of our Palestinian friends' for whom Gillies arranged meetings of the International Subcommittee and Parliamentary Labour Party.[52] It was a big success for the Labour Opposition when the House of Commons withheld endorsement of the partition policy.[53] Ben-Gurion again met the International Subcommittee in 1938 to protest against immigration restrictions.[54] As the situation worsened in 1938 and 1939, Gillies continued to provide practical support. He pulled strings on behalf of the Tel Aviv Municipal Council Labour Faction in 1938 when this group visited Britain to study local government, asking Creech Jones to help with travel and Herbert Morrison, who ran the London County Council, to offer support.[55] Gillies forwarded to Scott Lindsay, for the parliamentary Labour Party, increasingly lengthy and urgently phrased protests from around the world about immigration restrictions.[56]

Throughout the 1930s, the British Labour Party supported and came to share Labour Zionist utopian imaginings, furthering the Zionist cause wherever possible and gradually coming to accept not only the siting of a Jewish national home in Palestine, but also unrestricted Jewish immigration thereto. This was seen as an expression of *internationalism*, something to be dealt with by the international officer and Subcommittee, illustrating the complexity and the interrelationship of ideas of nationalism and internationalism. Had Labour Zionism not claimed to organise Arab people also, had Poale Zion not affiliated to the Labour and Socialist International, the British position might have been amended. However, the growth of British Labour as a *national* class party informed its sense that others needed a territorial identity. The belief in workers' representation, and achievement of power through reformist means, underpinned the strength of the relationship.

British Labour and the Labour and Socialist International

Partly because of its refusal of united and popular front collaboration with communists, British Labour relations with the International Labour Movement were more liable to fracture. The Labour and Socialist International offered collaboration to the Communist International, at executive level, in 1933. The communists refused, but sought to develop united front cooperation within European countries. Adler, with president Emile Vandervelde, succeeded by Louis de Brouckère, was moving towards a united-front position. Nazi coups in Germany and Austria meant a sharp limitation to international socialist imaginings; Utopia was redefined as restricting the fascist advance to the *status quo ante*-March 1933. As the International had no police force, was losing its strong parties and could not agree on sanctions, Communist collaboration became more attractive. However, by 1934, when the Communist executive was willing to listen to an approach and Adler started tentative meetings, Gillies had found allies to overturn any such proposals.[57] The International split into two camps, the 'Scandinavians' who opposed the united front and the 'Latins' who were in favour of talks. The International Executive allowed each country to make its own arrangements and the Spanish and French parties were, of course, amongst the first to operate popular fronts.

Germane to this chapter is the position held by the Polish Bund, which supported discussions with Communists and was amongst those who, with the British Independent Labour Party, sought international working-class unity. In 1931 the parties favouring unity had formed the International Labour Community within the International. This eventually split from the International, evolving into the International Bureau for Revolutionary Socialist Unity (also known as the London Bureau and, finally, the International Revolutionary Marxist Centre). Fourteen organisations joined this group but it was always fragile.[58] Supporting Labour Zionism at home, Gillies was doubly opposed to the united front/anti-Zionist activities of the Polish Bund abroad.

Of course, the position was complicated because persecution in Poland was one of the reasons for seeking unrestricted Jewish immigration to Palestine. It was not unrelated that Stafford Cripps, who was one of Labour's leading rebels seeking popular front activity in Britain, was the Labour parliamentarian who enunciated a pro-Arab position.[59] Gillies also caused a rift internationally by representing British Labour's reluctant commitment, from 1934, to national rearmament, in order to defeat fascism.[60] The British identity as mandator/persecutor of Jewish people in Palestine, in which the Labour government of 1929-31 was implicated, albeit contrary to the consistent Labour Party position thereafter, may have added to the perception of the British Labour as belligerent.

In addition, personal relations between Gillies and Adler broke down. The 'Scandinavian' bloc followed Gillies in criticising Adler's position; in at least one case, this led to anti-Semitism. Hendrik De Man, once secretary of the Youth International, was present at a meeting of the 'Scandinavian' wing in Britain in 1939, held at Hugh Dalton's flat. Hugh Dalton was a leading British parliamentarian; recalling the meeting he wrote:

De Man was very emphatic that the 2nd International must be cleared up, its scale of action greatly reduced, and, if possible, Adler got rid of and the staff, which now consists of Austrian Jews, diversified.

Dalton acknowledged that none of his colleagues much liked De Man, who afterwards as a government minister (1939-40) accepted the 'New Order' under the Nazis and was sentenced *in absentia* to 20 years imprisonment for war crimes.[61]

The Labour and Socialist International and Labour Zionists

The relationship between Labour Zionists and the Labour and Socialist International was the most complex of the three pairs. Labour Zionist utopianism, as we have seen, was both internationalist, in its affiliations and search for support, plus its imaginings of Jewish/Arab workers' solidarity; and nationalist, in its identification of a national homeland. To make this mix more accessible, we may benefit, from Sargisson's speculation on utopian interaction with postmodern philosophy, fluidity of subject and postulation of difference.[62] However, it was a difficult position to address politically. The Labour and Socialist International had a history not so much of support, as of discussion of the issues surrounding Zionism. For instance, the World Migration conference convened jointly by the International and the International Federation of Trades Unions held in London in May 1926 was attended by delegates from Palestine (Ben Zevie) and Poale Zion (Locker) and the Bund. The Bund resolution to this conference was that immigration should not be restricted by nation or race. The following month, Poale Zion held a second conference in London on *Das judische Wanderungproblem.*[63] In the 1930s, the 'Jewish Question', which Jarblum rightly described as: 'a world problem and one urgently requiring a solution'[64] was one of the many tragedies with which the International had to contend.

The Socialist Committee for Labour Palestine contained many of the leading figures of the Labour and Socialist International, including de Brouckère, Vandervelde, Huysmans, Bernstein and William Gillies. Its secretary, Jarblum, was based in Paris. Jarblum was Palestinian delegate to the Labour and Socialist International and kept the Labour Zionist position alive there, celebrating the activities of the Palestinian Labour movement. Nevertheless, reports of persecution, pogrom, arrest, kidnap and torture came from all sides. Resolutions from Palestine competed for time with those from Romania, Spain and other oppressed affiliates. The Internationalist Utopia receded with the fascist advance, although, as we have seen, for some such as Adler it remained an article of faith.

Adler was not a Zionist. When in London in the 1920s, he refused invitations to speak to the local Poale Zion, claiming that his English was inadequate. Later, he questioned the right of the League for Workers' Palestine to affiliate to the Labour and Socialist International. Leagues were groups in various countries, which gave material support to the Histadruth, but were not confined to organisations capable of affiliation to the International. Adler wrote to Jarblum in 1929 that he saw no need to modify his position on the League. Jarblum replied that he remained hopeful that the joyous day would arrive when Adler switched his sympathies. Always friendly, Jarblum several times invited Adler to dinner or tea. Adler was invited to Palestine, with others of the International but replied that he was unable to leave the International secretariat for a four-week period; others could go but could not commit the International ('*L'Internationale ne pourrant se charger d'aucune obligation de ce sujet*'). In 1934, when Austrian socialists were under attack from fascism, Jarblum sent Adler a letter of support, taking unusual care to be legible: '*je salve avec un emotion profonde la vaillante socialdémocratie autrichienne*' (I acknowledge with profound emotion the courage of Austrian social democracy).[65] Vandervelde, as we have seen, differed from Adler in his approach. Inspecting a variety of collective agricultural communities, he reported that Belgian cooperatives wished to establish economic relations with those in Palestine. Echoing Plavskin, Vandervelde spoke of Palestine as a window on Asia, a frontier between Europe and Asia; he gave his opinion that socialists should defend Asian people against bolshevism. It should be noted that Vandervelde had the experience of countering Belgian colonialism in the Congo. Here he had led the controversial but finally successful struggle for parliamentary annexation, in order to remove the Congo from the direct rule of the Belgian king and to enable welfare reforms.

With both Poale Zion and the Polish Bund as affiliates, in addition to differing views amongst its leaders, the International was presented with two approaches, not only to the 'Jewish Question' but also to Polish politics. Indicative of Poale Zion priorities were that body's 1936 reports of a meeting of socialists and Jewish workers in Lvov which protested 'their indignation and immense pain at the bloody and tragic events in Palestine'.[66] In contrast, The Bund was fighting discrimination in Poland, protesting government encouragement of widespread emigration as 'evacuation' and as propaganda which alienated Jewish people, 'with the object of representing the Jews to the masses of people as strangers'.[67] Noting Jewish people's 'historic service' in the liberation of Poland, the Bund perceived emigration proposals as an attack on working people, both diminishing their numbers and subverting their solidarity. In this context, the International recorded with satisfaction the solidarity of the *Polska Partja Socjalistyczna,* the Bund, the Polish–German socialists and the Free Trades Unions. It was, however, an indication of the worsening international situation that the annual fee of the Polish Bund was cancelled in 1936, as were all fees from 'countries without democracy or where democracy is in serious danger'.[68]

The International secretariat report for March 1937 noted that, despite Bund and Socialist Party successes in municipal elections, the Polish regime 'rests on bayonets alone'.[69] By mid-1937 the Bund and socialist parties were protesting government tolerance and press support for 'the frightful pogroms against the Jewish people'. Jarblum himself warned that racism was being introduced into Polish culture, before its inevitable introduction into the legal system and asked for support for those who fought against 'Hitlerism' and for democracy and equality for all citizens, for socialism and peace.[70] The emergency did not lead to breaking down the Socialist/Communist divide. The Polish Socialist Party conference in January 1937 adopted the slogan of a common front of all workers, peasants and intellectuals against fascism, but rejected cooperation with the Communists; it had found that: 'any loyal cooperation with people who are changing like a kaleidoscope, who represent such a muddled state of ideas and such impossible political and moral conditions, would be impossible'.[71] 'Anti-Semitic excesses are the order of the day', the International reported as the Bund celebrated its fortieth anniversary in November 1937. The following year the International reported a fragile stability. The catastrophe it had expected had not happened, but the left had failed to unite in the face of oppression.

The plan – known as the transfer arrangement – to allow Jewish emigration from Germany, in return for a portion of capital wealth being taken out of the country as goods, was discussed by the Labour and Socialist International in 1936. The problems were, first, that this broke the boycott on exporting Nazi goods which the International supported, although it had been difficult to arrive at a consensus International resolution on the boycott and the policy commitment was far from firm. Second, while emigration was obviously a vital and urgent matter, the limit on immigrés to Palestine remained, and the measure would disadvantage poorer prospective migrants. The British Labour Party had already discussed this, and Gillies sent the International Subcommittee memorandum to Adler, for information and to indicate which way the British would vote at the International. The Subcommittee memorandum suggested a compromise, that transfers be allowed provided they did not advantage the German regime. However, Poale Zion protested at the discussion of the transfer arrangement in this context, pointing out, with some justification, that many countries broke the boycott: Jews should not be singled out for reprimand, there should be no differentiation in moral judgement. Moreover, the measure was claimed as a success in the struggle against fascism. While the agenda item remained, Adler remarking that: 'the vast majority of Jews, with whom we as socialists are primarily concerned, cannot be robbed of any property ... they never had any to lose', Poale Zion was successful at having reference to Jewish people removed.[72]

As the political situation in Europe and Palestine worsened, the

International condemned the partition proposals for Palestine and, reflecting its own frustrations, perceived the Arab national movement as 'poisoned by German and Italian fascism'.[73] However, the International executive amended a Bund resolution that condemned anti-Semitism as a device of class oppression so that greetings were sent 'to all the socialist parties of the national minorities' whereas the original had been addressed to Bund members only.[74] This indicated the breadth of contemporary concern. When the Nuremburg anti-Semitic decrees were extended to Austria, the International accepted a Bund resolution which insisted on 'the *duty* of working class parties to support Jewish equal rights as part of the struggle against fascism'.[75] Such resolutions continued until the war, including condemnation of Hungarian anti-Semitism, but Jewish persecution was not singled out for international action. However, it is interesting that, in August 1939, when Gillies was attempting to force Adler's resignation, the Romanian, Luxembourg and Polish parties wanted Adler to remain in post because of his knowledge of Central and Eastern European politics, which obviously included treatment of Jewish people.[76]

Conclusion

Utopian imaginings provide powerful critiques. They allow different groups to share and inform each other's criticism, learning from each other's analysis. Thus the British Mandate actions in restricting Jewish immigration, setting up the legislative council and proposing partition were protested on the basis of workers' solidarity and anti-fascism. Anti-Semitism within Europe was condemned on the same criteria. However, national minorities were not fully integrated in national Labour Movements and British Labour remained ethnically exclusive. Ethnic exclusivity was also apparent in the Palestinian labour movement, despite its protests. Whereas some internationalists, Adler, the Polish Bund, preferred to work for assimilation of Jewish people in their national labour movements, others, Vandervelde, Poale Zion, had a different, Israeli Utopia. There could be no compromise between these two positions, but Adler, Jarblum and Vandervelde remained affectionate colleagues. Moreover, international resistance to fascism remained divided between reformist-Socialist and revolutionary-Communist approaches; it was appropriate that the Bund, seeking assimilation, should also seek working-class unity while the British, looking to Zion for a solution to 'the Jewish question', could afford to maintain the division. The dichotomy of nationalism and international socialism was not resolved but was glossed over, prohibiting effective international cooperation of workers, part of the continuing struggle in the open-ended Utopias envisaged by the three groups. Labour relations in Palestine were subject to consideration against a model of best British and international practice which was a myth, rather than a reality. Women were disadvantaged in both socialist and Zionist Utopias.

However, we are, perhaps, less effective at imagining international utopias now than our predecessors of the 1930s. We have lost Adler's belief in 'the final triumph of the fighting proletariat', discarded the utopian space for diverse imaginings as the home of hopeless romance. In Britain, New Labour has consciously jettisoned past pretensions and confined its visions to the Millennium Dome. If we allow no space for utopianism, fascism has truly triumphed. To look back and rediscover these visions may help us to rethink our idea of democracy to fully include women and ethnic groupings. Arthur Koestler wrote:

> In fifty years, when Israel's history is counted from the day of its birth on May 15 1948, few will take an interest in the struggles and shocks to which it was exposed in its pre-natal stages. Yet nations, like individuals, retain characteristic traces of these experiences.[77]

Notes

1. Sozialistische Arbeiter-Internationale papers, International Institute of Social History, Amsterdam, transcript of Vandervelde's speech, April 1928, SAI 2518/4. Biography of Vandervelde, Polasky, Janet (1995), *The Democratic Socialism of Emile Vandervelde*, Berg: Oxford.

2. Sargisson, Lucy (1996), *Contemporary Feminist Utopianism*, London: Routledge, *passim*. Cf. Gorni, Y. (1984), 'Utopian Elements in Zionist Thought', *Studies in Zionism*, **5** (1), 19: 'The idea of utopia is elusive, hidden behind the surface of reality. It is obscured by the tumult of everyday life and its hopes swallowed up in the turmoil of war'. Herman, D. (1994), 'Zionism as Utopian Discourse', *Clio*, **23** (3).

3. Collette, Christine (1998), *The International Faith: the British Labour Movement and Europe, 1918–1939*, Ashgate: Aldershot.

4. James and Lucy Middleton papers, the Ruskin Collection, Ruskin College, Oxford, Middleton to Charles Irving, 'an ex-Tory voter', 12 April 1929, MID 23/11. James Middleton was Assistant Secretary to Arthur Henderson until 1935. Kelemen, Paul (1996), 'Zionism and the British Labour party', *Social History*, **21** (1), 73 writes that Middleton pronounced himself sympathetic to Zionism because 'scripture lessons imprinted on his generation the story of the Israelites'.

5. Pettman, Jan Jindy (1996), *Worlding Women*, London: Routledge.

6. Collette, Christine (forthcoming), 'Questions of Gender', in Brian Brivati and Richard Heffernan (eds), *Labour's First Century*, London: Macmillan.
7. Tabili, Laura (1994), 'The Construction of Racial Difference in Twentieth Century Britain', *Journal of British Studies*, **33** (1). Ramdin, Ron (1987), *The Making of the Black Working Class in Britain*, Oxford: Wildwood House.
8. Collette, *The International Faith*, p. 92.
9. Braunthal, J. (1967), *The History of the International, 1914-1943*, vol. 2, London.
10. Levenberg, S. (n. d.), *Seventy Five Years*, Tel Aviv: World Labour Zionist Movement.
11. Ibid.
12. Labour and Socialialist International miscellaneous papers, National Museum of Labour history, Manchester. Kaplansky to Shaw 28 July 1924 confirmed the adherence of the World Conference of Poale Zion to the reconstituted International.
13. International Federation of Trades Union papers, International Institute of Social History, Amsterdam, International Conference of Women Trades Unionists 1936 IFTU 134.
14. Levenberg, op. cit.
15. Thanks to Arieh Lebowitz for his internet announcement of the 100th anniversary of the Jewish Labor Bund celebrated in New York January-March 1998.
16. Gorni, op. cit., p. 20.
17. Ibid., *passim*.
18. Sozialistische Arbeiter Internationale papers, notes on Jewish Labour and Socialist Federation 'Poale Zion' for LSI congress 1928, SAI 134.
19. Ibid., to LSI, signed by M. Perlmann for group, 17 May 1933, SAI 4461.
20. Koestler, Arthur (1983), *Promise and Fulfillment: Palestine 1917-1949*, London: Papermac, p. 29. Cf. Gorni (1984), op. cit., p. 10: 'Zionism was a revolution against the political and economic situation of the Jews in Europe – but not against the culture, lifestyle and political philosophy of European society'.
21. William Gillies Correspondence, National Museum of Labour History, Manchester, Plavskin to British Labour Party, 25 April 1934, WG/Pal/42.
22. Elboim-Dror, Rachel (1994), 'Gender in Utopianism: the Zionist Case', *History Workshop*, **37**, 99.
23. Ibid., p. 110.
24. William Gillies Correspondence, Rachel Katznelson-Rabashow to

Labour Party, 25 March 1934, WG/Pal/44.

25. Elboim-Dror, op. cit., p. 111.

26. William Gillies Correspondence, Cicely Craven to James Middleton, 24 January 1934; Cicely Craven, Howard League for Penal Reform to Labour Party, 24 January 1934, WG/Pal/29. The British position ignored the activities of the contemporary Turkish women's movement. For discussion of the latter and the effect of nationalism in confirming gender stereotypes see Baykan, Asequel (1994), 'The Turkish Woman: An Adventure in Feminist Historiography', *Gender and History*, **6** (1).

27. William Gillies Correspondence, Gillies to J. L. Cohen, 26 January 1934, WG/Pal/31, 17 April 1934, WG/Pal/38.

28. Rosenthal, Gabrielle (1991), 'National Identity as Multicultural Autobiography', in A. Lieblich and and R. Josselson (eds), *The Narrative Study of Lives*, London: Sage.

29. Sargisson, op. cit., p. 72.

30. Kelemen, op. cit., p. 7. See also chapter in this volume. William Gillies Correspondence, Minutes of National Executive 20 April 1920, WG/Pal/10.

31. The 1930 White Paper and MacDonald's proposal were repudiated by the extraordinary conference of the Palestinian and Jewish Labour Party, Sozialistische Arbeiter-Internationale papers. David Ben-Gurion to LSI 30 October 1930 and accompanying resolution, SAI 2525/5. This could help explain the diminution in the Labour vote in Whitechapel in the 1930 election: 63 per cent voted Labour in 1929, 39.2 per cent in 1930. See Radice, Lisanne (1984), *Beatrice and Sidney Webb*, London: Macmillan, p. 276 ff. I am indebted to Stephen Bird for this reference.

32. Ibid., Cooperative Wholesale Fruit and Vegetable Department, Spitalfields to Gillies 7 March 1933, WG/Pal/19 and Gillies to secretary, Palestine Joint Cooperative Society 8 March 1933, WG/Pal/20.

33. Ibid., Jarblum, Socialist Committee for Labour Palestine to Gillies, 11 December 1933, 3 January 1934, Gillies to Jarblum 12 January 1934: 'I am not willing to make such an avowal for Palestine' WG/Pal 23.

34. Ibid., Plavskin to British Labour Party, 5 April 1934, WG/Pal/34; Gillies to Cohen, 14 April 1934, 17 April 1934, WG/Pal/38/43; Cohen to Gillies 18 April 1934, WG/Pal/34.

35. Ibid., Plavskin to British Labour Party 25 April 1934, WG/Pal/34.

36. Sozialistische Arbeiter-Internationale papers, David Plavskin to SAI, Zurich December 1930 and Plavskin to 3rd International appealing for unity, copies to British Labour Party, SAI 2531/1 & 2.

37. William Gillies Correspondence, Locker to Gillies 14 June 1934, WG/Pal/46.
38. Ibid., Attlee's statement 8 November 1935, WG/Pal/61.
39. Ibid., I. Narodiczky notices 12 November 1935, WG/Pal/62/63.
40. Ibid., Poale Zion to British Labour Party, January 1936, WG/Pal/66.
41. Ibid., press report, 27 February 1936, WG/Pal/69.
42. Ibid., Locker to Gillies, 14 May 1936, WG/Pal/79.
43. Ibid., Dr. N. Rafalkes to Dear Comrade, 15 March 1936, WG/Pal/82.
44. Ibid., Advisory Committee for Imperial Questions report April 1937, WG/Pal/115.
45. Ibid., Arthur Creech Jones to Gillies 2 February 1937, enclosing Pumphrey's report, Autumn 1936 WG/Pal/113.
46. Ibid., Advisory Committee for Imperial Questions, memoranda November 1938, WG/Pal/158.
47. Ibid., statement from Mansur, 20 December 1938, WG/Pal/159.
48. Ibid., Mansur's report 1938, WG/Pal/188.
49. Ibid., Palestine Arab Workers' Society to Chair, British Labour Party, 27 June 1939, Locker to Gillies 31 July 1939, WG/Pal/195.
50. Collette (1998), op. cit., p. 62; William Gillies Correspondence, Joseph Cohen to Gillies 6 May 1937, WG/Pal/117.
51. William Gillies Correspondence, Gillies to Middleton 22 June 1939, WG/Pal/190.
52. Ibid., Gillies to International Subcommittee and 'representatives of our Palestine friends', 25 May 1937, WG/Pal/128.
53. Ibid., *Labour*, August 1937.
54. Ibid., International Subcommittee notes, January 1938, WG/PAL/138.
55. Ibid., General Federation of Jewish Labour, Labour Faction in Tel Aviv Municipal Council to Dear comrades, 20 December 1938, WG/Pal/160; Gillies to Creech Jones, 5 January 1939, WG/Pal/163; Gillies to Morrison, 5 January 1939, WG/Pal/164.
56. Ibid., Dov Hos to Labour Party, 19 April 1939, Dov Hos to Middleton 20 April 1939, Gillies to Scott Lindsay, 29 April 1929, WG/Pal/172; American trades unions to Labour Party 1939, WG/Pal/168; US and Canada Jewish Labor to Labour Party, 29 May 1939, WG/Pal/179; Poale Zion New York to Middleton 17 June 1939, WG/Pal/196.
57. Collette (1998), op. cit., p. 79.
58. Ibid., pp. 63-5.
59. Kelemen (1996), op. cit., p. 80.
60. Collette (1998), op. cit., p. 81 ff.
61. Ibid., pp. 89-97.

62. Sargisson (1996), op. cit., *passim.*

63. Sozialistische Arbeiter-Internationale papers, Bund resolution for conference, 18-21 May 1926, SAI 894; Poale Zion conference 22-25 June 1926, SAI 890/1.

64. Sozialistische Arbeiter-Internationale papers, secretary's report to executive, 17 January 1938; Jarblum succeeded Kaplansky as delegate, although there was much obscurity and correspondence about the identity of the official delegate and his address, Kaplansky to Jerusalem, Jarblum to secretary SAI 9 November 1924, SAI 2511/18; Jarblum to Dear Comrade, 16 January 1928, SAI 2512/44; Jarblum to Adler, 21 December 1928, SAI 2528/1.

65. Sozialistische Arbeiter-Internationale papers, Miss J. Rose, Poale Zion, England, to Dr Adler, 6 January 1925, 19 January 1925; Adler's replies, 17 January 1925, 19 January 1925, SAI 2516 /1-4; memo from Kaplansky 12 April 1930, SAI 2512; Adler to Jarblum 4 November 1929, SAI 2528/1; Jarblum to Adler, 12 January 1929, 9 February 1929, SAI 2528/3-5; Jarblum for Poale Zion re Austrian SDP, 15 February 1924, SAI 4461.

66. William Gillies Correspondence, Poale Zion to Labour Party, 29 August 1936, WG/Pal/93.

67. Ibid., Bund resolution for executive, 25 June 1937.

68. Labour and Socialist International miscellaneous papers, National Museum of Labour History, Manchester, LSI balance sheet 1936.

69. Ibid., LSI secretary's report for executive committee meeting, 8 March 1937.

70. Ibid., report by Jarblum for LSI executive, 25 June 1937.

71. Ibid., *Documents and Discussion,* 12 August 1936, 12 November 1926.

72. Sozialistische Arbeiter-Internationale papers, resolution on trans-fer, 29 February 1926, SAI 2523/2; Gillies to Adler, 27 February 1936, SAI 2523/7; Jaarblum to Adler, 12 March 1936, SAI 2523/11; Poale Zion to SAI, nd, SAI 2523/46; memorandum for LSI executive, 16-18 May 1936, SAI 2523/84; Adler to Jarblum, 4 May 1936, SAI 2523/84; Jarblum to Adler, 6 May 1936, SAI 2523/89.

73. Labour and Socialist International miscellaneous papers, secretary's report to executive, 11 January 1938.

74. Ibid., secretary's report to executive and Bund resolution, 17 January 1938.

75. Ibid., secretary's report to executive, 29-30 May 1938, my emphasis.

76. Collette (1998), op. cit., p. 90.

77. Koestler (1983), op. cit., p. 41.

CHAPTER FIVE

A Question of 'Jewish Politics'? The Jewish Section of the Communist Party of Great Britain, 1936-45

Jason Heppell

The concept of a modern 'Jewish politics' is used to describe and explain the participation of the Jewish people in the political arenas of nineteenth- and twentieth-century European society.[1] In an age of mass politics, the Jews came to play a significant role in the life of the nation states and to express their political aspirations on an unprecedented scale. The formation of a Jewish left represented the ideals and aims of a section of radicalised Jewish intellectuals and a largely secularised class-conscious Jewish proletariat. In the East European multinational states, the Bund and the various socialist-Zionist parties played a distinct and important part in the political life of the Jewish masses. However, whereas these clearly 'Jewish' groups seem to fit the criteria for entry into the realm of 'Jewish politics', it less apparent whether the activity of left-wing Jews in non-Jewish socialist parties does so. The greater integration and lack of explicitly Jewish political structures, especially in Western democratic Labour movements, makes differentiating between Jewish and non-Jewish politics particularly difficult. Exactly where the boundaries are set affects one's conclusions about the nature of the subject as it determines the range of source material available for study. Definition is, therefore, a fundamental aspect of 'Jewish politics' as it is with Jewish history in general. Delimitation is a complicated, sometimes tortuous, process, but in outlining the contours of the subject it can prove rewarding in revealing the nature of 'Jewish politics'.

The difficulties involved in the process of defining 'Jewish politics' can best be demonstrated through studies of the fringe elements of Jewish political behaviour, where inclusion or exclusion is contested the most. Subjects apparently peripheral can reveal much that is intrinsic to the core. The complex history of the Jewish Bureau (JB) of the Communist Party of Great Britain (CPGB) in the inter-war and war years, offers an opportunity for such a study. Communism poses particular problems for 'Jewish politics'. The traditional historiographical distinction which forms the basis for modern Jewish history, between 'Western' emancipated Jewry and the 'Eastern' Jewish nation, is not easily applied to communism. Communist parties were active and moderately successful in both spheres despite the supposed differences between 'East' and 'West'.[2] Communism also has a universal and class-based ideology which appears to be in contradiction to the ethnic particularism implied in the concept of 'Jewish politics'.

One solution as to whether Jewish involvement in communism represents 'Jewish politics' or not, is by applying an 'exclusive' definition that concentrates only upon the 'Jewish sections'. Nearly every communist party in a country with a major Jewish population had such a body. The Communist parties of the United States, Poland, the Soviet Union, Canada, Australia, Hungary, France, Austria and Palestine all had an official Jewish component at some time in their history.[3] Ezra Mendelsohn, while recognising the 'thorny problem' of deciding which organisations should be admitted to the domain of 'Jewish politics', does include these sections (including those found in socialist parties other than Communist) in his seminal work, *On Modern Jewish Politics*.[4] His own definition of modern 'Jewish politics' encompasses such sections alongside the Zionist, Orthodox and Bundist political organisations that developed from the nineteenth century onwards:

> The phrase Jewish politics as employed here refers to the programs formulated by these new movements , that is, the different ways in which they viewed the future of the Jewish people and their proposals for solving once and for all, the celebrated Jewish Question, and the competition among them for hegemony on what was sometimes called the 'Jewish street'.[5]

For Mendelsohn, Jewish sections and their programs were the sole examples of 'Jewish politics' within the Communist world. Jewish sections were 'halfway houses', temporarily located 'between the ultimately doomed ghetto and a future of universal brotherhood'.[6] However, the CPGB's own section shows that this conclusion is only half the story. The policies of the CPGB, the role of the Soviet Union, the influence exercised by the Jewish community, Palestinian developments and the dilemmas of Jewish-Communist identity are all part of the wider relationship between Jewish Communists and their party. A study concerned only with the policies of the Jewish section can limit as well as illuminate the phenomenon of Jewish communism.

Another alternative to the 'exclusive' focus upon the Jewish sections is the 'inclusive' approach of Henry Srebrnik in his study on London Jews and British communism.[7] The CPGB, although never a large party,[8] did have greater influence than its size would suggest, particularly in the trade unions. However, the doubling of its parliamentary contingent in the July 1945 general election only meant an increase from one MP to two. This one success was due to the election of Phil Piratin to the Mile End seat, a constituency in the heart of the Jewish East End. This event, along with Communist successes in the local municipal elections later in the year, has led Srebrnik to argue for its significance in terms of 'ethnic group politics';[9] the moment when the CPGB achieved 'political hegemony'[10] over the local Jewish population. The Mile End election, he believes, was the result of an

94

'ethno-ideological movement' based on the Jewish community acting as a self-contained group, separate socially, politically and culturally from the surrounding gentile society.[11] Established in the 1930s, and in which the party's own Jewish section came to play a leading role, Jewish communism, as 'social movement', went beyond class and institutional allegiances in an attempt to produce social change.[12] All dimensions of the relationship between Jews and communism can, therefore, be included within the realm of 'Jewish politics'.

Indeed, approximately 7 per cent of the CPGB's full-time workers, the 'cadres', those that staffed the party hierarchy and positions of leadership in its organisations, were Jewish.[13] As Jews formed less than 1 per cent of the population as a whole, the disproportionate numbers involved places British Jewish communists firmly within a general trend, noticed in the relationship between Jews and communism in other countries.[14] There can also be little doubt of the strong 'Jewish vote' for the Communist Party in Stepney or the CPGB's involvement in 'Jewish' issues such as combating anti-Semitism. However, whether one can argue that Communist success in the East End really represents a synthesis of ethnicity and politics or the domination of the ethnic over class, is questionable. The divisive impact of acculturation and party loyalty upon Jewish Communists alone casts doubt on an 'inclusive' unity thesis. A shared ethnicity can be a source of friction as well as understanding.

This chapter will seek to reassess the role of the ethnicity in the 1945 election as well as reconsidering the nature of the Jewish sections and the question of what 'Jewish politics' is. It will be suggested that politicised ethnicity, whether as institutional section or ethnic movement, cannot by itself explain the complex phenomenon of 'Jewish communism'. Instead, it is argued that Jewish left wing politics can only be understood through the intimate connections between political party, ethnic/non-ethnic identities and historical developments. To emphasise the paramount importance of the party, the actual structure of the CPGB will act as the framework of interpretation in order to clearly reveal the subjects parameters and the interdependency of ethnicity and political structure. Three sections outline the argument, each one representing in descending order the basic organisational and political levels of the CPGB: the party leadership, the district parties and the grass roots membership. This study spans the period of the Jewish Bureau of the CPGB from its foundation in 1936 through to its (non) involvement in the 1945 Communist election victory.

The Communist Party Leadership

The decisions of the Communist Party political leadership are the most important factors in understanding the creation of a Jewish section within the CPGB. Policy in the Communist Party was made under the guiding principle of 'democratic centralism'; decisions were taken by a small leadership élite and then relayed to the lower levels of the party structure where they were to be accepted without question. Rank and file involvement in decision-making was limited, although the ordinary members did have considerable scope in how they implemented these policies. The leadership itself was subject to the discipline of the Soviet Union as, technically, the CPGB was merely a subsection of the Comintern, the international organisation responsible for the development of world wide communism. This meant, in general, subordination to the policies of the USSR. Soviet intervention at various times in the CPGB was usually conclusive, often dramatic and certainly contentious. However, day-to-day interference on every issue was far from the norm. Party leaders were usually left to implement policy on their own, though strictly within perceived Moscow priorities. Other concerns, therefore, did influence decision-making, namely internal factors such as the Party's structural features moulded by its adaptation to British political life; and external pressures, including the attitudes of the British population and world events. The origins of the CPGB's Jewish Bureau can be seen within the interrelationships between these internal and external factors with an intermittent though decisive involvement by the Soviet Union.

Srebrnik has suggested that the change in Soviet policy introduced into world communism by the Seventh Comintern Congress of 1935 led the CPGB to adopt a favourable attitude towards Jewish concerns.[15] The success of fascism in Germany had led to the ending of the Class Against Class period where social democratic parties had been categorised as 'social-fascists' by the communists in a bid for leadership of the working class. The new strategy was the Popular Front whose aim was to build alliances among other 'progressive' forces in the fight against fascism. As well as changing the attitude towards other socialist parties, the middle class and the intellectuals, Srebrnik argues the Congress also affected their approach towards Anglo-Jewry as 'Jewish Communists were encouraged to assume political and moral leadership of a broad alliance within the Jewish community'.[16]

The Congress was influential in the formation of the Jewish Bureau, but not necessarily in the way one would expect. The Soviet Union's negative perception of Jewish interests rather than any positive steps it took towards 'ethno-politics' would be the key issue.[17] The Congress and its consequences were also not the only bridges between the Jewish community and communism, as the wider political and party context was particularly important.

The CPGB had always shown a limited awareness of Jewish concerns. The Unity Conference of 1920 which brought together various socialist groups to create the British Communist Party may not have involved organised Jewish elements, as was the case with the founding of its American sister party,[18] but it did issue a resolution condemning the murder of Jewish Communists by the Polish, Romanian and Hungarian governments, thus suggesting the activities of a Jewish contingent.[19] Moreover, the Communist-controlled front organisation, the League Against Imperialism, supervised a Jewish Workers Council which in 1930 published anti-Zionist propaganda.[20] There was to a limited extent an intrinsic 'ethnic' element to the CPGB which may have predisposed it favourably towards Jewish matters. Britain is a multinational and multiethnic state and the membership of the CPGB fully reflected this. The party leadership through the inter-war period, based in the Political Bureau and Central Committee, although containing only one Jew, Andrew Rothstein,[21] did have comrades of Irish, Welsh, Scottish, English and even Indo-Swedish background. The CPGB was politically involved in Ireland, in certain countries of the Empire (especially India) and had attempted to organise black workers in the docklands of Liverpool.[22] Jews had been members of the party from its foundation. The rise of fascism would bring many more into the Communist solar system, though the CPGB was active against the British Union of Fascists and aware of its anti-Semitism well before the 1935 Congress.[23] The party leader, Harry Pollitt, stated in November 1934 that the fight against fascism was to be 'the supreme task of our Party'.[24]

The Popular Front did reinforce the anti-fascist direction taken by CPGB, especially by placing a greater emphasis on drawing all sections of the national community into the fight, but it did not lead to the creation of the party's Jewish Bureau. The crucial aspect of CPGB policy which drew the party towards Anglo-Jewry was its desire to gain a foothold in a working class community, to create a 'little Moscow'. A small party with limited resources, the CPGB could concentrate only upon building its support within a few select areas. East London with its harsh socio-economic conditions and vibrant left-leaning local politics was an area well suited for the development of the Communist Party. Many senior party figures, including Harry Pollitt, had been politically active in London's East End and amongst its Jewish socialists for many years.[25] Although the Class Against Class policy turned the Communists against Labour, it did not turn the CPGB away from the *raison d'être* of British politics – parliamentary elections. In this respect, the by-election held late 1930 in the East End constituency of Whitechapel proved vital in Jewish-Communist relations. The party put forward Pollitt as its candidate. The need to adapt to local conditions meant that the CPGB produced election material and held meetings directly aimed at the Jewish workers. The Communists lost, but, due to the intense activity and positive reception the party received, the campaign had led to a consolidation of their position in the area and was duly seen as a 'success' and an 'inspiration' by the leadership.[26] Rajani Palme Dutt, the party's leading theoretician, presented a report on the by-election to the Political Bureau in which he stated that he now saw Whitechapel as Pollitt's 'permanent future local base' and that 'it is such local rooting of the party in a series of working class centres that we must now need to build up'.[27] This, in addition to the rise of fascism, made the 'Jewish Street' of the East End one of, if not the, most important regions for the party. The consequences of the party's desire for 'roots' was that progress in Stepney made the party stronger, but at the same time forced it to become more responsive to demands from the local population. The CPGB was not prepared for this, a weakness that led to the formation of the party's own Jewish Bureau.

In April 1936 a wave of Arab-Jewish violence swept through Palestine. It produced an emotive response from Anglo-Jewry as the fear of pogroms was revived. The Communist Party was caught off guard as little time had been spent developing its policy on Palestine. The CPGB normally treated the Yishuv or any aspects of the 'Jewish Question' as part of the wider Middle East Imperialist problem. Little had been said or done by the party when similar incidents had occurred in 1929. In 1936 things were to be very different. Warnings had already been given two years earlier by two Political Bureau members, Johnny Campbell and John Gollan, that the party was not prepared on this issue, but they were ignored.[28] The Seventh Congress had inaugurated the Popular Front policy, but, in the discussions on national conditions, it was the Palestinian Arab delegate position that held sway over any consideration of Jewish interests.[29] The CPGB maintained the Soviet line with its pro-Arab, anti-Yishuv bias.

Within a month of the outbreak of open conflict in Palestine, the leadership held its first ever detailed debates on the 'Jewish Question'. A resolution on Palestine was presented, but there was little doubt that the subtext was the Party's reaction to pressure from the Jewish community. As Ben Bradley, the Colonial Department secretary, admitted:

> we have been driven to the situation of discussion of this question because of the apparent revolt of the Jewish population against the line of the Party. It is not only something which has happened recently but since the 7th Congress. Since the delegates from the Arab countries made their contributions there, there has been a considerable discussion in Palestine and other countries against the line laid down by the 7th World Congress.[30]

Confusion and recriminations ensued among the party leaders. Those closely connected with the East End pointed out the need to move carefully because of the consequences it could have among Jewish workers, particularly with the success of fascist anti-Semitism on the Continent. Others accepted the Soviet line outright with little accommodation of Jewish concerns. General agreement was reached that there must be clarity on the 'Jewish Question'. The Political Bureau produced a package of measures to deal with the problem. One decision was to issue a press statement which deliberately ignored most of the Palestine controversy and concentrated instead on the fight against fascism and the role Jewish workers had to play in it. To avoid a repetition of the difficulties caused by the party's lack of preparation, it was also decided 'that an advisory board should be set up that can keep the Political Bureau in touch with current questions and advise upon what is taking place amongst the various Jewish organisations'.[31] This was the initial catalyst for the founding of the party's Jewish Bureau.[32] The setting up of a Jewish body in this way was not unique to the CPGB. The Palestinian Communist Party also set up its own Jewish section in 1936 in similar circumstances.[33] However, the party still maintained a largely pro-Arab position in its official publications. According to one of its correspondents in the *Labour Monthly* 'The present disturbances in Palestine are therefore unpleasant but reasonable'.[34]

With few Jews in the leadership elite and with no precedent for such a body, the party had to look elsewhere for interested and knowledgeable comrades to staff the section. The bureau's membership in fact came from a section of Jewish Communists based in a non-party association, the 'Hackney Study Group'.[35] Set up in 1932 by a small nucleus of Communists active since the late 1920s, the group's aim was to act as a 'centre for Marxist Educational work among the Jewish people'.[36] Most of its members, including its two main figures, Lazar Zaidman and Sam Alexander, were leading figures in the Workers' Circle, a left-wing Jewish Friendly Society, with its headquarters in Great Alie Street Stepney, London. Zaidman and Alexander had temporarily lapsed from party membership at the time of the Study Group's formation, which may explain the latter's non-party basis. However, they were both committed Communists as can be seen by their activity within a variety of Soviet-Jewish agricultural settlement committees[37] and both still 'sought a field of activity [with] which we could help the Party'.[38] As relatively well-known figures in the East End and with close links to the London District Committee, it is to them that the Party turned with its aim of setting up a Jewish section. Discussions were held in which Zaidman played a 'leading role' and which culminated in the formation of the Jewish Bureau.[39] He was elected secretary and remained so until 1939.

Limited to an advisory capacity in a few select areas and with sparse resources at its disposal, the JB proved to be largely ineffectual and irrelevant throughout the inter-war period. It was active only at an obscure level, publishing occasional articles for party journals alongside other (non-JB) contributors on the subject.[40] Eric Hobsbawm, the noted Marxist historian, recalls how, as a young Jewish student in the Cambridge University branch of the Communist Party in the late 1930s, he was instructed by the party to 'take up Jewish matters'. Zaidman was amongst those who came up from East London to meet him and the few other Jewish Communist undergraduates at Cambridge. Their discussions achieved nothing.[41] Hobsbawm showed little interest and the Jewish Bureau had no coercive power available to enforce its will. The bureau had no influential patrons at the party centre and remained an unimportant adjunct to London District activities. Joe Jacobs, the Stepney Communist Party branch secretary during the 1930s, does not mention the JB, Zaidman or Alexander once in his detailed autobiographical account of East London Communist politics.[42] The members of the JB were involved in London anti-fascist CPGB activities in the 1930s, especially in the communist dominated Jewish People's Council Against Fascism and Anti-Semitism (JPC). However, as an organisation, the bureau did not make any noticeable impact. There was no concerted drive to deal directly with Jewish problems, except on anti-Semitism, though even this was placed firmly within the context of the national and international struggle against fascism and capitalism, as much a threat to the Gentiles as it was to the Jews.[43]

Indeed, one should not exaggerate the extent to which the CPGB was involved in 'ethno-politics' or wished to be perceived as such even after the JB's formation. The party tried to avoid close association between its own policies and that of Jewish interests. Mindful of the anti-Semitic 'Bolshevism is Jewish' bogey and its use in the heartlands of East London fascism, the Political Bureau noted in 1937 that:

> We have to face the position where 5% of the Bethnal Green comrades are Jewish. When considering the fascist activity in the streets ... it is obviously necessary for the Party to arrange poster parades, [however,] large scale parades are needed with comrades who are not all Jewish.[44]

Although the JB had a limited degree of autonomy in its activities, there was little doubt that the party leadership had ultimate control and that Soviet policy would always be in the end the true guiding principle. At the outbreak of the war in September 1939 the JB was dissolved.[45] There is, unfortunately, little archival material to explain this development. However, one can assume that it is connected with the Nazi-Soviet Pact signed a few weeks before the invasion and the consequent desire of the CPGB to avoid the difficulties that the presence of a Jewish section might create once war began. It was certainly not the only area of party activity to be affected. As well as the resignation of Harry Pollitt as party leader, the JPC was reduced to a skeleton form and within a few months wound up altogether despite the continuing presence of anti-Semitism in the East End.[46] The party's 'Bright Shining Star' of anti-fascism imploded into a black hole.[47]

That the party viewed its Jewish section initially in terms of Soviet policy can again be seen by the reforming of the JB in 1941, 'at the request of the Party Centre',[48] following the invasion of the Soviet Union by the German army. The fight for the survival of the Soviet Union became the overriding concern of the British Communist Party. It sought to use the Anglo-Jewish community in line with the policies of the Soviet Jewish Anti-Fascist Committee (JAFC). Formed soon after the invasion and based in Kubyishev and Moscow, the JAFC's purpose was to promote a pro-Soviet policy for political and financial reasons amongst the world's Jewish communities, principally those of the USA, Canada and Britain.[49] The founding congress was reported on the 29 August 1941 by the main Anglo-Jewish community newspaper, the *Jewish Chronicle*,[50] and soon after by the CPGB journal, *World News and Views*.[51] The Soviet Embassy in London began immediately to make contacts with Anglo-Jewish groups, including the Orthodox Agudist

Organisation,[52] and to release propaganda material on Soviet Jewry through the *Soviet War News*, the daily bulletin of the embassy's press department.[53] Previously only a trickle of Jewish news from the USSR would reach the West; now a flood of articles on the heroic actions of Red Army Jews and the atrocities of the Nazis were published in the *Jewish Chronicle*. In turn, the paper adopted, along with large sections of the Jewish community,[54] a more sympathetic view of the Soviet Union than ever before, much to the satisfaction of the JAFC.[55]

It is in this context that Palme Dutt, the party leader most sensitive to changes in Soviet policy, summoned Zaidman to King Street, the party's headquarters in London, and re-established the JB with Zaidman as its first secretary.[56] This was not the only aspect of the British Party's change in approach to the Jewish community. Leading Jewish Communists were also brought in to propagate the new line: Ivor Montagu, son of a eminent Anglo-Jewish family and senior article writer for the *Daily Worker*, gave a talk in December 1941 to the Anglo-Palestinian Club on the need for Jews to fight with the Soviet Union and against Hitler.[57] This talk contrasted sharply with the one presented at the Workers Circle in February 1940 titled 'Jews Against the War'.[58] Alongside the *Jewish Chronicle*'s favourable reporting of the Soviet Union, the *Daily Worker* increased markedly its reporting of Jewish issues. In an attempt to spread the message of the JAFC, the communist Anglo-Russian Parliamentary Committee published the pamphlet *Jews Against Hitler: Appeal and Report of the International Conference of Jews held In Moscow August 24th 1941.*

Despite its refounding, the JB again had little impact within the CPGB or the Jewish community. It remained largely confined to only a limited sphere of activity, mainly the pro-Soviet fund raising organisations set up following the JAFC appeal: the Jewish 1942 Committee,[59] and its successors, the United Jewish Committee (UJC), and the Jewish Fund For Soviet Russia (JFSR).[60] In fact, the transformation of the UJC into the JFSR was due to the compromise forced on the JB by the Anglo-Jewish establishment. Because of its weak position within British Jewry, the JB had to cede control of this pro-Soviet group to the Board of Deputies and other senior community figures and organisations in order to gain their involvement.[61]

The next decisive event in the history of the Jewish section involved a direct contact with the JAFC. The committee's two leading figures, Solomon Mikhoels, director of the Moscow Yiddish Theatre, and Itzik Fefer, the famous Yiddish poet, embarked on a propaganda mission among the allied Jewish communities in October 1943. This was 'the high point of the new relationship between Soviet and world Jewry',[62] the first official contact between Soviet Jews and the Diaspora since the 1917 Revolution. The particular timing of the visit was an attempt to deflect attention away from the murder by the Soviets of the two Bundist leaders, Victor Alter and Henryk Erlich as well as an answer to the desperate war time predicament of the USSR.[63]

After visiting the USA, Canada and Mexico, Mikhoels and Fefer arrived in London on 30 October and stayed until 22 November. Touring and lecturing throughout the country on a pro-Soviet platform, they received an enthusiastic welcome from Anglo-Jewry, including such notables as Chief Rabbi Hertz and the full membership of the Board of Deputies.[64] However, Mikhoels and Fefer had another purpose as well as propaganda: making contact with the JB of the Communist Party. In a meeting at the Hyde Park Hotel, London, Mikhoels and Fefer discussed the situation in the Soviet Union with Zaidman and the other leading Jewish Communists, Alec Waterman, Chimen Abramsky and Hyman Levy. They encouraged the British Jewish Communists to become more involved in the Jewish community and to collect funds for the Soviet Union.[65] In turn, the JB along with the Soviet Ambassador in London sent reports to the JAFC on the progress of pro-Communist sympathies within the Anglo-Jewish community.[66]

The fact that these two senior Soviet officials had asked to see the members of the JB made a considerable impression on Dutt. He called the JB members to King Street and after discussions the Jewish section acquired a new status, signified by the allocation of a room for their work within the King Street building.[67] The JB now came under Dutt's personal supervision where it was made a subcommittee at the party centre responsible to the Colonial and International Bureaux. Previously, the JB had been supervised by the London District Committee and had held its meetings in members' homes. The physical relocation from the private sphere to the inner sanctum of the Communist Party represented an important symbolic and political movement upwards within party structures and consciousness. The removal of Zaidman as secretary and his replacement with Hyman Levy, Professor of Mathematics at the Imperial College London, was part of this profile raising process.

The twisted path of Soviet foreign policy had led finally to the creation of a fully functioning Jewish section at the heart of the party machine. The Bureau[68] now began a process of acquiring policy responsibility on Jewish matters from other areas of the party and developing and publishing its own proposals on subjects ranging from Zionism to the idea of a Jewish army. In 1945 the Bureau produced a statement, *The Jewish Question*, a detailed outline of their ideas and policy proposals. Nevertheless, the Bureau's primary aim during the Second World War was to raise support for the Soviet Union amongst the Jewish people through calls for a 'United Front' against fascism. The bureau members planned to engage other Jewish Communists in this effort under the name of 'Jewish Work'. Their results were to prove disappointing.

The District Party

In order for the re-established Jewish section to assert itself within the party and the Jewish community it had to develop its position in the areas of the country where the Jewish population lived, namely East London, Manchester, Leeds and Glasgow.

The JB organised, with the party's support, the first ever National Conference of Jewish party members on 31 January 1943. Forty-three Jewish Communists from throughout the country attended including representatives from most centres of Jewish life.[69] The JB's report on the conference set itself the key tasks of establishing and coordinating regional Bureaux.[70] By the time of the second conference in October this goal had been achieved.

To act on a national level, however, the Jewish section needed the support of the real power in the localities: the District and City party committees, the second tier of party organisation. There were usually 18 District committees, one for each of the main geo-political regions such as Scotland, Lancashire, Yorkshire and London. Some of these Districts would be closely connected with the City committees of its major population centres. These committees implemented party policy on a regional level, giving direction and guidance to local campaigns and party members. Their response to the JB was to prove critical in the success or failure of its provincial plans.

District and City committees were not passive recipients of King Street-imposed policy. They could negotiate to a limited extent with the Party Centre and they would generally interpret orders from there to match local conditions. What really mattered for the success of a policy was the amount of time and resources available that the local District leadership had to give to it and the political importance of the person or department giving the order. If a directive came from Harry Pollitt or the Industrial Department, for example, then it would have priority consideration. The difficulty for the JB was that it was a relatively new subcommittee of the International Department, with little real backing from its head, Palme Dutt. This meant that the establishment of JBs in their districts would be accepted, but only the bare minimum of support would be given to them. Problems would further arise if the JBs tried to draw on District resources, especially if they made any demands on the primary instrument for the advancement of the party in the localities: the party membership itself and in particular its activist core.

The Lancashire District shows these problems clearly. Manchester with the second largest Jewish community in Britain, estimated at 30,000, had the most active provincial JB and the worst relationship with its local party organisation. The Lancashire District committee complained in April 1943 over the demands from the JB for the release of a comrade from District responsibilities for activities in 'Jewish Work'. The Manchester Bureau turned to the national body for advice. Recognising its own lack of influence, the national bureau replied that the matter had to be dealt with locally.[71] It did not have the power to impose itself as there was too much risk in aggravating local power structures whose support they desperately needed. What caused concern for the JB in particular were the tensions that arose between the District and the local bureau over the establishment of a

103

Manchester Branch of the JFSR.[72] Relations deteriorated to such an extent that by mid-1943 the National JB was recommending a complete change in the personnel of the Manchester Bureau to improve the situation *vis-à-vis* its District organisation.[73] The situation did not improve in the short term.[74]

A similar experience was repeated in Leeds. The National Bureau sent comrades in 1943 to establish links with Jewish party members in the city. The Leeds comrades approached their local leader, the Yorkshire District secretary, Reuben Falber (who was also Jewish), over what they should do. Falber was hostile to the idea and although he did not block the setting up of such a bureau he recalled why he gave it little support:

> I was not keen on the project because I felt that these sub-committees tended to take the activists away from the work in the branches and that the work amongst the Jewish people in Leeds should really be in the hands of the Leeds city committee and particularly the North East Leeds branch which covered Chapeltown and Moortown, the principal Jewish areas in the city where there were synagogues, Jewish clubs, Jewish shops and where Jewish people in general lived and congregated.[75]

The fact that a District secretary would show so little concern with the JB shows how little importance the party assigned to it. When the second Jewish conference was being planned, its initial date was rejected by Harry Pollitt as it would coincide with District Conferences and a national recruiting campaign.[76] It was obvious to the party and to the JB where the political priorities lay.

The weakness of the JB within the CPGB led to two further problems. First, it was unable to control autonomous action by its provincial Bureaux. The Leeds JB issued a statement on the execution of Erlich and Alter. That a decision to release material on such a sensitive issue should be taken on a local level without the prior consent of the national body drew a sharp rebuke from the JB leadership against not only the Leeds comrades, but also the District committee for allowing the statement to appear in the first place.[77]

Second, uncertainty concerning the JB's status could be found throughout the CPGB, not just in the provincial areas. An attempt was made by the London District committee in May 1943 to merge the JB with the existing Colonial Bureau, effectively liquidating the Jewish section. If the JB's activities had been purely in connection with international Jewish concerns then its case for independent existence would have been weak. However, the bureau managed to survive by a direct appeal to the secretariat of the party's Central Committee. The bureau pointed out that 'the Jews of England, of which 260,000 live in and around the London area form a stable section of the population with organisations and problems deeply rooted in England' and that 'their problems are not of a Colonial character'. To merge the Jewish section with another bureau would have been 'grist to the mill' of the Zionists and others who claim that the Jews are an alien presence in this country.[78] Ironically, it was to be the visit of Mikhoels and Feffer a few months later which secured the bureau's position by making it a subcommittee of the party's International Department.

The JB recognised the problems it faced and tried to find reasons for them. In its own newsletter they argued that 'in the course of our work many difficulties are encountered which are basically due to the newness of Communist activities among Jews'. It complained about the absence of experienced cadres and knowledge 'from which to draw lessons and guidance' and criticised the party for failing to deal with 'Jewish Work' in the past.[79] It is apparent that despite the JB's formation in the mid-1930s it would take several years before the party dealt seriously with Jewish issues.

The situation did improve with time as the bureau began to embed itself within the Party structure particularly following the elevation in party status due to the Mikhoels and Fefer visit. A more positive assessment of its work was given at the Third Conference of Jewish Communists in January 1945. However, the opening statement by Palme Dutt addressed concerns still expressed over the JB's role in the CPGB. One weakness, the CPGB had, Dutt noted, when dealing with areas it had never really dealt with before was

> to try to solve the approach of the Party on the basis of wanting to set up our own special committees, special organisations and the like. The existence of the NJC [National Jewish Committee] of the Party is a perfectly straightforward and normal method of organising the Party's work in another particular sphere.[80]

By allaying doubts in the party concerning the JB, Dutt was seeking to give it credibility and authority within the party structure. He concluded that his statement was intended for the party as a whole and that:

> The Executive Committee desires, and it will require some pressure to ensure, that it be considered and discussed in the main general membership of the Party and especially by the District Committees of the Party, so that there is a clarity on the kind of questions and on our approach to them.[81]

District party opposition meant, however, more than just local obstruction to a 'Jewish policy'. It represented also the problematical relationship between political activity by Jews and the concept of 'Jewish politics'. The Districts and the JB did not have any history of dealing with each other. As the JB noted following the January National Conference, the provincial delegates had shown that 'they had never dealt seriously with Jewish work'.[82] One delegate from Salford declared at the conference that there were 20,000 Jews in his District but activities up to this point had been 'insignificant'.[83] This is despite the intense period of anti-fascist activity of the 1930s which brought into the Communist Party thousands of Jews. The Jewish involvement in the Aid-for-Spain movement, the International Brigades, the anti-Mosley demonstrations and the fight against anti-Semitism, set against the background of the rise of continental fascism, did not lead the CPGB at national or local level either to formulate any program for solving the 'Jewish Question' or to create any effective organisational structure sensitive to Jewish needs. The notion that an 'ethno-ideological movement' existed in the East End during this time has to be treated with caution. Just because Jews became politically active did not by itself result in a recognisable 'Jewish' political framework or ideology. Practically all political activity by Jewish Communists was through the Communist Party structure, its branches, front organisations, factory groups, its journals and its party hierarchy. Response to Jewish concerns was as much a result of external events and their interpretation by the party leaders, national and local, as it was to internal pressure from Jewish party members. Even when a response was forthcoming, it did not necessarily meet with success. The JB of the 1930s was ineffective and very localised in its activities. The JB of 1943 may have been of a different nature and acting at a time more favourable for Communist development in the Jewish community, but it was still in largely uncharted waters and making little headway. How much this was the case can be shown by the relationship between the JB and the ordinary Jewish party members.

The Grass Roots

The organisational difficulties the JB faced did impede but not altogether prevent its policies from filtering down to the lowest but crucial level of the CPGB structure, the ordinary branch membership. Once again, however, the Bureau received a response it did not want. The most severe setback the JB faced was the negative reaction of the grass roots to 'Jewish Work'.

At a London Jewish Committee meeting in November 1944, Alec Waterman remarked on their lack of success:

> The efforts of this committee to date, has failed, no comrades from East London having been found either capable or willing to do Jewish Work. Our role as advisors was sterile, since there existed not one comrade whom we could advise ... We had been plugging away for two years in advising and in efforts to get someone locally interested in Jewish work, with absolutely no result.[84]

The leadership of the Communist Party was well aware of this issue, as was apparent from a letter sent by Harry Pollitt to the first Jewish Communist conference:

> May I suggest that based on my own experience since our party was first formed and especially in the East End of London that the greatest stumbling block to doing effective work of a mass character amongst the Jewish people is the reluctance of our own Jewish comrades to recognise this as only possible for them to carry out and that it is their Party duty to do so.[85]

This was a constant theme throughout this conference and those that followed. But what accounts for this 'reluctance'? The critical factor is the problem of Jewish Communist identity. Jewish identity is a complex phenomenon. Historians approach the subject more with caution than confidence. Amorphous and ambiguous in some contexts, strikingly clear in others, Jewish identity is further confused in the political sphere by the competing claims of party loyalties. Jewish Communists' primary political loyalty was to communism. However, on the level of identity each would have a different relationship with his or her Jewishness, an identity developed mainly during the members pre-party lives. The question is: how did this manifest itself within the Communist Party and especially in relation to 'Jewish Work'? Henry Pelling has suggested that the influx of young Jews in the 1930s joined with the generation of Jewish communists from the party's earliest period to form a link between the old and the new Communist membership.[86] In fact, the very opposite was to prove the case as the Communist Party struggled to cope with inter-generational cultural differences translating into intra-party conflict.

The Communist Party's primary demand on its membership was for support for its policies and their assistance in their implementation. The party would have preferred a strong communist identity to facilitate effective party work and to prevent dissent. But the CPGB was a small party with limited resources available for a concerted drive to impose such an identity. In the spaces between party loyalty and party identity room existed for other elements, provided they did not conflict or interfere with party demands. Two sets of identities can be discerned amongst the British Jewish Communists in relation to 'Jewish Work'. One is a distinctive 'nucleus' and the other a broader less well-defined 'type'. The former I have called 'Jewish activists', the latter 'grass root Communist Jews'. Neither is hermetically sealed from the other, nor can these terms necessarily be used in areas of party and Jewish life outside of the context of the JB.

The Jewish activists were a small group, little more than a dozen with a handful of supporters in various institutions and localities. Nearly all were older, first generation immigrants whose language and early cultural background was non-British. They had a keen interest in Jewish history and a passionate concern for their fellow Jews in Eastern Europe. Many had actually started their socialist careers in Romania, Russia or Poland. The majority of them were members of the London Communist branches of the Workers' Circle. Issie Panner's book, published in 1942, *Anti-Semitism and the Jewish Question*,[87] dedicated to the members of the Hackney Study Group, was an attempt to place the Jews as a people within an historical Marxist analysis and it broadly reflects the groups ideological stance. It was this fairly well organised and coherent group which sought to actively improve the condition of the Jewish people through communism that came to form the backbone of the JB.

The vast majority of Jewish Communists, however, were second or third generation English-speaking Anglicised Jews who had joined the CPGB as youths during the great anti-fascist struggles of the 1930s. They were active in local affairs only, although a few were to rise to positions of authority within the Communist Party hierarchy. They were not organised in any way except through the CPGB structure of factory and local branches. The most important political difference was not between them and their fellow Communists but between them and other Jews and Gentile non-Communists. They were Communist Jews not Jewish Communists. Within the context of political activity, they were not 'Jewish' variants of a Communist, but were rather Jews separated from their ethnic community by their Communist beliefs. As individuals, a few Communist Jews would show an interest in specifically 'Jewish' activities, but most did not. It was here, on the 'Jewish Street', in the areas of Cheetham (Manchester), Leylands (Leeds), Stepney and Hackney, that the strongest resistance to 'Jewish Work' took place.[88]

Whereas the JB's problems with the District parties were about practical concerns over policy and its implementation, the tensions that arose with the grass root Communist Jews were related to identity issues. A particularly severe attack on the JB's views came from Alfred Sherman.[89] In an article titled 'Jewish Nationality: a Pernicious Illusion', he argued that Jewish national rights and culture had been rendered 'historically redundant' by the development of society.[90] There could be no 'centre path', it was either assimilation or segregation.[91] Jewish comrades were to work amongst Jews in order to 'break down the ghetto walls from inside' by encouraging assimilation, not by emphasising Jewish differences.[92] He reserved his real venom for the Jewish activists. In another article, 'Marxism and the Jewish Question', he remarked that the JB's *The Jewish Question*, though an advance on Panner's *Anti-Semitism and the Jewish Question*, still had 'glaring weaknesses' and that:

> It is always well to remember that the least assimilated of Jewish comrades in the UK who are alien to the majority of British Jewry tend to claim themselves to be representatives of Jewish comrades as a whole ignoring the fact that the majority of the Jewish comrades in the party think of themselves as communists rather than as Jews and do not claim any special hearing on the Jewish problem which the Rabbinical faction, as for example Zaidman, rather tend to think of as their own personal property in true petite-bourgeoisie style.[93]

The 'Rabbinical faction' understood the division between themselves and the younger Jewish communists very well. They stressed in their educational literature that the 'older generation [of British Jewry] has regard for Yiddish culture and feeling of kinship with Jewish workers abroad',[94] a feeling the majority of members of the JB shared. In their understanding of the problem, the Jewish activists emphasised the impact that joining the party had on Jewish Communists. In a confidential document, *Party Work Amongst the Jews in Britain: Presentation of the Problem,* supplied to the CPGB leadership by the Bureau in December 1943, its first point was:

> It is characteristic of Jewish Communists that they are largely isolated

from Jewish life and from Jewish organisations. This is due to their having broken away from these in their approach towards a revolutionary outlook and towards Party membership. Jewish Party members are mainly occupied in other spheres of party activity.[95]

The act of joining the party could lead to a separation from the Jewish community, though it was not necessarily an immediate consequence. It took several years before Dennis Angel's Communist beliefs led to his split from his family and the Jewish community. However, it produced a strong reaction against his past. A report on Angel in connection with allocation of party work stated that because of his Jewish background, 'Jewish Work' may be his forte, but the report noted, 'he expresses a strong distaste to the suggestion that he might work in this field and says that he has long ceased to have any contact with people in Jewish organisations'.[96]

The term applied by the party and the JB to the contentious relations with grass root Communist Jews was 'sectarianism'. This is one of the most pejorative terms in the Communist lexicon, though it is not easy to define. It touches on the fundamental problem that extreme political groups have in attempting to reconcile their ideological beliefs with the need to participate in the external world. Party members belong to an organisation that seeks to change fundamentally the society in which they live. A sense of insularity from that world is induced with the desire to prove their party loyalty, the failure of fundamental change, and personal discrimination in employment and other spheres of everyday life. Yet, this 'sectarianism' causes tension with the party authorities who realise that it is partly through involvement in the external world that the party can succeed and thus prove the truth of its convictions. The Jewish Communist had the additional burdens of the continuing process of integration into the national culture and away from the world of their fathers and mothers. The JB, by applying the term 'sectarianism' to the problems it faced with other Jewish Communists, sought to place its critique within this most critical form of intra-party discourse. It was not merely a 'Jewish' matter, it was first and foremost a communist problem. However, for the JB, in no other area of party work had Jewish Communists shown as great a degree of 'sectarianism' as they did towards 'Jewish Work'.[97]

It was not that Communist Jews became fanatical communist ideologues or that they had swapped one 'faith' for another. Most Communist Jews were neither particularly religious before joining the party nor did they become proficient Marxists after. Devotion to the Marxist ideology, which communists seldom showed, is not the same as loyalty to 'The Party', which most Communists did express. The creation of alternative social networks based on the CPGB provided adequate compensation for loss of ties to previous institutions and so reduced the incentive to remain in or become involved with Jewish institutions. The reaction of Communist Jews to calls for them to become involved in Jewish affairs was sometimes more of astonishment than ideological hostility. Reuben Falber explained his reluctance to become involved: 'because what would it mean? I wasn't going to join a Zionist organisation! So how do you take part in these activities? You join a synagogue?!'[98] Nor was this a question of 'self-hatred'. Falber later became chairman of the National JB in the 1950s. His initial resistance as Yorkshire District secretary to the Leeds JB was mainly due to his primary loyalty to his party position and the consequent need to allocate resources according to the present political situation and the strength or weaknesses of competing interests.

Differences between the grass roots Communist Jews and the Jewish activists were, therefore, not always related to questions of identity. As outlined already, there were organisational problems which hampered the Jewish activists: most Jewish Communists had never even heard of the JB. For those who had, the extra burden of 'Jewish Work' may have been too much to bear alongside other party commitments. The Communist Party did not throw its weight behind the Jewish activists, so Communist Jews were not forced to choose between their party and their past. If they had to, it would be more than likely they would have supported the party. There were very few resignations from the Jewish comrades following the Nazi-Soviet Pact.[99] This was an event of far more consequence than the policies of the JB and which would have involved personal dilemmas of greater significance than those posed by 'Jewish Work'. In the terms of political sociology, the formation of the JB did not cause 'social division' to translate effectively into 'political cleavage'.[100]

The Jewish activists did try to bridge the gap between themselves and the grass roots with lectures, party classes, articles, a specialist journal, the *Jewish Clarion* and by the limited amount of pressure they could exert through the party hierarchy. The main aim of the First Conference of Jewish Communists had been to forge 'a closer link between the Party, the Jewish Communists and the Jewish people'.[101] However, the patterns of socialisation were very different, a legacy the Jewish activists, despite all their efforts, found difficult to overcome. The integration of the younger generation into non-Jewish society was pervasive and continuous and was apparent in many areas of Jewish life in the 1930s and 40s. The increase in intermarriage, the decline in children attending *Cheder*, the regularity with which Jews broke the *mitzvot* concerning Sabbath work were all indicators of these deep-rooted social processes. The turn to communism and away from the Jewish community by a section of Jewish youth was just one echo of the impact of modernity. As the former Communist Raphael Samuel eloquently, if somewhat imaginatively, reflected:

> For my mother's generation Communism, though not intended as such, was a way of being English, a bridge by which the children of the ghetto entered the national culture. It was also, in some sense, a break from the hereditary upbringing, as my mother put it, 'to emancipate ourselves from the narrowness of a religious environment'. It served them as a surrogate for university, and a more spiritual version of it, a unity of theory and

practice, the discovery of a wider comradeship, an apprenticeship in learning and life.[102]

One could argue how far Communist Jews were already part of British society before they joined the party and to what extent the marginalised CPGB integrated them further, but Samuel's view does strike a chord in certain respects. In terms of introducing a section of the Jewish people to the traditions and practices of British politics, the CPGB certainly offered one path amongst many. Nevertheless, it was an unusual form of acculturation and one should not stress too far the idea that by joining the Communist Party Jews became 'English'.

Communist Jews had not lost their traditional ties completely; they still socialised with Jews, lived in Jewish areas and because of family commitments still celebrated the occasional festival. Most of them were not as hostile to Jewish culture as Sherman or Angel. The JB was also concerned about the small minority of Jewish Communists who were active in Jewish organisations but 'few of our comrades work in these as Communists, nor go beyond the limits of the administrative and organisational functions of these bodies'.[103] There was obviously an attempt at compartmentalisation; to separate political from social activities by some Jewish Communists who did not feel a need to reject their position within the Jewish community. All Jewish Communists would be particularly sensitive on the question of anti-Semitism, and many chose to square the circle concerning national rights by being sympathetic towards the Yishuv and yet declaring themselves anti-Zionist. Jewish identity was, therefore, not irrelevant to Communist Jews. They cannot simply be described as 'Communists of Jewish origin' or 'non-Jewish Jews'.[104] A recognisable Jewish identity did play an occasional part, to a lesser or greater degree, in several periods of their communist odyssey. However, few would pay much attention to their Jewish background and even fewer would have much sympathy for 'Jewish Work'. There was to be nothing in Britain to match the American Jewish Communist experience with its summer camps, Yiddish press and housing projects.[105]

The friction between the Jewish activists and the Communist Jews was a cultural conflict between East and West; between the heirs to the *Shtetl* and the modern hyphenated Jew. For the Jewish activists, the Jewish–Communist link was a bond, for the Communist Jews, it was a polarity which pushed apart without ever quite managing to break free.

The CPGB was not particularly preoccupied with the ethnic identities of its members. What mattered was whether you carried out party instructions or not and as a rule, Jewish Communists carried out their duties as well as any other Communists. What caused particular concern for the grass root Communist Jews, however, was the attempted coordination and labelling of their work as 'Jewish Work'. The political activity of Communists Jews especially before the post-war migration into the suburbs was generally amongst Jews, either in the clothing factories or on their doorsteps. But this was as Communists not as Jews. Just because they were aware of being

Jewish does not mean that they wished to act politically as Jews or to be seen to be doing so. Quite the opposite in fact. The policies of the JB appeared to represent what Communist Jews were actually doing in their local campaigning in Jewish areas or in the clothing or furniture trade unions. But, as Palme Dutt noted at the 1945 Conference:

> [There is] an old and still marked tendency to regard general party work and propaganda, and general work in the working class and democratic movement *as a substitute* for concern with Jewish questions and work in Jewish organisations. This is an old type of error familiar in many fields and characteristic of the early stages of work in new spheres. But it is most unsuitable when the Party has reached a strong basis and the leadership of the people in many-sided and wide spheres.[106]

In other words, it was a political mistake for Communist Jews to deny their roots especially as it would affect the development of the party. For the CPGB, the best way to be a good Communist was to be a good Jew.

For the Communist Jews, the JB's policies crossed a crucial mental threshold and put their own identity in doubt. By emphasising particularism rather than universalism, Jewishness rather than Britishness, 'Jewish Work' raised questions that many preferred to ignore rather than answer. It is because of the reluctance of Communist Jews to confront their ethnicity that the JB quoted despairingly in their information circular 'the country is full of [Jewish] English-speaking communists engaged in all kinds of Communist work, but not as Jews, not as Jewish Communists'.[107]

Conclusion: Towards a Redefinition of 'Jewish Politics'

The 1945 Mile End general election victory was a consequence of the inter-war and wartime local activist struggles of Communists and Communist Jews amongst a predominantly working-class community. However, one should be cautious in linking votes cast with commitment to that party's ideology or to the notion of the Jewish population's 'powerful group consciousness'.[108] The 'Jewish Street' went 'Red' but sympathy does not mean synthesis or hegemony. Nor should one exaggerate the Communist Party's attachment to ethnicity. Jewish motifs were used in party propaganda but one must be wary of seeing this as other than local strategies required for electoral success. The only explicitly 'Jewish' policy pursued by the CPGB during this time, the JB, played no significant part in the election campaign.[109] An event in 1936 of far more importance to the election result than the creation of the JB was the formation of the London Stepney Tenants' Defence League. As Michael Shapiro, the League's founder and successful Stepney CPGB candidate in the November council elections, recounted in a report to the party authorities:

> It was a genuine united movement of the people drawing together Jews

and Christians at a time when anti-Semitic propaganda was being stepped up, helping to isolate and expose both Fascists and right wing local Labour leaders, drawing in and building unity with sections of the Church and winning the warm approval of the organised Labour movement ... Our victories in the 1945 Parliamentary and Municipal elections were based primarily on the reputation and following we had built up in the great pre-war struggles. In the general swing to the Left people saw us as the real leaders.[110]

Note the emphasis on Communist activism, historical circumstance and the ability of the local party to go beyond the Jewish community. An 'inclusive' approach towards Jewish Communism and its place in 'Jewish politics' may fuse the 'ethnic' with the 'movement' but in doing so confuses the general and the particular. Ethnicity is only one element in a complex matrix uniting party, locality and historical circumstance. Srebrnik's movement away from a purely class-based analysis is welcome, but not all the answers can be found in the ethnic. The party was its own driving force in the East End of London. It benefited from local factors but it also led and organised the protests that it helped create, not for 'ethnic' purposes but for its own policy reasons. By 1945, the Communists finally had their base; 'roots' that fed the party tree, not a frame that bore a tabernacle.

Is the London Mile End election then a case of 'Jewish Politics'? Does the failure of the JB to have an impact illustrate the fragility or strength of the concept 'Jewish politics'? Is in fact the JB an example of 'Jewish Politics' at all? Its successes and failures as well as its very existence owed as much to the involvement of the Soviet Union and the structure of the CPGB than the activities of its Jewish members. Indeed, the very people who were to carry out 'Jewish Work', the ordinary Jewish membership, were reluctant or even hostile to involvement in anything that might be described as 'Jewish politics'. Conversely, it is obvious 'Jewish politics' is involved in some way with the Communist Jews, as they were the focal point for the JB's activities, and indeed, their resistance to the Bureau reveals a great deal about the modern Jewish condition itself. But, is the link between Jewish identity and Jewish politics self-evident? Where does Communist politics end and Jewish politics begin? When is a Jew acting politically as a Jew and when is he or she acting as a socialist, a proletarian or a Briton?

Mendelsohn's 'exclusive' concentration upon the Jewish sections as clear examples of Jewish politics within the context of communist history seems also, therefore, to require revision in the case of the CPGB's own bureau. The conceptual boundary of Jewish versus non-Jewish politics that split the JB from the Communist Jews is undermined by both questioning the 'Jewish' dimension of the JB and by the rethinking of the 'Jewishness' of the Communist Jews. Where Srebrnik might have gone too far in his analysis of Jews and Communism, Mendelsohn may not have gone far enough. The change in perception from separation, of Jewish Communist from party structure, to relationship, between party and Jews, necessitates a re-

113

evaluation and redefining of what is 'Jewish politics'.

The difficulties involved in judging where the boundary lies between Jewish and non-Jewish politics is not merely an obstacle in the way of the search for greater understanding, but is of significance in revealing a paradox of modern 'Jewish politics': modernity creates both unity and disunity, it fashions collective political will and establishes party division, it mobilises the masses and yet turns them away from each other. Alongside the unifying methods of mass mobilisation lie the ruptures produced by class, gender, nationality, generation, ideology and, above all, party loyalty. With the greater access to the non-Jewish world comes a obfuscation of the distinction between the Jew/non-Jew dialectic, not just between political structures, but within individuals as well. Beside institutional formation comes identity fragmentation. 'Jewish politics' is thus a multilayered and multifaceted phenomenon whose focus can shift according to the observer's and subject's perspective. A definition that avoids these complexities and tensions risks missing the point.

Nevertheless, a recognition of multiplicity and ambiguity within the field of 'Jewish politics' only helps us so far. One has still to decide which parts of identity are involved and how and why they relate to each other. Nor is it simply a question of personal choice but also one of power, coercion and control. An overall structure that could enable a viable definition of 'Jewish politics' to be developed may be offered by grounding our understanding in historical and institutional context. As well as a balanced appraisal of the importance of ethnicity and society, particular importance must be attached to the dominant form of political activity in the twentieth century: the political party. Lying between section and movement, the party is more than just a backcloth for the actors of Jewish identity to be viewed against, but has instead an integral role in the whole play. Most political activity by Jews in the modern era, 'East' and 'West', was channelled through political parties, Jewish and non-Jewish, and/or party systems. Trapped between state and society, Jews had little alternative but to act within the intermediary political arena of the party. Political parties are as much products of modernity as Jewish integration and it is no coincidence that the histories of both are closely intertwined.

Jews did not take political decisions in a vacuum but usually within the context of party politics. Without an understanding of how the party operates, what language it uses, how it forms its policies, how it implements them and the consequences for its Jewish members, little can be gained from the application of the term 'Jewish politics' to the political activities of Jews in the modern era. Rather than starting within the ambiguities of the Jewish community and Jewish identity and seeking to explain Jewish political activity from an internal perspective, one can use the clearer institutional boundaries and structure of the party to bring a wider external political and social environment to bear upon the actions of its Jewish party members. This is not to derogate the part Jewish identity has in explaining Jewish political activity, but rather to reveal its relative importance and rich complexity through the prism of political structure. Party is both framework and factor; without it no understanding of the Jews and the left, and maybe even modern 'Jewish politics', is possible.

Notes

1. For an introduction to this subject see, Frankel, J. (1981), *Prophecy and Politics: Socialism, Nationalism and the Russian Jews 1862-1917*, Cambridge: Cambridge University Press; Mendelsohn, E. (1993), *On Modern Jewish Politics*, Oxford: Oxford University Press; Lederhendler, E. (1989), *The Road to Modern Jewish Politics: Political Tradition and Political Reconstruction in the Jewish Community of Tsarist Russia*, Oxford: Oxford University Press.

2. For the debate over 'East' versus 'West' Jewish politics see the articles Hyman, P. (1992), 'Was there a "Jewish Politics" in Western and Central Europe?', and Frankel, J. (1992), 'Modern Jewish Politics East and West (1840-1939)', both in Z. Gitelman (ed.), *The Quest for Utopia: Jewish Political Ideas and Institutions Throughout the Ages*, London: Sharpe.

3. See, for example, Dothan, S. (1975), 'The Jewish Section of the Palestine Communist Party, 1937-1939', pp. 234-62 in D. Capri and G. Yogev (eds), *Zionism: Studies in the History of the Zionist Movement and of the Jewish Community in Palestine*, Tel Aviv: Tel Aviv University; Gitelman, Z. (1972), *Jewish Nationality and Soviet Politics – The Jewish Section of the CPSU 1917-1930*, Princeton: Princeton University Press; Zucker, B. (1991), 'The Jewish Bureau: The Organisation of American Jewish Communists in the 1930s', in M. Cohen (ed.), *Bar-Ilan Studies in History III*, Bar-Ilan: Bar-Ilan University Press.

4. Mendelsohn, *On Modern Jewish Politics*.

5. Ibid., preface.

6. Ibid., p. 28.

7. Srebrnik, H. F. (1995), *London Jews and British Communism, 1935-45*, Ilford: Valentine Mitchell.

8. Its membership never exceeded 20,000 before the Second World War and indeed struggled to reach half that throughout most of the inter-war period.

9. Srebrnik, *London Jews*, p. 1.

10. Ibid., p. 151.

11. Ibid., p. 4.

12. Ibid., pp. 11-19. Srebrnik was unfortunately not granted access to the archives of the CPGB during his research in the 1970s and

115

1980s. Since the completion and publication of his thesis the Communist Party Archives (CPA) have become available for study in the National Labour History Museum, Manchester, and much of what is presented in this chapter has been taken from them.

13.   Figures taken from an analysis of CPGB's biographical collection held at the Labour history Museum, Manchester. Note that this figure only applies to cadres not the ordinary membership so one must be cautious in extrapolating the exact numbers of Jews within the party as a whole from this 7 per cent figure.

14.   For example, in the Polish Communist Party's youth section Jews constituted 51 per cent of its membership in 1930. The proportion of Jews in the party never fell below 22 per cent in the inter-war period and was significantly higher in the cities: Schatz, J. (1991), *The Generation: The Rise and Fall of the Jewish Communists of Poland*, Berkeley: University of California Press, p. 96.

15.   Srebrnik, *London Jews*, pp. 13-14.

16.   Ibid.

17.   Srebrnik does not mention the Jewish Bureau of the 1930s even though he references an article written by it in 1937, ibid., p. 122. Srebrnik does discuss the National Jewish Committee (NJC) during the war period though he does not address any connection with the earlier Jewish Bureau. The NJC, he argues, was established in April 1943 (p. 72) although he later quotes a NJC document from February 1943 (p. 79).

18.   Zucker, 'The Jewish Bureau', *Bar-Ilan Studies in History III*, Ramat-Gan, pp. 135-47. The Jewish Federations were an integral part of the American CP's two founding parties, the Communist Labor Party and the Communist Party of America.

19.   Communist Party of Great Britain (1920), *Communist Unity Convention, London July 31 & August 1 1920: Official Report*, London: The National Labour Press Ltd, pp. 21-2.

20.   CPA CI reel 11 Political Bureau 1930, 17/18 August.

21.   Although, according to Jewish religious law, he was not Jewish as his mother was a non-Jew.

22.   CPA CI reel 11 Political Bureau 1930, 21 August.

23.   CPA CI reel 14 Political Bureau 1933, 18 May and in connection with Lancashire, reel 5/6 Central Committee 1934-35, 1 February 1935.

24.   CPA CI reel 15 Political Bureau 1934-35, 15 November 1934.

25.   Pollitt showed a considerable understanding of the Jewish community in the secret meeting called by Neville Laski, the head of the Board of Deputies of British Jews, to discuss with the important Labour Party figure, Herbert Morrison, joint action against the fascists. See Holmes, C. (1976), 'East End Anti-Semitism, 1936', *Society for the Study of Labour History*, (32)

Spring, pp. 26-33

26.   CPA CI reel 11 Political Bureau 1930 12 December. The Communists achieved 2106 votes. The success here was contrasted with the failure in the recent Shipley by-election where the party was seen as isolated from the masses. In the general election of 1931 the Communist vote went up by a further 500.

27.   Ibid., 11 December. Pollitt, though, shifted his candidature from Stepney to Rhondda, South Wales, for subsequent elections.

28.   CPA CI reel 15 Political Bureau 1935-1935, 4 May 1934.

29.   *Imprecor* (1935), **15**, 17 October, no. 54, pp. 1344-5; 21 November, no. 62, p. 1541; 2 December, no. 65, pp. 1617-18. See also Budeiri, M. (1979), *The Palestine Communist Party 1919-1948*, London: Ithaca Press, pp. 80-83; Dothan, op. cit., pp. 244-5, p. 259.

30.   CPA CI reel 7 Central Committee 1936, 5 June.

31.   CPA CI reel 16 Political Bureau 1936-1937, 21 May 1936.

32.   Note, however, that the first secretary of the Jewish Bureau, Lazar Zaidman in his own account (CPA CP/CENT/PERS/8/14) gives the date of the founding of the bureau as 1935, a year before the riots in Palestine. However, the Political Bureau obviously had no knowledge that such a body existed within its party in 1936 which makes it highly unlikely that it did exist before the May/June meetings as only the Political Bureau had the authority to set up such a body. Zaidman's account was written in 1952 so he may have given the wrong date by accident. The Jewish Bureau was also referred to occasionally as the Jewish Advisory Bureau/Committee which appears to reflect the original intentions of the May/June meetings.

33.   Budeiri, op. cit., p. 99.

34.   British Resident, 'The Events in Palestine', *Labour Monthly*, 18 July 1936, (7), p. 412.

35.   CPA CP/CENT/PERS/8/14 Lazar Zaidman and CP/CENT/PERS/01/01 Sam Alexander. Hackney is an area of East London north of Stepney.

36.   CPA CP/CENT/PERS/8/14 'Lazar Zaidman – An appreciation (speech by John Mahon)'.

37.   These included ICOR an organisation linked to Biro-Bidzjan, the Soviet Union's own Jewish 'homeland'.

38.   CPA CP/CENT/PERS/01/01 Sam Alexander.

39.   CPA CP/CENT/PERS/8/14 Lazar Zaidman.

40.   See 'A reply to S. Townsend Warner by the Jewish Bureau of the Communist Party' (1937), *Discussion*, 1 (14), 22-4. In the same journal see articles by 'Zionist Socialist' and Bridgeman, R. (1937), 1 (10), 17-22, and three articles under the heading 'Communism, Zionism and the Jews', 1 (13), March 1937, 14-24.

41.   Letter from Eric Hobsbawm to author, 30 September 1997.

42.   Jacobs, Joe (1978), *Out of the Ghetto: My Youth in the East End: Communism and Fascism 1913-1939*, London: Janet Simon. He does however mention 'the people in the Workers' Circle' (p. 229) who were members of the CPGB including Issie Rennap and Alf Holland both of whom were either members of the Hackney Study Group or close to it.

43.   See for example the article by Campbell, J. R. (1939), 'Why the Jews are victimised', in the *Daily Worker* (*DW*), 8 August, p. 2: 'Anti-Semitism is thus the road to anti-English treachery. The universality of anti-Semitism in the capitalist world is the expression of the universality of the capitalist crisis and is used by German Fascism as a weapon in its drive for world conquest.'

44.   CPA CI reel 8 Central Committee 1937, 10 September.

45.   CPA CP/CENT/PERS/8/14 Lazar Zaidman.

46.   'Jewish People's Council to be Dissolved. But Need for Defence Remains' (1939), *Jewish Chronicle* (*JC*), 22 September 1939, p. 17. Julius Jacobs, the JPC's organising secretary, denied in a letter to the *JC*, (6 October, p. 9) that the council was to be dissolved just that recommendations were to be made to affiliated organisations. It continued to exist in name only and was finally dissolved in January 1940: 'End of the Jewish People's Council' (1940), *JC*, 12 January, p. 21. The official reason for closing down the JPC was because of government restrictions and lack of 'financial resources'. The Board of Deputies Defence Committee had also reduced its London activities after the outbreak of war though within a few months it had re-established them: 'Defence Meetings Again' (1940), *JC*, 23 February, p. 26. This is not to say that local CPGB branches were not active against the fascists in this period though this is an area of Communist activity we know surprisingly little about.

47.   For a description of CPGB anti-fascism in Lancashire see Barrett, N. (1997), 'A Bright Shining Star: The CPGB and Anti-Fascist Activism in the 1930s', *Science and Society*, **61**, (1), 10-26.

48.   CPA CP/CENT/CTEE/8/14 Lazar Zaidman.

49.   Redlich, S. (1995), *War, Holocaust and Stalinism: A Documented History of the Jewish Anti-Fascist Committee in the USSR*, Luxembourg: Harwood Academic Publishers.

50.   *JC*, 29 August 1941, p. 8. A manifesto issued by the Moscow Jewish leaders urging Soviet Jews to resist Hitler had been reported earlier in the *JC*, 11 July 1941, p. 1.

51.   'Jewish Congress Appeal' (1941), *World News and Views*, 6 September, **21** (36), p. 573.

52.   *JC*, 12 September 1941, p. 9.

53.   *JC*, 3 October 1941, p. 8.

54.   Srebrnik, H. (1986), 'Communism and Pro-Soviet Feeling Among

the Jews of East London 1935-45', *Immigrants and Minorities*, 5 November.

55. Redlich, *War, Holocaust and Stalinism*, 287.
56. CPA CP/CENT/PERS/8/14 Lazar Zaidman and interview by author with Chimen Abramsky, 16 October 1996.
57. *JC*, 12 December 1941, p. 19.
58. *DW*, 21 February 1940, p. 4.
59. This was formed after the second JAFC congress on May 24 1942. See the letter to the editor by its secretary, Simon Blumenfield, *JC*, 19 June 1942, p. 13. See also the support given to it by the *JC*, 26 June 1942, p. 8.
60. According to the *JC* direct contact was established between the UJC and the JAFC. Reports about Soviet Jewry were to be sent to the UJC, *JC*, 31 July 1942, p. 13. The JAFC gave radio broadcasts in Yiddish once a week on Saturday 8.30pm.
61. CPA CP/CENT/CTEE/02/02 Discussion Material for the Enlarged Meeting of the National Jewish Committee (1943), p. 5. The UJC had been very much a child of the JAFC as its secretary, Joseph Leftwich, expressed in a letter to the *JC*, the UJC 'exists to answer the appeal of the Jewish Anti-Fascist Committee in Kubiyshev', *JC*, 16 October 1942, p. 6. However, the JFSR was more an establishment body, an integral part of Mrs Churchill's Red Cross Aid to Russia Fund, see *JC*, 25 December 1942, p. 8.
62. Redlich, *War Holocaust and Stalinism*, p. 74.
63. Ibid., and interview with Chimen Abramsky, 25 March 1998.
64. Srebrnik, 'Pro-Soviet Feeling', pp. 295-7.
65. Interview with Chimen Abramsky, 16 October 1996.
66. Redlich, *War, Holocaust and Stalinism*, p. 288.
67. Ibid.
68. The Jewish Bureau was renamed the National Jewish Committee in 1943. This was due to the dissolution of the Comintern and the dropping of Comintern terminology such as 'Bureau' and substitution with less Soviet-sounding alternatives. This applied throughout the party not just to the Jewish Bureau. It did not signify any change in the nature of the Jewish section. To avoid confusion, I will continue to refer to the Jewish section as the 'Jewish Bureau' (JB) throughout the article.
69. CPA CP/CENT/CTEE/02/02 Report (National Conference of Jewish Members of the CPGB, 31 January 1943). William Rust, the editor of the *Daily Worker*, was the party's Central Committee representative at the conference. His wife, Tamara Rust, was of partly Jewish descent.
70. CPA CP/CENT/CTEE/02/02 The Jewish Bureau, Circular No. 2, 18 February 1943.
71. CPA CP/CENT/CTEE/02/02 National Jewish Bureau minutes, 20

April 1943.

72.   CPA CP/CENT/CTEE/02/02 National Jewish Bureau minutes, 4 May 1943. See also letter from Zaidman to the Manchester Jewish Bureau, 14 May 1943, concerning this matter and offering guidance on the relations between the DPC and the Bureau.

73.   CPA CP/CENT/CTEE/02/02 National Jewish Bureau minutes, 8 June 1943.

74.   CPA CP/CENT/CTEE/02/02 National Jewish Bureau minutes, 3 August 1943. No JFSR branch had been set up yet. No effective leadership existed and there was, according to the JB, a danger of the bureau 'falling away'.

75.   Reuben Falber reply to questionnaire sent by the author, 1 March 1996.

76.   CPA CP/CENT/CTEE/02/02 Pollitt letter to the National Jewish Committee, 6 August 1943.

77.   CPA CP/CENT/CTEE/02/02 National Jewish Bureau minutes, 20 April 1943, p. 2.

78.   CPA CP/CENT/CTEE/02/02 Letter from the National Jewish Bureau to Secretariat of the Central Committee, 30 May 1943.

79.   CPA CP/CENT/CTEE/02/02 Newsletter, 10 October 1943, p. 1.

80.   Zaidman Collection, (ZC) The Communist Party National Jewish Committee, Third Annual Enlarged Meeting, 13-14 January 1945.

81.   Ibid.

82.   CPA CP/CENT/CTEE/02/02 Minutes Jewish Bureau, 15 February 1943.

83.   CPA CP/CENT/CTEE/02/02 Report (31 January 1943), p. 3.

84.   ZC London Jewish Committee minutes, 11 November 1944.

85.   CPA CP/CENT/CTEE/02/02 Report, p. 2.

86.   Pelling, H. (1975), *The British Communist Party*, London: A. and C. Black, p. 82.

87.   Rennap, I. (pseudonym) (1942), *Anti-Semitism and the Jewish Question*, London: The Camelot Press Ltd.

88.   Note that similar differences are evident in other national Communist Parties. For the 'non-Jewish Jews' versus the 'Jewish Jews' in the Polish Communist Party see Schatz, J., op. cit., pp. 55, 100, 118-27.

89.   He later became a leading and influential supporter of the Conservative Prime Minister, Margaret Thatcher.

90.   ZC, 'Avis' (Alfred Sherman) (1946), 'Jewish Nationality: A Pernicious Illusion', April, p. 7, an unpublished article in the Zaidman collection archive at the University of Sheffield.

91.   Ibid., p. 10.

92.   Ibid., p. 16.

93.   ZC, 'Avis' (Alfred Sherman), *Marxism and the Jewish Question*, n.d., p. 7.

94. ZC, 118/9f/11 'Notes for Session (Third) of School on Jewish Affairs'.

95. ZC (1943), *Party Work Amongst the Jews in Britain: Presentation of the Problem*, 9 December.

96. CPA CP/CENT/PERS/01/01 Dennis Walter Angel.

97. CPA CP/CENT/CTEE/02/02 Letter of the National Jewish Committee of the Communist Party, 10 October 1943, p. 1.

98. Interview with Reuben Falber, 1 May 1996.

99. Not that this did not cause difficulties for some. See Mindel, M. (1986), 'Socialist EastEnders', *Jewish Socialist*, **2** (6), p. 27, for his reaction to the pact.

100. For a brief overview of the theory of political and social cleavage see Maor, M. (1997), *Political Parties and Party Systems*, London: Routledge, pp. 18-30.

101. CPA CP/CENT/CTEE/02/02 Report (21 January 1943), p. 1.

102. Samuel, R. (1985), 'The Lost World of British Communism', *New Left Review*, (154), p. 51.

103. ZC (1943), 'Party Work Amongst the Jews in Britain: Presentation of the Problem', 9 December.

104. For the classic account of the 'non-Jewish Jews' see Deutscher, I. (1968), *The Non-Jewish Jew and other Essays*, London: Oxford University Press.

105. Zucker, op. cit. and Liebman, A. (1979), *Jews and the Left*, New York: John Wiley and Sons, pp. 305-25.

106. ZC, The Communist Party National Jewish Committee, Third Annual Enlarged Meeting, 13-14 January 1945. Emphasis added.

107. CPA CP/CENT/CTEE/02/02 Letter, 6 November 1943, p. 7.

108. Srebrnik, *London Jews*, p. 151.

109. See Piratin's own account (1948), of the election and the earlier years of communist activity in *Our Flag Stays Red*, London: Thames Publications (reprinted 1978, London: Lawrence and Wishart). He does not mention the Jewish Bureau once.

110. CP/CENT/PERS/6/7 Michael Shapiro.

CHAPTER SIX

Szmul Zygielbojm, the British Labour Party and the Holocaust

Isabelle Tombs

Szmul Zygielbojm, a leading member of the Jewish Bund,[1] killed himself in London on 12 May 1943 by taking poison. His suicide was a protest against what he perceived as the world's indifference to the fate of the Jews, and a gesture to move them into action.[2] In his farewell letter to the Polish Prime Minister, Wladyslaw Sikozski, and President, Wladyslaw Rackiewicz, he explained his gesture:

> The responsibility for this crime of murdering the entire Jewish population falls in the first instance on the perpetrators, but indirectly it is also a burden on the whole of humanity, the people and the governments of the Allied states who thus far have made no effort toward concrete action to halt the crime.[3]

Zygielbojm's act has been mentioned – although not in detail – in major works on the Warsaw Ghetto uprising and the Holocaust. However, the reactions on the part of the British Labour Party to Zygielbojm's action have been largely neglected. Yet the Labour Party was directly mentioned by Zygielbojm in one of his three farewell letters.[4] During the time he was in London, Zygielbojm had informed Labour officials and prominent personalities of the fate of the Jews in Poland and – through him – news of the Holocaust had been revealed to Labour circles.

I shall concentrate on the reactions on the part of the Labour Party to the news of the Holocaust provided by Zygielbojm and to his growing despair. The first part will highlight his initial successes in publicising the news of the extermination of the Jewish population and will analyse the reactions of key Labour figures. This will then lead to the reactions to his death in Labour circles. My conclusions will assess his relative success and failure and suggest explanations.

Zygielbojm's Publicity

Zygielbojm arrived in London from the USA in March 1942, to represent the Bund on the Polish National Council[5] – a quasi-Parliament in exile. He substituted for Henryk Erlich – the original choice – who had been arrested in Russia.[6] Another Jewish representative had been sitting on the National Council from the beginning, the Zionist, Ignacy Schwarzbart. In pre-war

Poland, Zygielbojm had been active in the Bund Central Committee, in trade unions and in local politics, and was a 'seasoned politician'.[7] He took part in the first battle of Warsaw in September 1939,[8] and was the Bund representative in the first *Judenrat*, and in this capacity opposed the involvement of the *Judenrat* in the establishment of the ghetto. In spite of the threat of the death penalty he then resigned and escaped from Poland for America, via Germany, Belgium and France, in the most perilous conditions.[9] Some Bundists had reached America at the beginning of the war, where they established the American Delegation of the Bund, to whom Zygielbojm would regularly report when he was in Britain. Earlier in the war the Labour Party International Secretary, William Gillies, had tried unsuccessfully to help four Bund leaders to come over to Britain. The Bund intended that 'when the Labour Party will formulate a programme concerning the millions of Jews in Europe, she [*sic*] will find a way of hearing the viewpoints of the Socialist party of the largest Jewish Community in Eastern Europe'.[10]

In the third week of May 1942, Zygielbojm received a key report from Leon Feiner, a member of the underground Bund in Poland, which revealed the 'physical extermination of the Jews on Polish soil'. It gave precise details on the scale – a death toll of 700,000 Polish Jews – location and killing methods; gassing in Chelmno was mentioned, at an average rate of 1,000 Jews and Gypsies a day: 'A special automobile (a gas chamber) was used.'[11]

Zygielbojm swiftly publicised the May report; in the Polish National Council; through the BBC, for example on 2 and 25 June and 2 July, and the press; only the *Daily Telegraph* published the report on 25 June 1942.[12] On Zygielbojm's and Schwarzbart's initiatives the Polish National Council had issued an appeal to the parliaments of the free world.[13] The coordinated action of Zygielbojm and Schwarzbart was somewhat unusual as they were not on friendly terms. A Zionist contemporary, Rafael F. Scharf, who played the role of go-between, recalled that Zygielbojm was disparaging and that 'Zionism was a red rag to a bull ... . The war between the Bund and the Zionists was still going on in London'. When the news of the Holocaust arrived, their main aim was to arouse public opinion, but they continued to disagree on methods of action and which of the two was the best representative of Polish Jewry.[14] On 30 June 1942, Zygielbojm sent extracts to the Labour Party, with an appeal 'in a matter of the most urgent importance' and begged them:

> to undertake immediately all possible steps to secure the initiation of a special action by the Government of Great Britain, the United States of America and all other Allied Nations to bring pressure on the German Government to stop the slaughter ... These are facts without precedent in human bestiality.[15]

Arthur Greenwood, chairman of the parliamentary Labour Party, spoke on the BBC of the massacres of the Jews in June.[16]

Also, together with Adam Ciolkosz,[17] Zygielbojm approached the Labour

Party via Gillies, George Dallas of the International Subcommittee (ISC) and James Middleton, the Labour Party General Secretary, and they spoke to a special committee of the ISC.[18] This resulted in a series of steps on the part of the National Executive Committee (NEC), after a decisive meeting of the ISC on 17 July. On 22 July the NEC approved and published a protest resolution drafted by the ISC and an additional joint protest resolution was then issued by the National Council of Labour (NCL), that is, the joint body that included members from the TUC General Council and members from the NEC and the Parliamentary Executive. Thus trade union members and MPs were associated. The NEC also endorsed the idea of a joint deputation to convey the resolution to Anthony Eden, the Foreign Secretary and to John Winant, the American Ambassador. The protest resolution stressed the necessary retribution for 'bestial' atrocities, that 'cast infamy on those who have perpetrated them and dishonour upon the nation which has acquiesced in them'. However, it remained silent on the Bund's vital point: 'the physical extermination of the Jewish population on Polish soil'.[19] At this stage it is worth noting that the Labour Party was concerned with atrocities both in Poland and Czechoslovkia, not the fate of Jews specifically.[20] Zygielbojm's suggestion to put pressure on the Allied governments had nevertheless been adopted by the Labour Party.

In the summer of 1942, together with three Polish Socialists – Ciolkosz, Jan Kwapinski and Jan Stanczyk – Zygielbojm sent the Labour Party another document entitled 'Poland', largely based on the underground report of May, describing the destruction of the Polish nation, with nearly half of the document entitled 'mass slaughter of the Jews'. 'Gas chambers' – a paragraph heading – were given prominence: 'According to reports subsequently received by the Polish Government, the poisoning of people by gas is going on not only in Chelmno but also in several other localities.' While information about the start of the liquidation of the Warsaw Ghetto did not appear in that document, a special section dealt with the Lwow and Warsaw ghettos. Between 22 July and 12 September 1942, over 265,000 Jews were transported from Warsaw to Treblinka. It stated that, given that the Jews in Warsaw were used as slave labour, 'the biggest Jewish centre in Poland has not yet come into orbit of mass slaughter by shooting and the use of poison gas'. On the other hand, it mentioned that:

> Quite recently ... however, [it] has also been affected by the wave of deportations and executions. German posters announcing that 6,000 Jews must register immediately for deportations appeared on the walls. Two train-loads of Jews have already been despatched from Warsaw to an unknown destination, and nothing further has been heard of them.

On 11 August 1942, the Labour Party circulated the joint protest resolution of 22 July together with the document prepared by the four Polish Socialists, which declared:

> Every voice raised in protest against those crimes will be a tremendous

encouragement to our people ... Any sign of fraternal sympathy and solidarity on the part of the British Labour Movement will resound throughout our country as a message of hope from those with whom history has linked our fate, both now and in the future.[21]

Middleton made the information available to trade unions, constituency Labour parties, local Labour parties and women's sections, and asked them to send Eden and the American Ambassador similar resolutions to the one adopted by the NEC and the TUC.[22]

The planned deputation of Labour Executive representatives and Walter Citrine (for the TUC) was received by Eden on 24 August:

Replying Mr Eden referred to the Prime Minister's statement that "retribution for these crimes must henceforth take a place among the major purposes of war". The Government was in full sympathy with the resolution and with the spirit which has prompted it.

As planned they then met the American Ambassador. On Harold Laski's proposal, supported by Greenwood, it was also decided to press Attlee to make a strong declaration on the subject.[23] This would not be done before his statement in the House of Commons on 19 January 1943.

Following another ISC recommendation on 17 July, the Labour Party organised a protest meeting on 2 September against German atrocities in all occupied countries and more specifically in Poland and Czechoslovakia – for which 'the assassins have reserved their bestial cruelties in the greatest abundance'.[24] According to Ciolkosz this 'was the only public protest organised by the Labour Party during the war'.[25] The executive decided to invite British representatives and socialists from occupied countries.[26] The meeting was chaired by A. J. Dobbs, Chairman of the NEC. Herbert Morrison, the Home Secretary, and Mary Sutherland, the Chief Women's Officer, were the two other British representatives.

Zygielbojm reiterated at the meeting the unique fate of the Jews, mentioning it no less than 16 times: 'From the beginning the Nazi officials frankly declared that while foreseeing for the Poles a future as slaves of the "Herrenvolk" they could see no future whatsoever for the Jews'. He summarised all previous news and described the mass deportation from Warsaw and the resulting suicide of the Mayor of Warsaw, L. M. Czerniakov, when ordered to prepare a list of 100,000 Jews to be deported, at a rate of 7,000 daily. Appealing to his socialist audience, he said:

If we do not find the means to rescue the people of Poland and of the other occupied countries in time, there is going to be neither a Socialist Europe nor any other Europe. My people ... raise their hands to you from their lethal chamber, and they raise their voice to you in faith and confidence.[27]

The focus of most speeches was not specifically the Jews; they concerned the fates of the various occupied countries. However, the British delegates who concentrated on Poland and Czechoslovakia, made clear that such organised atrocities concerned specifically the 'Jewish population'. The word 'extermination' was used. For Dobbs, one of the answers was hastening victory. Morrison, on the other hand, concentrated on Czechoslovkia. In the light of his key position as Home Secretary, a remark he made is significant:

> We Britons want to assure all Poles and all Czechoslovaks ... that we know well that protests are not enough. For the waiting has been long ... We wait the day when the chance to strike home will first present itself ...[28]

No immediate solutions were put forward by any representative.

In the following months, Zygielbojm received further messages from the Bund in Poland; 'one dated 2 October said that 300,000 Jews from Warsaw had been killed and that half a million remaining in the whole of Poland faced the same lot'.[29] On 2 December, previous news was confirmed face-to-face by Jan Karski. His information was based on firsthand observation and on a message from two Jewish representatives in Warsaw, one of them a Bundist, Feiner, who was Zygielbojm's main source throughout. Although the information was not altogether new for Zygielbojm, the demands from the underground leaders to those in free countries probably came as a shock:

> Let them go to all important English and American offices and agencies. Tell them not to leave until they had obtained guarantees that a way has been decided upon to save the Jews ... Let them die. This may shake the conscience of the world.

Zygielbojm rejected the suggestion of a hunger strike on the doorstep of the government as 'they would take me to some institution for a psychiatric examination'.[30]

Five days later, Zygielbojm sent the Labour Party a Bund report from Feiner dated 31 August.[31] Rafael Scharf makes the point that the Polish government had prepared another version of Karski's report; he argues that the original references to Polish anti-Semitism had been replaced so 'the whole Polish population was portrayed as being united to a man in their condemnation of German anti-Jewish activities'.[32] The seven-page report reiterated the mechanisms and methods of the systematic extermination of the Jews: 'this problem – the slaughter of the Jews – is without precedent'. It described deportations from Warsaw with Jews 'packed into trains ... and liquidated at their place of destination'. Three extermination camps – set up in spring 1942 – were mentioned: 'Trains pass on their way to Tremblika [*sic*], Belzec and Sobibor.' The Bund emphasised: 'There is no point or meaning in passing resolutions to punish the German scum after the war ... *There is a need for action for immediate and effective action!*'.[33]

In his covering letter of 7 December, Zygielbojm asked for immediate 'extraordinary steps ... in order to rescue the very small number of Jews in Poland who possibly have survived'. He also recorded three motions he had put to the Polish National Council, which were the subject of conversations between the British and the Polish governments. Two of them were directly drawn from the five proposals of the underground Bund. The first was a joint retaliation against Germany by the USA and Britain to stop mass murders in Poland. The second was the dropping of leaflets from planes, and radio broadcasts to Germany, on the 'wholesale massacre of the entire Jewish population'. A third was added later: that a special inter-Allied conference with the participation of Britain, the USA and the USSR should issue a protest and a stern warning to the German nation and government.[34]

The information Zygielbojm had given to the Labour Party was confirmed to them by reports from the Polish Ministry of Information which also described in detail murder and extermination. In the winter of 1942, several Labour leaders also met Karski, who later recalled that he met Greenwood, Hugh Dalton and Ellen Wilkinson.[35] With time Zygielbojm's appeals became increasingly pressing and desperate: 'It will actually be a shame to go on living, to belong to the human race' he said in a BBC broadcast, 'if steps are not taken to halt the greatest crime in human history'.[36]

Therefore, largely through Zygielbojm's initial efforts, by mid-December 1942 the Labour Party possessed facts regarding the extermination of Jews and the demands for help from the Bund. They had also learnt from Eden the steps taken by the British government to bring about a response by the United Nations. On 4 December, a Labour deputation had again visited the Foreign Secretary, officially to discuss the food situation in Belgium, but they 'also raised the question of atrocities perpetrated by the Germans on Jews in Poland and other occupied countries'.[37]

There is no explicit record that the Bund report was discussed by the Labour Party Executive. However, although it is not attached to any specific NEC or ISC minutes, on the basis of the date of Zygielbojm's letter and the way it is paginated in the minutes, it is likely that it was distributed at the NEC meeting of 15 December. It was precisely on that day that the Labour Party issued another resolution to the press, entitled 'The Massacre of the Jews', appealing

> to the conscience of civilised mankind to arise in passionate protest against the bloodiest crime in history ... within a short time the Jewish people ... will have been exterminated. This ... act of barbarism will always be associated with the name of modern Germany ... And we appeal to those who still have power and influence in Europe at least to make an effort to save the children.[38]

Concrete measures were not however suggested. Of the proposals made by the Bund and relayed by Zygielbojm, only the appeal to other nations had been retained. Retaliation, the dropping of leaflets and radio broadcasts did not feature in their resolution.

Nevertheless it is clear that Zygielbojm had succeeded in evoking some response on the part of the Labour Party. In fact, Zygielbojm's initial successes appear to have been helped by a specific group in the Executive around the International Subcommittee. Two of the ISC members played an instrumental role: Dallas, its Chairman, and Gillies, its Secretary. Both were at the centre of a group of British and exiled socialists who have become known as 'hard liners' regarding Germany. They believed that Germany as a whole shared responsibility for Hitler's crimes and that stern punishment should be applied after the war. Gillies was a go-between for the Labour Party and exiled socialists in the group, and in this capacity played a significant role in publicising news of the Holocaust given by Zygielbojm. He was the editor of the *International Supplement* of the *Labour Press Service* set up as a 'medium of communication between the representatives in this country of the Labour and socialist parties in occupied territories and the British Labour Movement'.[39] Gillies, in his position as editor of the *International Supplement* of the *Labour Press Service*, publicised the plight of the Polish Jews. As early as 8 July 1942, the title of an article could not be any clearer: 'Germans in Poland Use Poison Gas'. On the basis of the Bund's May report, it gave a precise account of gassing in vans in Chelmno and described the Lodz ghetto. It ended: 'According to recent information, many hundreds of thousands of Polish Jews have been slaughtered by the Germans'. In September 1942, it reprinted extracts from several speeches made at the protest meeting of 2 September.[40] Also published was a long article by Zygielbojm in December 1942, based on the report sent at the end of August by the underground Bund.[41]

In February 1943, Zygielbojm exposed two new German decrees, interpreted as 'final steps to complete the extermination of Polish Jews'. They concerned the resettlement of Polish Jews in 53 'Jewish Residential Areas'. He renewed his appeals: 'what has been done so far to rescue these people has proved to be ineffective, and further effective steps must be taken immediately'.[42] But even if Zygielbojm continued to have access to the *International Supplement* and remained in contact with his first supporters, it became clear to him that there was little prospect of exercising real influence through them. Other players had entered the scene, among them Zionists and personalities such as Victor Gollancz, who did not belong to Zygielbojm's original circle of supporters.

The Labour Party resolution of 15 December had marked an important turning point in Zygielbojm's influence, as his first success was then to recede. It was followed by a campaign in Parliament and in the press in favour of 'refugees', a euphemism for Jews in occupied Europe. The most visible signs of the mounting campaign appeared in the House of Commons on 17 December 1942, when the Foreign Secretary and Leader of the House, Eden, read the declaration of the governments of the United Nations denouncing the 'bestial policy of cold-blooded extermination'.[43] This had been prearranged in meetings between Richard Law, Parliamentary Under-Secretary in the Foreign Office, and the MPs Sidney Silverman and Alexander Easterman, of the World Jewish Congress.[44] It marked the public involvement of British Zionists – especially in the House of Commons – in recognising and protesting against the systematic extermination of the Jews.

By this time the initial news transmitted by Zygielbojm was corroborated and relayed by others, Zionists in particular. This diminished his influence and increased that of Zionists. Thus Poale Zion, the Jewish Socialist Party which was affiliated to the Labour Party, was very much in the forefront of talks with the Labour Party. It published a pamphlet – *Under Sentence of Death* – with a foreword by Middleton. It gave a similar account to that given by Zygielbojm and the Bund, who were not, however, mentioned. Also, it reprinted the Labour Party's resolution of July 1942 on the atrocities in Poland and Czechoslovakia,[45] which had been largely prompted by news given by Zygielbojm. Yet there was a significant addition advocating a Jewish homeland with the inclusion of a speech by Ben-Gurion, Chairman of the Jewish Agency Executive at the National Assembly of Palestine Jewry.

Gollancz, one of the editors and founders of *Left News*, as the honorary secretary of the National Committee for Rescue from Nazi Terror set up by Eleanor Rathbone, had played an active role in the campaign for aiding refugees by mobilising public opinion and MPs. After having met Karski,[46] he published *Let My People Go*, of which 250,000 copies were sold in three months. He had written to Middleton: 'I have just read your introduction to the pamphlet on Jewish horror. I am trying to write a pamphlet myself over Christmas with a view of getting it on the bookstalls, where there is nothing.'[47]

Zygielbojm continued to play a role, but more as a spreader than as the provider of information. Thus the press and publicity department of the Labour Party invited him to take part in a series of meetings throughout Britain, at the end of 1942, on the massacres of the Jews.[48]

Now that the matter had been publicly discussed in Parliament, it was the government which was directly concerned. Subsequently the Labour Party Executive tended to withdraw behind government declarations. For example it answered a letter from Berl Locker of the World Zionist Organisation,[49] suggesting rescue actions, merely by saying that they welcomed the declaration that Attlee as Deputy Prime Minister had made in the Commons on 19 January, which stated that Britain was in consultation with other governments 'with a view to seeing what further measures of rescue and relief it is possible to take'.[50]

Labour members of the government appear to have felt that their room for manoeuvre was restricted. Two examples are representative. When Attlee was contacted by Kwapinski to transmit a message from the Underground Polish Socialists asking for reprisals, he contacted the Foreign Office for further advice. The reply was to include the statement made by Attlee in the Commons; as to 'reprisals against German civilians ... We have consistently taken the line that we cannot undertake reprisals as such and that our air bombing of Germany must be governed by strategic considerations'.[51] Philip Noel-Baker, MP, who was sympathetic to Zionism and who was often pressed by his constituents for further action, would give similar answers.[52] He adopted the line that he was sure that the government was doing all it could, but that he was not in a position to put pressure on the Foreign

Secretary and that as a member of the government his freedom for manoeuvre was limited.[53]

This helps explain the diminution of Zygielbojm's influence. Up to December 1942, he had, via the vehicle of the Labour Party Executive, especially a few of its active personalities, exercised some influence. This receded when the debate shifted to the Commons and became more public. In such circumstances, the government, including Labour Ministers, was in a better position to channel and control the discussion. The executive was also restricted in any action it might have contemplated which could have contradicted the government's position. This was especially true for Labour ministers in a coalition at a time when the outcome of the war was still uncertain. Thus Bernard Wasserstein has claimed that the Labour Ministers'

> failure to press the matter in government induced Harold Laski ... to write to the Prime Minister in 1943: 'What hurts me so deeply is the realisation that among my own colleagues in your Government Dr Goebbels has induced a spirit of caution [on the Jewish refugee problem] when you have so amply shown that audacity is the road to victory.'[54]

While the ghetto uprising, which started on 19 April 1943, was in full swing, Zygielbojm wrote of his 'intolerable feeling of helplessness ... I can't even console myself that my work here was of significance or that I rescued anyone from a merciless death'.[55] And in another letter: 'It breathes with the fact that all is ending ... It is impossible to work or to live with this knowledge'.[56] He was also shocked while addressing a trade union meeting in Leeds: 'Comrade Arthur reported what was going on in Poland. When he finished, one of the delegates present stood up and said to him these words: "Comrade Zygielbojm, was it really necessary for you to undertake such a dangerous journey from Poland to here in order to tell us such funny stories?"'[57] It would seem that the reality had still not been comprehended by all rank and file socialists.

Spring 1943 was crucial on the battlefield, and so the Warsaw Ghetto uprising does not appear to have been at the top of Labour circles' agenda. Neither the NCL's May Day resolution or Morrison's May Day message to the Workers of Poland mentioned Jews or the ghetto uprising.[58] The NCL's message is somewhat ironical in retrospect:

> We rejoice in every fresh manifestation ... among the people in the occupied countries, who are daily gathering strength and courage from the military victories won by the Armed Forces of the Allies.[59]

Gillies informed Morrison:

> A message has just been received from Poland that the number of Jews remaining is no more than 10% of the pre-war figure.[60]

Simultaneous to the ghetto uprising, was a meeting of UK and USA representatives in Bermuda. On 10 March – after long pressure in Parliament – Eden had made a statement that the massacre of Jews in Poland was

130

continuing and announced that the government welcomed the suggestion of 'a preliminary informal discussion' between Britain and America.[61] This has been interpreted rightly as the best way of avoiding taking real decisions. Certainly, the Bermuda conference produced no immediate and effective solutions, and may have contributed to Zygielbojm's final decision; no Jewish representative was invited.[62] The War Cabinet on 10 May – attended by Attlee, Bevin and Morrison – had decided that there would be no public declaration 'at this stage' on the number of refugees Britain could receive and that given signs of anti-Semitism, it would be better 'to avoid implying that refugees were necessarily Jewish'.[63]

Zygielbojm's growing despair at the obvious impending crushing of the uprising and the lack of effective measures to be found at the Bermuda conference led to his suicide.

Reactions to Zygielbojm's Death

Schwarzbart had asked the Polish government to distribute Zygielbojm's last letter to the British Cabinet and to the leaders of both Houses, but according to David Engel 'the Polish Government made no effort to influence the course of the Commons debate'.[64] On 19 May, a week after his suicide, the Commons finally debated the refugee problem following the Bermuda conference. As the Labour Party stated in its annual report,

> It was announced that the United Nations could do little in the immediate present. The rate of extermination was such that no measures of rescue or relief could be commensurate with the problem, but the Bermuda Conference had agreed on a number of definite and practical recommendations. As these involved military questions, however, the report of the Conference had to be kept confidential.[65]

Zygielbojm was not mentioned. A remark made by George Ridley, Labour MP for Clay Cross and member of the Labour Party Executive, was somewhat ironical in retrospect: 'The size of our contribution to the general refugee problem is warmly recognized by the leaders of world Jewry.'[66]

The Labour press reported Zygielbojm's death. The *Daily Herald* on 13 May reserved one factual 18-line column for the Bund leader 'well-known in international socialist circles ... depressed recently because he felt powerless in face of the mass murder by the Germans of Polish Jews'. It was complemented by a fuller article by Hannen Swaffer on 18 May, urging that his death 'may shock the Commons into action'. Swaffer interpreted Zygielbojm's suicide as a reply to the Bermuda conference: 'He saw his own race being exterminated but heard only "sympathy" and regret'. After his funeral, the *Daily Herald* also reproduced his last words, as quoted by Schwartzbart at the cremation ceremony: 'Polish Jewry is dying in the ghettoes. The Jewish Community in Warsaw has just fought the last battle against the Germans. They are finished and I have no more to live for.'[67]

Lucjan Blit wrote a long obituary in the *International Supplement* of the *Labour Press Service*. He recalled: 'The democratic world was told more than once of the terrible facts which the Jewish Socialist Movement in Poland sent through Zygielbojm'.[68]

Tribune, which had reported the ghetto uprising in several articles, published an obituary:

> To live in London ... among people who refuse to be unduly disturbed by the greatest and most irrevocable massacre in history, he could not bear ... ·The international labour movement has lost one of its most courageous and most uncompromising fighters.[69]

The desperate fight of the Warsaw Ghetto was reported in the *New Statesman*. Kingsley Martin, its editor, wrote: 'What broke him ... was the seeming impossibility of rousing Christendom to any comprehension of the fate which has overwhelmed the Jewish race in Europe, or to any effective measure of rescue ...'.[70]

However, if the Labour and left-wing press did report his death, there was no strong reaction or resulting action in the Labour leadership. The NEC does not appear to have discussed his suicide and did not go beyond reproducing a letter to the Bund signed by exiled socialists and Labour Party members. The letter recalled:

> Upon the platform, in the Press, and on the wireless, he had given eloquent and convincing testimony ... as to the suffering of the Jews in Poland, victims of a barbarous German persecution ... The Labour Movement throughout the world mourns for the loss of a loyal comrade and co-worker.[71]

Only one Labour official, Gillies, gave an address at Zygielbojm's funeral. He recalled that he had kept in close touch with him, and in unmistakable words: 'Our comrade is one of the victims of the "foulest crime known in any land or age" ... by the leaders of the German people ...'. He then made an important comment in the context of the ongoing controversy of what could be done:

> Was he unjust to us? We were calm in face of the greatest danger in our history. But we were not indifferent ... We have never ceased to fight ... But until we can measure our strength against the enemy citadel, and destroy it, we cannot save Europe. This he understood. He also understood that we had not the means of retaliation, and that retaliation in kind was not a weapon which we could use. It would be a denial of the very purposes for which we were fighting ... But his service to Socialism, to Poland, his country ... – I am a Pole, he always said to me – ... will live in our memories and in our hearts ... Anti-semitism is a mark of the beast ... the dawn of liberation – retribution – is slowly breaking.[72]

This is a good summary of the Labour Party's position. They were in agreement with the government that the priority was to win the war, as all other questions depended on the final victory.

Conclusion

In conclusion, it therefore appears that, from the summer to the winter of 1942, prominent Labour officials took the first news of the extermination of Jews in Poland seriously and disseminated it. The key personalities in this were the respective secretaries of the NEC and of its international committee, Middleton and Gillies and the Chairman of the ISC, Dallas. Awareness on the part of Labour personalities resulted in a protest meeting and in several protest resolutions in the summer and autumn of 1942, culminating in the resolution of 15 December 1942 entitled, 'The Massacre of the Jews'. It was followed by the debate in the House of Commons and the United Nations' declaration of 17 December.

From mid-December, after Karski's visit and with news received and relayed by Zionist organizations, Zygielbojm's initial information was confirmed and the campaign for help to refugees mounted. However, this process reduced Zygielbojm's role, and increased that of the Zionists. But Labour and exiled-socialist circles did not adopt or suggest any concrete measures, as they believed – together with the coalition government – that victory was the only way of putting an end to the extermination of the Jews. Immediate retaliation against German nationals and direct propaganda in Germany – suggested by Zygielbojm – had been discounted. On the other hand, post-war retribution was favoured, and supported by an increasing number. Many of those active in disseminating the Holocaust news transmitted by Zygielbojm had long favoured stringent measures towards Germany as a whole – not only towards the Nazis – which entailed the punishment of war criminals. The news of the extermination of the Jews reinforced their point.

Zygielbojm felt increasingly isolated, especially when the ghetto uprising passed almost unnoticed by his socialist comrades and when no concrete measures were announced after the Bermuda conference. War strategies superseded other considerations, especially suggestions that had been put to Zygielbojm by the Bund in Poland.

In summary, I have tried to show that Zygielbojm's presence in London was not met with indifference by the Labour Party but that many of them felt as powerless as he did, short of a final victory. Whether any effective action was possible or not is, of course, still a matter of deeply felt controversy, and will perhaps never be resolved.[73] It is that terrible question that caused Zygielbojm's despair, and to which he responded with his ultimate act of self-sacrifice.

An epilogue is provided by the Labour Party's conference a month after Zygielbojm's suicide. It voted for severe punishment of Germany after the war, and in this context the fate of the Jews was mentioned, even though it was not at the centre of the debate. Dobbs invited the conference to remember 'the devotion and sacrifice of our comrade, Zygielbojm. We have a debt to pay'. Thereafter, there was also an important resolution supporting a Jewish homeland in response to 'this policy of race hatred germinated and ... put forward by Germany against the Jewish people of the world'. James Walker who moved the resolution – backed by Laski – was supported by Maurice Rosette of Poale Zion, who referred to the courage of the Warsaw ghetto fighters and appealed to assurances of 'national rights' for the Jews and a reaffirmation of the party's plea for a Jewish National Home in Palestine.[74] It was a pyrrhic victory for the Zionist stand and a defeat for the Polish and Bundist ideal defended by Zygielbojm and his vision of international socialism.

Acknowledgements

I would like to thank contemporaries to the events for having given me interviews: Majer Bogdanski, Esther Brunstein, Nora Henry, Rene Saran, Rafael F. Scharf, and Perec Zylberberg; Dr Lidia Ciolkoszowa and Wladka Robertson for having given me interviews and access to their papers; Mieczyslawa Waszacz for having shown me her filmed interview with Jan Karski together with the first version of a film she is preparing on Zygielbojm. I am grateful to Professor Iain Begg, Mark Minion and Sarah Glynn for their comments.

Notes

1. The Bund, founded in 1897 in Vilnius, fought against the Tsarist regime and was later proscribed by the Soviet Union. Based in Poland in the inter-war years, it fought for the Jewish people to have equal rights and opposed the Zionists on the principle of *Doykeyt* (hereness) – a specific Jewish presence in Poland. It increased its political influence in the 1930s, especially in municipal elections in 1938, in which it gained the largest numbers of Jewish seats. It became a member of the Labour and Socialist International in 1930, after long controversies with those who would have preferred to join the Comintern. This consolidated close relations with socialist parties in the West and with the Polish Socialists. (For the history of the Bund, see Johnpoll, Bernard K. (1967), *The Politics of Futility: The General Jewish Workers Bund of Poland, 1917-43*, Ithaca, NY: Cornell, and Minczeles, Henri (1995), *Histoire générale du Bund, un mouvement révolutionnaire juif*, Paris: Editions Australie.

2. There are several spellings of his name. The Polish version used while he was in London, will be retained hereafter. He wrote two letters and one telegram respectively to explain his gesture: to the Polish President and Prime Minister; to two Bundists Leon Oler and Lucjan Blit; to Emanuel Nowogrodski for the American Delegation

of the Bund. They all appear in Nathan Weinstock (1997), 'Sur Shmuel Zygielbojm' (II), *Revue d'Histoire de la Shoah Le Monde Juif*, January-April, pp. 152-8.

3. Ravel, Aviva (1980), *Faithful Unto Death: The Story of Arthur Zygielbaum*, Montreal: Arthur Zygielbojm Branch, Workmen's Circle, p. 178.

4. Letter to Oler and Blit, Blit papers, Wladka Robertson papers. Zygielbojm asked Oler and Blit to send the Labour party a translation to his letter to the Polish Prime Minister and President.

5. He was appointed to the National Council by President Raczkiewicz in February 1942 (Adam Romer to Zygielbojm, 24 January 1942, and Raczkiewicz to Zygielbojm, 3 February 1942, Polish Institute, A 5/72, Zygielbojm file).

6. Wladyslaw Sikorski to Schwarzbart, 27 February 1942, Schwarzbart's diary, YVA M-2/766, as quoted in Blatman, Daniel (1990), 'On a Mission against all Odds: Samuel Zygielbojm in London' (April 1942-May 1943), *Yad Vashem Studies*, **20**, 240.

7. Interview with Majer Bogdanski, 10 July 1997. Manuscript entitled 'Szmul Zygielbojm by Blit,' (apparently Blit's funeral oration), Wladka Robertson papers.

8. Edelman, Marek and Krall, Hanna (1993), *Mémoires du Ghetto de Varsovie, un dirigeant de l'insurrection raconte*, Paris: Liana Levi Scribe, Paris, p. 31.

9. For a detailed account of his escape see Ravel, *Faithful Unto Death*.

10. Memorandum for the British Labour Party given to Mr Attlee by the American representation of the General Jewish Bund of Poland, enclosed with letter from Nowogrodski to Attlee, 22 November 1941, and Nowogrodski to Gillies, 26 March 1941; Rosner to Gillies (n.d.) Gillies to Alex Maxwell (Home Office), 22 April 1941; and Maxwell to Gillies, 31 July 1941; Labour Party Archives (LPA), Manchester, J. S. Middleton Papers, box 12 (JSM 12), file 'Poland and the Jewish Bund in the USA'.

11. Bauer, Yehuda (1968), 'When did they Know', *Midstream*, April, 52; 'Report of the Bund regarding the persecution of the Jews', (full translation of the original document), pp. 57-8. Feiner was the Bund representative in the Polish underground. He originated most reports to London and America.

12. Laqueur, Walter (1980), *The Terrible Secret*, London: Penguin, pp. 73-4.

13. Pazner, Chaim (1977), 'Debate', *Rescue Attempts During the Holocaust, Proceedings of the Second Yad Vashem International Historical Conference, Jerusalem, April 8-11, 1974*, Jerusalem: Yad Vashem, p. 458.

14. Interview with Rafael F. Scharf, 18 December 1997.

15. Attached to International Subcommittee (ISC) Minutes, 17 July

1942, *The Archives of the British Labour Party, Series 3, General Correspondence and Political Records, 1917-43*, Part 8, International Committee, 1940-43, Microfilm Reel 002 (Hassocks, 1985).

16. Laqueur, *Terrible Secret*, p. 74. Greenwood having left the War Cabinet in February, may have felt freer to take a position.

17. Ciolkosz was a member of the Polish National Council and the representative in London of the underground central committee of the Polish Socialist Party. He was a former Member of the Polish Parliament and Chairman of the District Labour Committee in Cracow.

18. Ciolkosz, Adam (1965), 'Im London Mit Arthur Zygielbojm', *Unzer Zeit*, May, 23; I would like to thank Dr Miri Rubin for her help in translating this article. ISC Minutes, 17 July 1942.

19. ISC Minutes, 17 July 1942, National Executive Committee (NEC) minutes and Records (Hassocks, 1976), 22 July 1942 and *Labour Party Conference Report* (LPCR), 1943, 'Report of the international department', p. 38.

20. Lidice in June 1942 had been a symbol of atrocity when its population was slaughtered and the village razed in reprisal for the assassination of Reinhard Heydrich.

21. Undated statement entitled 'Poland', LPA, file 'War, Nazi responsibilities for atrocities, 1942-43', International Department Correspondence (IDC) 9. Kwapinski and Stanczyk, well-known Polish socialists and trade unionists, were Minister of Industry and of Labour and Social Welfare respectively. As Mayor of Lodz, Kwapinski had come in person to Zygielbojm's house to warn him of the imminent danger to Jews with the German invasion (videoed interview with his son, Joseph Zygielbojm kindly lent to me by Mieczyslawa Waszacz).

22. Middleton to Trade Unions, Constituency Labour parties, Local Labour Parties, Women's sections, 11 August 1942, file 'War, Nazi responsibilities for atrocities, 1942-43', Labour Party Archives, IDC 9.

23. ISC Minutes, 2 September 1942 and LPCR 1943, p. 39. The delegation was composed of Dallas, Walker, Tom Williamson and Gillies for the Labour Party and Citrine for the TUC.

24. Dobbs's speech; speeches were published 'by Polish friends' in *German Atrocities in Poland and Czechoslovakia: Labour's Protest* (1942), London: privately published; extracts were also reprinted in the *International Supplement* of the *Labour Press Service*, 16 September 1942.

25. Ciolkosz, 'Im London', p. 24.

26. ISC Minutes, 4 August 1942.

27. *German Atrocities*, pp. 4-6. For background information on the

attitude of Polish circles towards Jews and the Holocaust see Engel, David (1987), *In the Shadow of Auschwitz: The Polish Government-in-Exile and the Jews*, Chapel Hill: University of North Carolina Press; and a subsequent debate between Engel and Dariusz Stola in *Polin*, **8**, (1994), 330-81. See also, Stola (1997), 'Early News of the Holocaust from Poland', *Holocaust and Genocide Studies*, **7** (1), 1-27.

28.   Dobbs's and Morrison's speeches, *German Atrocities*, pp. 2 and 12.

29.   Laqueur, *Terrible Secret*, p. 118, from information in the Studium Polski Podziemnej.

30.   Karski, Jan (1945), *Story of a Secret State*, London: Hodder and Stoughton, p. 275. Karski's memoirs provide the most valuable source on this meeting. As to its precise date, the consensus among both protagonists and historians appears to point in the direction of 2 December. In a recent interview with Karski by Mieczyslawa Waszacz, he mentioned again 2 December.

31.   Memorandum from the Underground Labour Groups in Poland to Mr Zygielbojm, 31 August 1942, *Archives of the British Labour Party, Series 3*, Part 8, International Committee, 1940-43, Microfilm Reel 002, pp. 816 and 826-32, and Noel-Baker papers (NBKR) 4/578 (Churchill College, Cambridge), and CHA, (D51a/46).

32.   Scharf, Rafael (1986), 'In Anger and In Sorrow', *Polin*, **1**, 274.

33.   Memorandum from the Underground Labour Groups in Poland, pp. 6 and 3 (emphasis in the original).

34.   Letter from Zygielbojm, 7 December. Zygielbojm and the Bund report did not specify the kind of retaliation the United Nations should apply.

35.   See Maciej Kozlowski (1990), 'The Mission that Failed: A Polish Courier Who Tried to Help the Jews', in Antony Polonsky (ed.), *'My Brother's Keeper', recent Polish Debates on the Holocaust*, London and New York: Routledge, p. 91. For Zygielbojm's information see 'Extermination of the Polish Jewry: What Happened in the Warsaw Ghetto', *Polish Fortnightly Review*, 1 December 1942, *Archives of the British Labour Party*, pp. 830-40.

36.   BBC broadcast, 13 December 1942, in Ravel, *Faithful Unto Death*, p. 171.

37.   NEC Minutes, 15 December 1942 and LPCR 1943, p. 39. The deputation consisted of Dallas, Harold Clay, Walker, T. Williamson, Gillies and Middleton.

38.   'The Massacre of the Jews', resolution of the British Labour Party, 15 December 1942, NEC Minutes, 15 December 1942 and LPCR 1943, p. 39.

39.   The position of Dallas and Gillies is confirmed by Ciolkosz: 'There was one man in this country who really did his best to help

Zygielbojm ... Gillies. He publicised in the "Labour Press Service" all the alarming news Zygielbojm brought to his notice' (Ciolkosz to the Editor of the *Observer*, 21 May 1968, Adam Ciolkosz papers [ACZ], file 'Zygielbojm', 260). Labour Party, *Conference Report* (LPCR), 1941, p.31.

40.   *International Supplement, Labour Press Service*, 16 September 1942.

41.   Ibid., 'Am I my brother's keeper', 16 December 1942.

42.   Ibid., 3 February 1943. This information was also sent to some Labour leaders as attested by its presence in Noel-Baker papers (Szmul Zygielbojm to 'Dear Friend', n.d.; with an enclosed document: 'Official Gazette for the General Government, issued at Cracow, 1 November 1942' signed by Krueger on 28 October 1942; and 'Enactment for the General Government', issued at Cracow, 14 November 1942, No. 98, p. 683, NBKR 4/578).

43.   On debates in the Commons on this issue at the end of 1942 and beginning of 1943 see Gilbert, Martin (1981), *Auschwitz and the Allies*, London: M. Joseph/Rainbird and Bernard Wasserstein (1979), *Britain and the Jews of Europe 1939-45*, Oxford: Clarendon Press.

44.   Gilbert, *Auschwitz,* p. 93. On 27 November Easterman and Noah Barou of the World Jewish Congress had asked Raczynski that the Polish Government 'initiate among the Allies ... a declaration that "Germans ... would be held responsible for all deeds leading to the mass murder of Jews"' (Engel [1994], 'Readings and Misreadings: A Reply to Darisz Stola', *Polin*, **8**, 357).

45.   Poale Zion, *Under Sentence of Death*, p. 7, n.d., London: Poale Zion.

46.   Edwards, Ruth Dudley (1987), *Victor Gollancz, A Biography*, London: Gollancz, p. 372.

47.   Gollancz to Middleton, 21 December 1942, Middleton papers 94 (Ruskin College, Oxford).

48.   Zygielbojm to the American Representation of the Jewish Labor Bund of Poland, 17 December 1942, Weinstock, 'Sur Shmuel Zygielbojm' (II), p. 141.

49.   During the war, Locker headed the political bureau of the Jewish Agency for Palestine in London. There had been some competition between Locker and Zygielbojm, as the latter reproached Huysmans for having shown a document on Belgian Jews in France first to Locker (Blatman, 1.251).

50.   ISC Minutes, 26 January 1943, NEC Minutes, 27 January and LPCR 1943, p. 39.

51.   Millard to Garner, 9 April 1943, FO 371 34550, C3736/34/55 (Foreign Office papers, Public Record Office). Guy Millard was Assistant Private Secretary to Eden.

52. NBKR 4/578. Noel-Baker, Parliamentary Secretary at the Ministry of War Transport, was in contact with pro-Zionist organizations, which he supported.

53. Noel-Baker to Barrington Whitlaw, 8 March 1943, NBKR, 4/578.

54. Laski to Churchill, 1 July 1943, PRO PREM 4/51/8/476 in Wasserstein, *Britain and the Jews*, p. 33.

55. Letter to his brother, 30 April 1943, Ravel, *Faithful Unto Death*, p. 173.

56. 'Arthur' (Arthur was Zygielbojm's pseudonym) to American Representation of the Bund, 30 April 1943, *Zygelboym Bukh*, p. 40 in Bernard K. Johnpoll (1967), *The Politics of Futility, the General Jewish Workers Bund of Poland, 1917-1943*, Ithaca, NY: Cornell, p. 257.

57. Interview with Majer Bogdanski, 10 July 1997 and 'The Bund and the Anti-Nazi Resistance' at 'A day to relate, debate and celebrate: 100 Years of Jewish Socialism', London, 16 November 1997.

58. 'May Day Message to the Workers of Poland from the Rt Honorable Herbert Morrison, M. P., JSM 13, file 'Poland 1941-45, Polish Socialist Party, 1941-45'.

59. *Daily Herald*, 30 April 1943.

60. Gillies to Morrison, 3 May 1943, LPA, JSM 13, file 'Poland 1941-45, Polish Socialist Party'.

61. 'Nazi Massacre of the Jews: What is the Government Doing?', *Left News*, April 1943, p. 2437.

62. See for example Gilbert, *Auschwitz* and Rubinstein, William D. (1997), *The Myth of Rescue, Why the Democracies Could Not Have Saved More Jews from the Nazis*, London: Routledge.

63. War Cabinet Minutes WM (43) 67 (CAB 65, War Cabinet Conclusions, Cabinet Records, Public Record Office).

64. Engel, David (1993), *Facing the Holocaust*, Chapel Hill: University of North Carolina Press, p. 76.

65. Parliamentary Report, LPCR 1944, p. 57.

66. *Hansard*, Parliamentary Debates, House of Commons, 19 May 1943, columns 1120 and 1144.

67. *Daily Herald*, 22 May 1943.

68. 26 May 1943.

69. 'Zygielbojm defender of Warsaw', *Tribune*, 21 May 1943.

70. Critic, 'A London Diary', *New Statesman*, 29 May 1943, p. 348.

71. NEC Minutes, 18 May 1943, letter dated 14 May signed by: Louis de Brouckère and Huysmans for Belgium; Joseph Belina and Gustav Winter for Czechoslovakia; Louis Lévy for France; J. W. Albarda for Holland; Pierre Krier for Luxembourg; Locker for Palestine; Ciolkosz and Adam Pragier for Poland; F. J. Burrows, Dallas, Dobbs, Gillies, Eleanor Stewart, Mary Sutherland, Walker, Williamson for Britain, LPA, Labour and Socialist International

papers, LSI 25/1/114.

72. Funeral for Szmul Zygielbojm, 21 May 1943, Address by Gillies (ID/JD/210543), ACZ, correspondence, 1943 and also in Polish Institute, A 5/72, Zygielbojm file. See also programme of the burial ceremony, ACZ, file 'Zygielbojm', 260.

73. See for example, Rubinstein, *Myth of Rescue.*

74. LPCR 1943 pp. 117 and 188.

CHAPTER SEVEN

Looking the Other Way: The British Labour Party, Zionism and the Palestinians

Paul Kelemen

Towards the end of 1949, most of the Palestinians who had fled, or were expelled, during the previous year's war between the Israeli and Arab forces, faced their second winter in the camps of neighbouring countries and in the Gaza strip. The Red Cross had reported a general improvement in the health of the refugees over the previous 12 months but the camps were overcrowded, medical provision was rudimentary and the food ration per head had had to be reduced because of supplies running low.[1] In the Egyptian controlled Gaza strip, the per capita ration of the 245,000 refugees was 1,500 calories per day. The camps were heaving with a traumatised, destitute people:

> Simple village folk who fled in their summer garment, unable to carry anything with them but their children, in some cases robbed of their jewelry and small sums of money as they fled. They fled in the heat of the summer, hoping to return to their home within a few weeks.[2]

Uncertainty about the future and the daily humiliation of living from handouts were taking their toll. 'With few exceptions', the American Friends Service Committee reported, 'the slowly declining morale of the refugees is upheld by one dominating idea, namely, that they shall be allowed soon to return to their former homes.' But it suggested that there was little prospect of that or, even, of significantly improving the refugees' material conditions:

> In spite of large contributions of tents from various nations it is still true to say that many thousands of refugees are living in dugouts or under pieces of threadbare sacking, or other conditions of over-crowding and squalor to which no human being should be subjected ... If the refugees were to spend another winter in their present circumstances their suffering would be terrible.[3]

A letter from the London-based Refugees' Defence Committee gave a stark summary of the situation:

> After more than a year's cessation of hostilities there are still 710,000 Palestinian Arab Muslim and Christian refugees – 430,000 under canvas (three families to a tent), 30,000 actually in caves reminders of our pre-historic ancestors.[4]

In November 1949, with Foreign Office encouragement, a handful of prominent individuals, headed by Ernest Bevin, and representatives of the British Council of Churches, launched a public appeal to support the refugees in the name of a committee called 'Christian Relief to the Holy Land'.[5]

While the refugee crisis was still unfolding, the Labour Party sent a delegation to Israel led by Alice Bacon, the vice-chairperson of the Labour Party and the Durham miners' leader, Sam Watson, in his role as chairperson of the NEC. The visit, as the party secretary Morgan Phillips indicated, was intended as a signal to Israeli leaders that the Labour government desired to begin a new chapter and establish friendly relations with Israel.[6] The three thousand word report that Bacon and Watson submitted on their visit reflected this intention. It recommended that Britain 'give full recognition to Israel' and 'should assist in its economic recovery'.[7] It made no mention of the Palestinians. Until 1973, the Labour Party did not address itself either to the plight of the refugees or to the question of how Palestinian national aspiration might be satisfied.

Through what ideological prism did the party view the Arab–Jewish conflict, that the Palestinians' fate held such little significance? Was this an unfortunate effect of the Labour Party's 'socialist humanistic tradition' which, according to Yosef Gorny's *The British Labour Movement and Zionism*, underpinned the party's endorsement of the Zionist as against the Arab case? The view that Zionism had, by the criteria of socialist humanism, a stronger case than the Palestinian Arabs is essentially a political judgement. In any case, Gorny's claim that socialist humanism was the ideological basis of Labour's policy on Palestine does not stand up to historical examination. His view, nevertheless, may be considered a plausible explanation for the Labour party's pro-Zionist tilt towards the end of the war, when the scale of the Nazi extermination of Jews became fixed in the party's consciousness. The party's strong emotional support for Zionism, in this period, manifested, claims Gorny, 'the more human and attractive aspects of the Party's image'.[8] His argument implies that, whatever injustice and suffering the establishment of Israel entailed for Palestinians, in Labour's humanist perspective, this would have been outweighed by the need to recompense European Jewry for the six million exterminated by the Nazis. However, the view that the Palestinians should bear the cost of making some amends for the Holocaust was predicated, as had been the Balfour Declaration, on Britain's imperial relation to Palestine: on the power to decide over the land and future of a colonial people. In part, the Attlee government's role in the final phase of the Mandate which, in upholding British imperial interests in the Middle East, collided with the Zionist objectives has helped to eclipse the imperial inspiration of the Labour Party's traditional support for Zionism. But the historical connection between Labour's pro-Zionism and British imperial politics and ideology is, none the less, close and it is a connection that Gorny's work elides. The Holocaust made a deep impression on the Labour Party but that, in itself, does not explain why the leadership, in its 1944 post-war settlement proposal, saw the appropriate response to be the formation of a Jewish state in Palestine.

The linking of the Holocaust to the setting up of Jewish state was neither as self-evident nor as uncontested in the immediate post-war period as has been subsequently represented.[9] A Mass Observation survey on public attitudes to the Palestine conflict, in 1947, while finding general indifference to the issue noted: 'Jewish sufferings during the war are not often mentioned as a reason for sympathising with Zionist aims'.[10] Among political élites, too, in this period, the Holocaust was not the main consideration in discussions on the future of Palestine. 'With regard to the deliberations in the United Nations and its commissions in 1947-48,' Friesel notes, 'it is difficult to find evidence that the Holocaust played a decisive or even significant role'.[11] The Labour Party's commitment to a Jewish state in Palestine, as a recompense to Jews for the Holocaust, emerged out of a perspective on the Palestine conflict that was formed in the inter-war years.

The Bacon-Watson report extends, seamlessly, the dominant theme in the party's inter-war discourse on Palestine. It portrays Zionism as a social democratic force bringing enlightenment to the Arab world.

> A new Social Dynamic based on progressive democracy and Socialism is being created in a manner akin to that of Britain and the Scandinavian countries. This social force is something new in the Middle East, and is the most outstanding development in that part of the world for centuries.[12]

Nearly 30 years before, Ramsay MacDonald had written about Zionist activity in Palestine in similar terms. Like the Bacon-led delegation he had visited the country as guest of the Histadruth and had been similarly unconcerned about the views of the Arab inhabitants. They appear in his desert scenes, in which the narrative switches between the viewpoint of the pilgrim and of the intrepid explorer. At the end of his journey he recounts:

> Our mud-caked Ford cars are being scraped and repaired after their heroic journeys; our ruts are being trodden down by donkeys and camels; no more will the Bedouin scurry at our hoots, and shoulder his ass to the side of the road.[13]

The sleepy, stagnant Orient is the foil to the dynamism of the Zionist settler.

> The Jewish town spreads on the sand. The foundations of a new garden city have been laid; in the middle of the sand dunes a big factory is at work turning out stones everyday sufficient to build a house.[14]

MacDonald perceived the Jews of Europe extending progress into a hithertoneglected corner of the world: 'the Arab population do not and cannot use or develop the resources of Palestine'.[15] Its rulers, argued MacDonald, unable to deliver development feared the progressive political influence of Zionism on the masses.

> Socialism and trade unionism came with the immigrants, and the Jewish workmen demanded a higher standard of life than the Arab. The old Arab leaders saw their position threatened.

By consequence, he saw the Arab hostility to Zionism as an aspect of 'the conflict between the Middle Ages and the Twentieth Century'.[16] The 1936 Arab rebellion provided the opportunity for these arguments to be rehearsed and to entrench them in Labour Party thinking on Palestine.

The rebellion began with a general strike that lasted for six months and involved most of the urban population. From the Arab motor transport and the Jaffa port workers the strike spread to the railways, petrol companies and public sector. As Lockman has documented, the British authorities and the Zionist trade union movement collaborated closely to try to break the strike. For Zionist leaders, the strike offered an opportunity to advance their 'conquest of labour' strategy which aimed at replacing Arab with Jewish labour. This had been partially effective in the Jewish-owned private sector but the British authorities had until then largely resisted the displacements of Arabs in the state run sector in order to avoid increasing labour costs.

> Now, however, the Arab revolt created circumstances in which the government had a strong political and security interest in backing the Histadruth's drive for Hebrew labour, in order to keep vital enterprises functioning and weaken the nationalist revolt.[17]

In the House of Commons, the Labour Party leadership denied the legitimacy of the strike and called for the government to resist its demands, which were aimed at halting further Zionist settlement activity. From the front bench Tom Wlliams explained: 'these disorders in Palestine can scarcely be characterised as the result of a strike in the sense in which that term is generally understood in this country'.[18] The *Daily Herald* commented:

> In Palestine the strike has been purely political, having its roots and its purpose in the same supercharged nationalism which is rapidly setting Europe by the ears: its methods have been those of the gunmen of Mussolini and Hitler.[19]

The Arab Higher Committee, formed by the political leaders of the various parties, had put itself at the head of the strike movement which had been initiated from below. But the Labour Party echoed the Zionist movement's claim that the strike, and the armed struggle it had triggered had no popular base or progressive content. Labour politicians insisted that there was no contradiction between the interest of Jewish workers and the Arab labouring

144

classes, on the basis that Zionism, and particularly Labour Zionism was introducing not only economic development but also new forms of working-class social and political organisation. 'The policy of the Zionist movement', claimed Creech Jones:

> has not been to create an army of landless Arabs but, rather, to build up the Arab people by safeguarding to them the use of land. By Jewish immigration new markets have been created, new land has been reclaimed and the Arab peasant has gained by being released from the money lender because of the capital which has become available.[20]

The Arab industrial worker also gained from Zionist settlement, according to Morrison: Jewish trade unions were 'assisting in the formation of Arab trade unions under Arab leadership'.[21] The Labour leadership's generally uncritical endorsement of the Zionist interpretation of the Palestine conflict was challenged, on a few occasions, from within the party. At the 1936 Labour Party conference, Alex Gossip, a leader of the National Amalgamated Furnishing Trades' Association, moved a motion ostensibly critical of the Mandate and the British government but, in reality, targeting the party's position. He told the conference:

> The Arabs have been in Palestine for over 1000 years. Their consent has not been asked. What right has Great Britain to go there, or any number of countries to say to Great Britain: You go into Palestine?' It is not the land of the British people at all. What would you or I say, what would we all say, if the Arabs or any other nationality came into this country and started to dominate and deal with us as the British Government is dealing with those who are under their control at the present time?

Gossip's resolution was defeated, while that put by Poale Zion was 'carried by an overwhelming majority'.[22] A discussion paper drafted by Tom Reid, in January 1942, for the party's Advisory Committee on Imperial Questions also diverged from the leadership's position on Palestine. Reid had been a member of the Woodhead Commission which investigated the feasibility of implementing the Peel Commission's partition proposal and in that task, he explained, 'spent six months on end at this subject alone with all documents and persons concerned (except Arabs)'.[23] Reid's paper challenged the frequently affirmed Labour Party view that Zionist settlement was congruent with Arab interests. Land bought by the Jewish authorities, he pointed out, could not be sold to the Arabs and where possible Arab labour was excluded from Jewish enterprises. Jewish immigrants he argued 'who come to stay in Palestine must throw in their lot with Palestinians instead of trying to set up an exclusive racial or communal economic system for themselves alone'. He recommended that both land sales and Jewish immigration be restricted since they were intended by the Zionists to give Jews a majority and political domination over the Arabs.

> The transference of political power from the people of Palestine to Jews, mostly recent immigrants, against the wishes of the majority of the people of Palestine cannot be justified by the promises made, nor by any fair principle of politics.[24]

Reid's paper ran into objections in the committee from Bentwich, a member of Brit Shalom and from Creech Jones. The exercise was, in any case, largely academic since the committee wielded little influence on the party's executive, where the Zionist case had several determined advocates.

Although a Poale Zion leader judged, in 1942, that Zionist lobbying 'had not penetrated very far beyond the top layer of the Labour leadership',[25] by this time few party activists could have been unaware where their sympathy was expected to lie on this issue. Most articles on Palestine in the Labour press – and particularly in the *Daily Herald*, the *New Statesman* and *Tribune* – and party conference statements and resolutions on seven occasions between 1921 and 1945, were favourable to Zionism. Morrison, the deputy leader from 1935, Gillies, the party secretary, Creech Jones, Noel Baker, Wedgwood and Laski frequently intervened in favour of Zionism, while the Arab case did not have a single prominent Labour Party advocate in the 1930s.

Poale Zion, the socialist Zionist party which acted as the propaganda arm of the Zionist Labour movement, was highly effective in lobbying British labour leaders. At various stages such prominent figures as Ben-Gurion, Dov Hoz and Berl Locker assisted its work in London. On at least one occasion, this involved drafting the contributions for a Commons debate on Palestine of sympathetic MPs. Ben-Gurion wrote to his wife from London: 'The speeches by Lloyd George, Leopold Amery, Tom Williams, Creech Jones, Herbert Morrison, James de Rothschild and Victor Cazalet were wholly or partly prepared by us.'[26] British Labour Party figures who visited Palestine as guests of the Histadruth also helped its work by addressing meetings, writing articles and providing contacts. Nevertheless, British membership of Poale Zion was limited to around 450 until 1939. It grew during the war to 1,500. Its work focused on lobbying the parliamentary party to which it was affiliated. On developments in Palestine it was one of the Labour Party's main source of information. It was frequently consulted by the Advisory Committee on Imperial Questions and briefed MPs. No similar access was available to George Mansur, the former Secretary of the Arab Workers' Society in Jaffa, who from 1936 ran the Arab Centre in London. It took nine months for him to obtain a meeting with the Advisory Committee. Poale Zion was able to acquire influence because the party was favourably predisposed to Labour Zionism. There are four main factors that account for this.

First, the Labour Zionist project appeared to represent a benign, social democratic form of colonisation. Instead of instituting a capitalist system involving the exploitation of the indigenous people it aspired to introduce cooperative forms of economic organisation and trade unionism. It was seen by Labour as embodying the ideals of 'trusteeship', which required reform rather than the dismantling of the Empire. The Labour Party was committed to the 'humane' management of the colonies, to the notion that it was the duty of the imperial power and, by extension, of Western civilisation to develop the resources of the colonial world, while attending to the interests of 'the natives'. 'The Jews have proved to be first-class colonisers', enthused Morrison, 'to have the real, good, old, Empire qualities, to be really first-class Colonial pioneers, and I do not object in any way, on the contrary, I welcome it'.[27] The Jew as coloniser, as the bridge between the West and the East, is redeemed not by discarding the categories of anti-Semitism but by reascribing them to the urban Jew – whom Morrison still disdained – and to the Arab. 'The Jews I saw in Palestine', commented the Labour MP, Commander Fletcher, 'were young, virile, vigorous, full of health, whereas many of the young Arabs seemed to me to be sickly, stunted and diseased.'[28]

Second, as the above indicates, an integral part of Labour's 'humane' imperialism, was a racist view of the Arab world which could not sustain the notion that development could come in any other way than through outsiders. Accordingly, Arab opposition to Zionism was castigated as hostility to progress. 'No people', opined Brailsford, 'enjoys the process of being shaken out of its medieval slumbers: the camel hates the bustling motor car.'[29] Wedgwood, the most vocal advocate of Zionism in the Labour Party, also believed that the Palestinian Arabs were merely paying the price of progress: 'every change in cultivation or in civilisation does injure some people, and these wondering Bedouin have suffered and must suffer as civilisation advances'.[30] Building on the image of a world trapped in biblical times in which Bedouins wandered over a limitless desert, Labour helped to insert into public consciousness the figure of the *effendi*. The latter was depicted not merely as a rapacious landlord and religious fanatic but also as the sole figure of Arab politics. This vision of the Middle East in which the wandering Bedouin could always move on (and the *effendi* needed moving on), contributed to the party's proposal on Palestine, in 1944. The National Executive Committee's report, after noting the Nazi atrocities against the Jews, stated:

> Here too in Palestine surely is a case, on human grounds and to promote stable settlement, for transfer of population. Let the Arabs be encouraged to move out, as the Jews move in. The Arabs have many wide territories of their own; they must not claim to exclude the Jews from this small area of Palestine, less than the size of Wales.[31]

Third, from the mid-1930s the Zionist goal of gathering Jews in Palestine was seen increasingly, by at least some Labour leaders, as a solution to the growing number of refugees from fascist persecution in Germany and

Eastern Europe. In this, perceptions of self-interest, humanitarian concern and anti-Semitic prejudices were intermingled. Between 1933 and 1939 about 50,000 Jews sought refuge in Britain. Although Labour politicians interceded on behalf of individual Jews seeking refuge in Britain, the Labour Party did not advocate a mass entry of Jews. Following the *Kristallnacht* pogrom in November 1938, Noel-Baker called on the government to 'consider the principle of large-scale settlement in Palestine, where there is work ready to be done'.[32] Zionism enabled Labour to reconcile its humanitarian concern for the Jewish victims of fascism and anti-Semitism with its own unease over immigration in to Britain. Morrison, as Home Secretary in the coalition government, apparently believed that anti-Semitism inevitably accompanied the presence of Jews and the greater their number, the more intense the anti-Semitism. He warned his Cabinet colleagues in 1940: 'If there were [*sic*] any substantial increase in the number of Jewish refugees or if these refugees did not leave this country after the war we should be in for serious trouble.'[33]

Fourth, the right wing of the Labour Party saw in Labour Zionism a counter-model to Soviet communism, useful in its political struggle against Communist influence in working-class politics. Labour Zionism proclaimed the priority of the national interest and it played down the role of class struggle, claiming to build socialism in collaboration with rather than through the violent overthrow of the bourgeoisie. In 1922, MacDonald contrasted the 'constructive work' of the cooperatives in Palestine with Lenin's approach and concluded: 'we cannot begin with the creation of an agricultural settlement, but if England were in a similar position to Palestine, we should also have to follow the same course'.[34] And Morrison, who had been active in driving out Communists from the Labour party, argued that the Zionist cooperatives were giving rise to 'a finer thing than is happening in any part of Russia. Here are colonies in which people are working on a voluntary basis, with no element of dictatorship or compulsion behind them'.[35]

In the 1930s, the Labour Party's support for a Jewish national home in Palestine drew on a humanitarian concern for the victims of fascism. This concern was generally linked to nationalist and pro-imperialist sentiments, to which Labour Zionism often explicitly appealed. To the Labour Movement, Zionist colonisation – the term used, at the time, by Zionists – held out the prospect of extending socialism into the Middle East without dismantling the British Empire and of providing refuge to Jews, without social cost or political risk to British society. In this sense, Zionism was the perfect ideological supplement to the social democratic parties of the Second International, which in their policy towards the colonial world had moved away from a commitment to national self-determination and, in their own countries, sought to defend their political base in the face of right-wing and, in some cases, fascist parties by vaunting their nationalist credentials.

The Labour party's response to the Nazi extermination, which precipitated its 1944 proposal that the Arabs move out of Palestine, was largely defined by the ideological ascendancy that Zionism had acquired in the Labour movement in the 1930s. But with the election of a Labour government in 1945, the party leadership, as the guardians of British imperial interests. became subject to different pressures and entered into a bitter confrontation with Zionism. Out of this clash, the Labour Party did not come to a new understanding of the Palestine conflict. Bevin and Attlee pursued a policy in the Middle East in which ultimately the Palestinian Arab case for self-determination went by default just as it had done in the party's traditional, pro-Zionist stance.

The foreign policy of the Labour government that took office in 1945 has been closely identified with Ernest Bevin and much discussion has been devoted to determining whether Bevin was anti-Semitic or not. The term 'Bevin's foreign policy' is a useful shorthand designation. It is however misleading to interpret it in relation to Palestine as defined by his attitude to Jews. As Louis points out, Bevin's 'anti-Semitic' reputation developed from policy, not personal sentiment'.[36]

A paper submitted by Bevin to the Cabinet, in August 1949, summarised the importance of the Middle East for British interests:

> Strategically the Middle East is a focal point of communications, a source of oil, a shield to Africa and the Indian Ocean, and an irreplaceable offensive base. Economically, it is, owing to oil and cotton, essential to United Kingdom recovery.[37]

Bevin perceived Britain's position in the Middle East as under threat mostly from Russia and Arab nationalism, and to a lesser extent, from US commercial rivalry. In so far as he sought to add a distinctly Labour slant to Middle East policy, it was to give Britain a role in the region's economic development and to place London's political relations to Arab governments on a more equal and cooperative basis.

On the economic front, Bevin was prepared to recognise that past British policy had been of little benefit to the mass of the peasantry and he aspired to what he called a 'peasants, not pashas' policy. In economic terms, however, the post-war Labour government lacked the resources to deliver. The government faced, at the end of the war, an enormous debt and far from being able to fund an investment programme, it sought to cling on to the Middle East countries' sterling deposits, by opposing sterling's convertibility and thereby forcing these countries to be de facto creditors to Britain. The assistance Bevin offered was largely restricted to the provision of technical and scientific experts to be operated by the British Middle East Office in collaboration with Arab governments. Technical assistance, it was thought,

149

could underpin British influence with a broader social base than in the past. The development work of the BMEO was limited, however, not only by resources – including a shortage of technical experts – but more seriously by the political constraints within which it operated. It could do little to improve the position of the *fellaheen* within the prevailing system of land ownership but Britain's strategic position depended on the conservative rulers who upheld that system. To retain British influence in the Middle East, Bevin needed the 'pashas' and in the face of the Palestine conflict none more than Abdullah, the King of Transjordan.

Bevin's close alliance with Abdullah has never been in doubt but it is only since the late 1980s that Ilan Pappé and Avi Shlaim – who belong to a new school of Israeli historians – have challenged the traditional Zionist account of 1948. Using documents released after 30 years by the Foreign Office, Pappé and Shlaim have shown that the British–Abdullah connection did not form a united front with the Arab nations aimed at thwarting the formation of a Jewish state. Rather, the connection operated, from an early stage of the 1948 war, on the understanding that the Zionist objective would have to be accommodated.[38] Bevin's support for Abdullah during the war prevented not the formation of a Jewish state but of the sovereign Arab Palestine, which the UN had also decreed. This was to set the limit of the Labour government's 'pro-Arab' leaning. Bevin's foreign policy was, in essence, as Elizabeth Monroe has pointed out, pro-British: its primary objective was to preserve the allegiance of rulers on whom British power in the Middle East depended.[39]

Bevin's initial aim had been to reconcile Jewish and Arab claims by proposals for various forms of unitary state, under continued British tutelage. When this proved unsatisfactory to both sides, and the British presence in Palestine was put under pressure by a campaign of terrorism by Zionist armed groups, the Labour government decided to put Palestine's future status before the UN. The Foreign Office had believed that the international community would merely reaffirm Britain's responsibility in finding a solution to the conflict. Successful Zionist lobbying, however, and American pressure led the General Assembly to partition Palestine into two states, an Arab and a Jewish, with Jerusalem accorded a separate, international status. To the Palestine Arab leadership, as to the Arab states, the partition was unacceptable. On 15 May 1948, on the termination of the British Mandate, the Arab states declared war on the newly established Israeli state. Abdullah was the supreme commander of the Arab offensive, a position that was more than nominal by virtue of his control of the Arab Legion, the strongest of the Arab forces. The legion received its funding, arms and a cohort of officers from Britain. Abdullah's objective was however more than the proclaimed liberation of Palestine. He saw the war as an opportunity to expand his impoverished kingdom by incorporating the more developed Palestine.

150

Pappé and Shlaim argue that Abdullah had an understanding with the Zionist leadership that, in tandem with the formation of the Jewish state, Transjordan would annex the UN-designated Arab part of Palestine. Only over Jerusalem could the two sides not accommodate each other's territorial ambitions. Elsewhere Abdullah adhered to the 'tacit understanding', as Shlaim describes it. The Arab Legion clashed with Zionist forces around Jerusalem but otherwise kept to the UN partition line. With Bevin having accepted, by early 1948, that a Jewish state was a *fait accompli,* the Abdullah-Zionist understanding was broadly in accord with his priorities: it promised to retain a part of Palestine under the control of Britain's most pliant ally. Bevin wanted to gain from the war only a change in the UN proposed boundaries of Israel, principally, in order to bring the Negev under Transjordan control. It was over this region of Palestine alone, Pappé argues, which Britain regarded as providing an important corridor between Egypt and the rest of the Arab world, that British and Israeli interests directly clashed.[40] In the event, Israeli forces occupied the Negev, in accordance with the UN partition plan, and Galilee, in defiance of it, but central Palestine was divided between Israel and Transjordan. The Gaza strip came under Egypt's control, where the Mufti briefly headed the 'National Palestine Council'. By the end of 1948 Egypt had no further use for him and all semblance of a Palestinian Arab government ceased. The 'main aims of the British Palestine policy in the post-Mandatory period were achieved', notes Pappé. 'What had begun as an act to prevent a larger Jewish state turned into almost a crusade against an independent Palestine state by the British, the Jordanians and the Israelis'.[41]

Bevin's 'pro-Arab policy' did not, therefore, introduce to the Labour Party, or to the wider public, the Palestinian Arab claim to self-determination or, any sense, that here was a nation in the making. Both a bi-national state under British control, which Bevin first favoured, and the Transjordan annexation of the UN-defined Arab part of Palestine, precluded Labour ministers arguing for an Arab Palestine as a sovereign, independent nation. Nevertheless, the Labour government's pursuit of a conventional imperial policy in the Middle East necessarily led it to articulate some of the Arab world's opposition to Zionism. Thus for the first time since the 1930 Passfield White Paper controversy, an anti-Zionist case was put to, and had to be seriously considered by, Labour Party members. At the 1946 party conference, Bevin spoke about Palestine against the background of the government's decision to slightly relax restriction on Jewish immigration. The government opposed the Zionist demand of mass entry into Palestine of 100,000 Jews from the displaced persons' camps in Europe: 'I do not believe in absolutely racial States' reasoned Bevin.

> I really do not, because you cannot sort the world out that way, however you try. It is too disturbing to move people who have been living there for centuries and make a racial state. You might just as well try to do that

in England with the Welshmen and the Scotsmen, or, what is worse, try to make Glasgow completely Scotch and see how you would get on, or Cardiff completely Welsh. It is impossible.[42]

In Palestine it was none the less attempted. Bevin again evoked the rights of the indigenous people when he discussed the plight of the Palestinian refugees who fled from, or were expelled by, Zionist forces during the 1948 war.

> The Arabs believe that for what they regard as a new and an alien State to be carved out of Arab land by a foreign force, against the wishes and over protests of its inhabitants, is a profound injustice. They point to the fact that since Britain gave up the Mandate – and I repeat the figure I gave just now – 500,000 Arabs have been driven from their homes. In Jaffa which was an Arab town of 70,000 allotted to the Arabs by the Assembly Resolution of 1947, there are now, so I am informed, only 5,000 Arabs.[43]

The publisher Victor Gollancz who, in 1943, had written *Let My People Go*, pleading for the Allies to rescue European Jewry from extermination was one of the few, on the left, moved to speak out on behalf of the Palestinian refugees. He felt, as a Jew, a particular responsibility and unhesitatingly identified the Arabs as the victims of the establishment of the Israeli state. Appealing to the Jewish community for financial contributions for the Palestinian refugees, he wrote:

> ... imagine that you are yourself one of these starving and dying people – just as, five years ago, some of us tried to imagine that we were our own fellow Jews who were being gassed and cremated in Auschwitz and Buchenwald, or a few years later, that we were Germans on starvation rations in the cellars of Cologne. Have we then no responsibility in the face of this horror – no extra, no specially Jewish responsibility, over and above our common human responsibility? ... I am very far from implying that all this misery is the result, either immediately or in the final analysis, solely of Jewish actions. But two things are certain. These women and children would not be dying of starvation and exposure if the Israeli State had never been founded; and the Israeli state was founded exclusively for the salvation and rehabilitation of Jews.[44]

More bluntly, a woman who identified herself as a Labour supporter wrote to Bevin in response to a *Picture Post* report:

> I was shocked and disgusted to read of the plight of several thousand Arab refugees camped in the Transjordan. To quote the reporter who reported these facts with pictures, lost, disillusioned people are waiting for a lot of 'shiny, pink men, sitting around a table' to make up their minds. Well have you?[45]

More common from Labour Party ranks, were expressions of support for Israel. These generally blamed the Palestinians' fate on the Arab states' rejection of the UN partition and on their subsequent attack on the newly established Jewish state. Crossman, who became a fervent advocate of Zionism, nevertheless expressed the hope that Israel would allow the refugees to return, though he argued that it would be better to provide them with alternative housing in their 'own' communities:

> They [the Israelis] say how stupid it would be to move them back. After all, these villages were only mud huts anyway. They were terribly bad villages full of vermin. Give them better houses in their own Arab community either in the Arab triangle of Arab Palestine or in Transjordan.[46]

The destruction of Palestinian society and the dispersal of its people caused little interest either in the Labour Party or among communists. The Communist Party had some influence on the left of the Labour Party but it had abandoned its earlier hostility to a Jewish state, in line with the change in the Soviet Union's position. After 1945, the Communist movement saw Zionism as a force that could weaken British imperialism in the Middle East. In consequence, apart from a few individuals, the left neither embraced the Palestinian Arabs' right to self-determination, nor evinced much humanitarian concern for the Palestinian refugees. Bringing their plight to the attention of the British public was left almost entirely to the government, the mainstream press and a few voluntary organisations. 'The striking fact about the Palestine situation', noted *Tribune* in October 1949, 'is the manner in which it has dropped out of the news'. In December, however, Palestine was again newsworthy, as result of a UN appeal on behalf of the refugees. A few months later a *Guardian* editorial claimed: 'The plight of the Arab refugees from Palestine is slowly burning itself into the conscience of the country'.[47] But this followed a House of Lords debate and the leader writer appears to have drawn the unlikely conclusion that its deliberation reflected the public mood. The 'Christian Relief in the Holy Land' appeal disappointed the expectations of its sponsors as had a similar, earlier, attempt by Catholic voluntary societies. A Foreign Office official noted that though the organisers had hoped to raise between £200,000-500,000, they collected £1,800.[48] The chairperson of the organising committee explained to Bevin:

> We have raised a certain amount of money and sent some goods out to the Middle East but generally speaking there has just not been the interest in the Appeal'. He attributed the indifference to 'the political implications' and to the impression that 'the United Nations was dealing with the matter.[49]

A more probable reason was the political parties' near silence on the refugees. A Mass Observations survey of attitudes to the Palestine conflict found, in 1947, from its sample of artisan and middle class respondents, that: 'Personal sympathy with the Arabs is very rare; for most they seem to be a rather shadowy people, whose rights, must in principle be upheld.'[50]

After 1949, the Palestinian Arabs rarely figured in Labour Party discourse on Israel or on the Arab–Israeli conflict. The fate of the Palestinians as a result of Israel's establishment clearly did not tally with one of the main arguments in the party's past defence of the Zionist project, namely, that it benefits the Arab population of Palestine. Crossman, in a lecture to celebrate the tenth anniversary of Israel, explained that this had been an illusion of Weizmann, the pioneer of modern Zionism, though without admitting that the Labour Party had subscribed to it.

> One of the central themes of his Zionist philosophy was that the National Home was not only a Jewish need – it was essential also to the renaissance of the Arab world. It was his notion that Israel should become the pilot plant in which should take place those experiments in agriculture, in the re-conquest of the desert, in the industrialisation of a backward area and in collective living required to revive the vanished glories of Middle Eastern civilisation.

Crossman concluded: 'Not one tittle of this vision has come true.'[51] Yet he attributed this failure not to the vision – or to its implementation – but to the Arab world's response, to its hostility to Israel. About the Palestinians he had little to say. Most of the refugees, he cursorily remarked, 'sit idly in the UNRWA camps today', while the Arab population remaining in Israel which he had described, in 1949, as 'a privileged and pampered minority',[52] he now considered to be justifiably discriminated against: 'Ten years after the war ended, these Arab villagers are still a "fifth column" inside Israel, and one cannot be surprised that the Army and police insist on treating them as such.'[53]

Two decades after the publication of Crossman's lectures on Israel, Harold Wilson published his tribute to Zionism, *The Chariots of Israel*. In the intervening period and particularly during the 1970s, there had developed a current of opinion in the party critical of Israeli policies towards its Arab neighbours and the Palestinians. In 1973, the party's annual conference adopted a resolution which pointed to 'the failure to find a fair and humane solution to the problems of the Palestinian community' as the root cause of the Arab–Israeli conflict. A few months later, the party leadership's insistence on a pro-Israeli stance towards the 1973 Arab–Israeli war provoked dissension in the parliamentary party.[54] Wilson's book was characteristic of the dominant view in the party. In 400 pages devoted to recounting the British involvement in Palestine, Wilson omits to mention the 1948 war's impact on the Arab inhabitants, even from the narrow angle of the Attlee government's effort to provide humanitarian assistance to the refugees. No leading Labour Party figure seems ever to have glimpsed, as Kurtz did in Conrad's *Heart of Darkness*, the horror of what had been done in the name of a doctrine that had claimed to bring progress to the 'natives'.

Notes

1. *Report of the British Red Cross Commission*, 23 February 1949, FCXII Dr. 4, p. 53, British Red Cross Archives, Wonersh, Guildford.
2. Warburton, M. C., 'The Arab Refugee Situation', approx. March/April 1949, G2/P1 Church Missionary Society Archives, Birmingham University.
3. *Report of the Secretary of the United Nations Relief for Palestinian Refugees,* 30 September 1949, FO371/75442, Public Records Office.
4. *The Times*, 10 October 1949.
5. *The Times*, 18 November 1949.
6. Morgan Phillips to D. Weitzman, 2 February 1950, Box Palestine/Israel, Labour Party Archives, Manchester Labour History Museum.
7. Alice Bacon and Sam Watson, *Report*, Labour Party Delegation to Israel, 29 December-13 January 1950, p. 10.
8. Gorny, Y. (1983), *The British Labour Movement and Zionism, 1917-1948*, London: Frank Cass, p. 188.
9. Arnov, D. (1994), 'The Holocaust and the Birth of Israel: Reassessing a Causal Relationship', *Journal of Israeli History*, **15** (13).
10. *Report on Attitudes to Palestine and Jews*, September 1947, File Reports 2515, p. 58, Mass Observation Archives, University of Sussex.
11. Friesel, E. (1979), 'The Holocaust and the Birth of Israel', *The Wiener Library Bulletin*, **32** (49/50), 57.
12. Bacon and Watson, op. cit., p. 8.
13. MacDonald, J. R. (1922), *A Socialist in Palestine*, London: Poale Zion.
14. Ibid., p. 2.
15. Ibid., p. 19.
16. Ibid., p. 13.
17. Lockman, Z. (1976), *Comrades and Enemies, Arab and Jewish Workers in Palestine, 1906-1948*, Berkeley: University of California Press, p. 243.
18. *Hansard,* 19 June 1936, vol. 313, col. 1326.
19. *Daily Herald*, 12 October 1936.
20. *Hansard,* op. cit., col. 1354.
21. Ibid., col. 1388.
22. *Labour Party Annual Conference Report*, 1936, pp. 220-21.

23. Labour Party Advisory Committee on Imperial Questions, 17 January 1942. Letter from Tom Reid, International Department, Box Palestine/Israel.

24. Reid, T. 'The Palestine Problem', 238B, September 1941.

25. Berl Locker to Histadruth, 30 November 1942, *Kaplansky Papers*, A137/75, Central Zionist Archives, Jerusalem.

26. Ben-Gurion, D. (1971), *Letters to Paula*, London: Valentine Mitchell, p. 100.

27. *Hansard*, 24 November 1938, vol. 341, col. 2005.

28. *Hansard*, 20 July 1939, vol. 350, col. 846.

29. *New Leader*, 2 January 1931.

30. *Hansard*, 24 March 1936, vol. 310, col. 1084.

31. 'The International Post-War Settlement' NEC, Labour Party, 1944, London.

32. *Hansard*, 21 November 1938, vol. 341, col. 1438.

33. Quoted in Wasserstein, B. (1979), *Britain and the Jews of Europe, 1935-1945*, Oxford: Clarendon Press, p. 179.

34. MacDonald, op. cit., p. 24.

35. *Hansard*, 19 June 1936, vol. 313, col. 1387.

36. Louis, W. R. (1986), 'British Imperialism and the End of the Palestine Mandate', in W. R. Louis and R. Stookey (eds), *The End of the Palestine Mandate*, London: I. B. Tauris, p. 1.

37. Quoted in Northedge, F. S. (1984), 'Britain and the Middle East', in R. Ovendale (ed.), *The Foreign Policy of the Labour Government*, Leicester: Leicester University Press, p. 149.

38. Pappé, I. (1988), *Britain and the Arab-Israeli Conflict, 1948-51*, Basingstoke: Macmillan; Shlaim, A. (1988), *Collusion Across the Jordan*, Oxford: Clarendon Press.

39. Monroe, E. (1961), 'Mr Bevin's "Arab Policy"', *St. Antony's Papers*, no. 11, p. 23.

40. Pappé, op. cit., p. 58.

41. Ibid., p. 114.

42. *Labour Party Annual Conference Report*, 1946, p. 166.

43. *Hansard*, 26 January 1949, vol. 460, col. 933.

44. Gollancz, V., 'Jewish Aid for Arab Refugees', MSS.157/3/JS/2/1, *Gollancz Papers*, Modern Records Centre, University of Warwick.

45. J. H. Chubb to Bevin, 22 June 1949, FO371/75430.

46. *Hansard*, 26 January 1949, vol. 460, col. 995.

47. *Tribune*, 29 October 1948; *Guardian*, 31 March 1949.

48. J. T. Sheringham, 11 April 1950, FO371/82235.

49. R. Williams-Thompson to Bevin, 6 April 1950, FO371/82235.

50. *Report on Attitudes to Palestine and Jews*, p. 47.

51. Crossman, R. (1960), *A Nation Reborn*, London: Hamish Hamilton,

p. 104.

52. *Hansard*, 26 January 1949, vol. 460, col. 995.

53. Crossman, op. cit., p. 95.

54. Watkins, D. (1984), *The Exceptional Conflict*, London: CAABU, p. 37.

CHAPTER EIGHT

Jews and the Trade Union Movements in the UK and US: Select Bibliographical Sources

Arieh Lebowitz

Part 1: The United Kingdom

General works/background (including items covering both the UK and the USA)

Abramsky, Chimen (1971), 'The Jewish Labour Movement: Some Historiographical Problems', in *Soviet Jewish Affairs*, vol. 1, no. 1, June.

Alderman, Geoffrey (1983), *The Jewish Community in British Politics*, Oxford: Oxford University Press.

Alderman, Geoffrey (1992), *Modern British Jewry*, Oxford: Clarendon Press.

Antonovsky, Aaron (1961), *The Early Jewish Labor Movement in the United States* [chapter on London as the cradle of the US Jewish labour movement], New York: YIVO Institute.

Barou, Noah (1945), *The Jews in Work and Trade: A World Survey*, London: Trades Advisory Council.

Beloff, Max (1991), 'Anglo-Jewry Revisited', *Jewish Journal of Sociology*, vol. 33, June.

Bentwich, Norman (1960), 'The Social Transformation of Anglo-Jewry, 1883-1960', *Jewish Journal of Sociology*, vol. 2, June.

Berrol, Selma Cantor (1994), *East Side/East End: East European Jews in London and New York, 1870-1920*, Westport, CT: Praeger.

Black, Eugene C. (1988), *The Social Politics of Anglo-Jewry, 1880-1920*, Oxford: Basil Blackwell.

Bross, J. (1950), 'The Beginning of the Jewish Labour Movement in Galicia', in *YIVO Annual*, vol. 4.

Bunzl, John (1975), *Klassenkampf in der Diaspora: Zur Geschichte der judischen Arbeiterbewegung*, Vienna: Europaverl.

Burgin, Hertz (1915), *Die Geshichte fun der Idisher Arbayter Bavegung in America, Rusland, un England*, New York: Fareynigte Idishe Geverkshaften.

Carrier, J. W. (1967), 'A Jewish Proletariat', in M. Mindlin and Chaim Bermant (eds), *Explorations: An Annual on Jewish Themes*, London: Barrie & Rockliff.

Carrier, J. W. (1973), 'Proletarian Yehudi B'Britania', *Tefutsot Israel*, vol.

11, no. 4.

Cesarani, David (ed.) (1990), *The Making of Modern Anglo-Jewry*, Oxford: Oxford University Press.

Cesarani, David (1992), 'The Remaking of the Jewish Immigrant Working Class in England', paper delivered at the conference, Jewish Workers: Integration and Jewish Movements: A Comparative Approach, Amsterdam, 27 March.

Cohen, Stuart A. (1982), *English Zionists and British Jews: The Communal Politics of Anglo-Jewry, 1895-1920*, Princeton: Princeton University Press.

Dyche, John A. (1898), 'The Jewish Workman', *Contemporary Review*, vol. 73, January.

Dyche, John A. (1899), 'The Jewish Immigrant', *Contemporary Review*, vol. 75.

Elman, Peter (1951-52), 'The Beginnings of the Jewish Trade Union Movement in England', *Transactions of the Jewish Historical Society of England*, vol. 17, pp. 53-62.

Englander, David (ed.) (1994), *A Documentary History of Jewish Immigrants in Britain, 1840-1920*, London: Leicester University Press.

Feldman, David (1983-84), 'The Role of Trade Unions among Jewish Immigrants', *Jewish Quarterly*, vol. 31, no. 1.

Feldman, David (1994), *Englishman and Jews: Social Relations and Political Culture, 1840-1914*, New Haven, CT: Yale University Press.

Fine, J. L. (1953), 'The Jewish Trade Unions', *Jewish Vanguard*, no. 123, 31 July.

Frankel, Jonathan (1981), *Prophecy and Politics: Socialism, Nationalism and the Russian Jews, 1862-1917*, Cambridge: Cambridge University Press.

Garrard, John A. (1970), 'Trade Unionism and the Jewish Immigrant', *Wiener Library Bulletin*, New Series, no. 24.

Gartner, Lloyd P. (1960), *The Jewish Immigrant in England, 1870-1914*, London: Allen & Unwin.

Gartner, Lloyd P. (1994), 'The Jewish Labor Movement in Great Britain and the United States', in Tamar Manor-Friedman (ed.), *Workers and Revolutionaries: the Jewish Labor Movement*, Tel Aviv: Beth Hatefutsoth, the Museum of the Jewish Diaspora.

Gorny, Joseph (1983) *The British Labour Movement and Zionism, 1917-1948*, London: Frank Cass.

Gould, Julius and Esh, Saul (eds) (1964), *Jewish Life in Modern Britain*, London: Routledge & Kegan Paul.

Green, Nancy L. (ed.) (1998), *Jewish Workers in the Modern Diaspora*, Berkeley: University of California Press.

Gross, Feliks and Vlavianos, Basil J. (eds) (1954), *Struggle for Tomorrow: Modern Political Ideologies of the Jewish People*, New York: Arts Inc.

Helfgott, Roy B. (1961), 'Trade Unionism among the Jewish Garment Workers of Britain and the United States', *Labor History*, vol. 2, no. 2.

Hofmeester, Karin (1990), *Van Talmoed tot Statuut: Joodse arbeiders en arbeidersbewegingen in Amsterdam, London en Paris, 1880-1914*, Amsterdam: Stichting beheer IISG.

Hofmeester, Karin (1999), '"Als ik niet voor mijzelf ben ...". De verhouding tussen joodse arbeiders en de arbeidersbeweging in Amsterdam, Londen en Parijs vergeleken, 1870-1914', PhD Thesis, University of Amsterdam.

Infield, Henryk F. (1962), *Essays in Jewish Sociology, Labour and Cooperation in Memory of Dr. Noah Barou, 1889-1955*, London: Thomas Yoseloff.

Kushner, Tony (ed.) (1992) *The Jewish Heritage in British History: Englishness and Jewishness*, London: Frank Cass.

Lerner, Shirley W. (1961), *Breakaway Unions and the Small Trade Union*, London: Allen & Unwin.

Levin, Nora (1978), *Jewish Socialist Movements, 1871-1917*, London: Routledge & Kegan Paul.

Lipman, Vivian David (1954), *A Social History of the Jews in England, 1850-1950*, London: Watts & Co.

Lipman, Vivian David, ed. (1961) *Three Centuries of Anglo-Jewish History*, Cambridge: W. Heffer.

Lipman, Vivian David (1975), 'Jews in British Urban Society, 1880-1914: From Ghetto to Suburb', paper read at the Economic History Society Conference, Leeds.

Lipman, Vivian David (1990), *A History of the Jews in Britain since 1858*, Leicester: Leicester University Press.

Mendelsohn, Ezra (1964), 'The Jewish Socialist Movement and the Second International, 1889-1914: the Struggle for Recognition', *Jewish Social Studies*, vol. 26.

Menes, Abraham (1955), 'The Jewish Labor Movement', in *The Jewish People Past and Present*, vol. 4, New York: Jewish Encyclopaedic Handbooks.

Mishkinsky, Moshe (1969), 'The Jewish Labor Movement and European Socialism', in H. H. Ben Sasson and Shmuel Ettinger (eds), *Jewish Society through the Ages*, New York: Schocken Books.

Patkin, A. L. (1947), *The Origins of the Russian-Jewish Labour Movement*, Melbourne: F. W. Cheshire.

Pollins, Harold (1977), 'Anglo-Jewish Trade Unions, 1870-1914', paper delivered to the Jewish Historical Society of England, 16 March.

Pollins, Harold (1982), *Economic History of the Jews in England*, Rutherford, NJ: Fairleigh Dickinson University Press.

Prager, Leonard (1990), *Yiddish Culture in Britain: A Guide*, Frankfurt am Main: Peter Lang.

Reutlinger, Andrew S. (1977), 'Reflections on the Anglo-American Jewish Experience: Immigrants, Workers, Entrepreneurs in New York and London, 1870-1914', *American Jewish Historical Quarterly*, vol. 66, no. 4.

Rollin, Aaron R. (1956), 'Industry and Commerce', *Jewish Chronicle Supplement: Tercentenary of British Jewry*, 27 January.

Rollin, Aaron R. (1966), 'Bletlech zu der Geschichte fun der Yiddisher Arbeter-Bevegung in England', *YIVO Bleter*, vol. 43.

Rollin, Aaron R. (1968), 'Russo-Jewish Immigrants in England before 1881', *Transactions of the Jewish Historical Society of England*, vol. 21.

Samuels, Leon (1956), 'The Jewish Labour Movement', *Jewish Quarterly*, vol. 3, no. 3, winter.

Schloss, D. F. (1891), 'The Jew as Workman', *Nineteenth Century*, vol. 29.

Tcherikover, Elias (1929), *Der Onheyb fun der Yiddisher Sotsialistisher Bavegung (Lieberman's Tekufeh)*, Warsaw.

Weinstock, Nathan (1984), *Le Pain de misère: Histoire du mouvement ouvrier juif en Europe* [volume II: *L'europe Centrale et Occidentale jusqu'en 1914*, which has a chapter on London], Paris: La Decouverte.

Wischnitzer, Mark (1965), *A History of Jewish Crafts and Guilds*, New York: Jonathan David.

Local studies

Adler, Henrietta (1934), 'Jewish Life and Labour in East London', in H. Llewelyn Smith (ed.), *New Survey of London Life and Labour*, vol. 6, London: P. S. King.

Alderman, Geoffrey (1989), *London Jewry and London Politics, 1889-1986*, London: Routledge.

Alderman, Geoffrey and Holmes, Colin (eds) (1993), *Outsiders and Outcasts: Essays in Honor of William J. Fishman*, London: Duckworth.

Bermant, Chaim (1975), *Point of Arrival: A Study of London's East End*, London: Eyre Methuen.

Booth, Charles (ed.) (1889, 1891), *Life and Labour of the People of London* (2 vols), London: Williams & Norgate.

Booth, Charles (ed.) (1892-97), *Life and Labour of the People of London* (9 vols), London: Macmillan.

Bush, Julia (1984), *Behind the Lines: East London Labour, 1914-1919*, London: Merlin.

Buckman, Joseph (1968), 'The Economic and Social History of Alien Immigration to Leeds, 1880-1914', PhD dissertation, University of Strathclyde.

Buckman, Joseph (1980), 'Alien Working-Class Response: The Leeds Jewish Tailors, 1880-1914', in Kenneth Lunn (ed.), *Hosts, Minorities and Immigrants: Historical Responses to Newcomers in British Society, 1870-1914*, Folkestone: Dawson Press.

Buckman, Joseph (1983), *Immigrants and the Class Struggle: The Jewish Immigrants in Leeds, 1880-1914*, Manchester: Manchester University Press.

Cesarani, David (1987), 'The East London of Simon Blumenfeld's Jew Boy', *London Journal*, vol. 13, no. 1.

Collins, Kenneth E. (1990), *Second City Jewry: The Jews of Glasgow in the Age of Expansion, 1790-1919*, Glasgow: Scottish Jewish Archives Committee.

Englander, David (1989), 'Booth's Jews: The Presentation of Jews and Judaism in "Life and Labour of the People in London"', *Victorian Studies*, vol. 32.

Feldman, David (1985), 'Immigrants and Workers, Englishmen and Jews: Jewish Immigration to the East End of London, 1880-1906', PhD Dissertation, University of Cambridge.

Feldman, David (1989), 'Jews in London, 1880-1914', in Raphael Samuel (ed.), *Patriotism: The Making and Unmaking of British National Identity*, vol. 2, London, Routledge.

Fishman, William J. (1975), *East End Jewish Radicals, 1875-1914*, London: Duckworth.

Fishman, William J. (1985), 'Morris Winchevsky and the Poilishe Yidl: First Chronicle of the East London Immigrant Ghetto', in Christiane Harzig and Dirk Hoerder (eds), *The Press of Labor Migrants in Europe and North America, 1880s to 1930s*, Bremen: Universität Bremen.

Fishman, William J. (1985), *Morris Winchevsky's London Yiddish Newspaper: One Hundred Years in Retrospect*, Oxford: Oxford Centre for Postgraduate Hebrew Studies.

Fishman, William J. (1986), *The Condition of East End Jews in 1888: Reflections in Retrospect*, London: West Central Counselling and Community Research.

Fishman, William J. (1988), *East End 1888, A Year in a London Borough among the Labouring Poor*, London: Duckworth.

Friedman, S. (1899), 'Condition of the Jewish Workers of Leeds', *Trade Unionist*, August.

Friedman, S. (1899), 'Sketch of the Leeds Jewish Tailors' Union', *Trade Unionist*, July.

Gillespie, J. A. (1984), 'Economic and Political Change in the East End of London in the 1920s', PhD dissertation, University of Cambridge.

Green, Joseph (1991), *A Social History of the Jewish East End in London, 1914-1939: A Study of Life, Labour and Liturgy*, Lampeter: E. Mellen.

Hall, P. G. (1962), 'The East London Footwear Industry: An Industrial Quarter in Decline', *East London Papers*, vol. 5, no. 1.

Halpern, Georg (1903), *Die Judischen Arbeiter in London*, Stuttgart: J. Cotta'sche.

Hendrick, June (1970), 'The Tailoresses in the Ready-Made Clothing Industry in Leeds, 1889-1899: A Study in Labour Failure', MA thesis, University of Warwick.

Holmes, Colin (1973) 'The Leeds Jewish Tailors' Strikes of 1885 and 1888', *Yorkshire Archaeological Journal*, vol. 45.

Hourwich, I. (1904), 'The Jewish Labourer in London', *Journal of Political Economy*, December.

Howard, Walter S. (n.d.), 'Jews in the Furniture Trade, 1880-1920', MPhil thesis, University of Southampton.

Kershen, Anne J. (1990), 'Trade Unionism amongst the Jewish Tailoring Workers of London and Leeds, 1872-1915', in David Cesarani (ed.), *The Making of Modern Anglo-Jewry*, Oxford: Oxford University Press.

Kershen, Anne J. (1995), *Uniting the Tailors: Trade Unionism amongst the Tailoring Workers of London and Leeds, 1870-1939*, Ilford: Frank Cass.

Krausz, Ernest (1964), *Leeds Jewry: Its History and Social Structure*, Cambridge: W. Heffer.

Kushner, Tony (1986), 'The Manchester Jewish Museum', *Bulletin of the Society for the Study of Labour History*, vol. 51, no. 3, pp. 18-19.

Lerner, Shirley W. (1966), 'The Impact of the Jewish Immigration of 1880-1914 on the London Clothing Industry and Trade Unions', [summarized in] *Bulletin of the Society for Labour History*, vol. 12, summer.

Lerner, Shirley W. (1966), 'A Voice from the Aliens about the Anti-Alien Resolution of the Cardiff Trade Union Congress (1895)', *Bulletin of the Society for Labour History*, vol. 12, summer.

Lestchinsky, Jacob (1907), *Der Idisher Arbayter*, Vilna: Tsukunft.

Levy, Abraham Bernard (1951), *East End Story*, London, Constellation Books/Vallentine Mitchel.

Litvinoff, Barnet (1950), 'Zangwill's Ghetto Is No More: The Passing of Whitechapel', *Commentary*, vol. 10, October.

Maitles, Henry (1991) 'Jewish Trade Unionists in Glasgow', *Immigrants and Minorities*, vol. 10, no. 3.

Massil, William I. (1997), *Immigrant Furniture Workers in London, 1881-1939: And the Jewish Contribution to the Furniture Trade*, London: Jewish Museum.

Meltzer, Albert (1976), *Anarchists in London, 1935-55*, Orkney Islands: Cienfuegos Press.

Mindel, Mick (1986), 'Socialist Eastenders', *Jewish Socialist*, vols 6/7, summer/autumn.

Newman, Aubrey (ed.) (1981) *The Jewish East End, 1840-1939*, London: Jewish Historical Society of England.

O'Brien, Rosalind (1975), 'The Establishment of the Jewish Minority in Leeds', PhD dissertation, Bristol University.

Oliver, J. Leonard (1961), 'The East London Furniture Industry', *East London Papers*, vol. 4, October.

Poulson, Charles (1988), *Scenes from a Stepney Youth*, London: THAP Books.

Rollin, Aaron R. (1949), 'A Jewish Tailors' Strike of 60 Years Ago', *Jewish Chronicle*, 14 October.

Rose, Millicent (1951), *The East End of London*, London: Cresset Press.

Schmiechen, James A. (1984), *Sweated Industries and Sweated Labour: The

London Clothing Trades, 1860-1914, London: Croom Helm.

Schonenbohm, Dieter (1987), *Ostjuden in London: der Jewish Chronicle und die Arbeiterbewegung der judischen Immigranten im Londoner East End, 1881-1900*, Frankfurt am Main: Peter Lang.

Selitrenny, L. (1896), 'The Jewish Working Woman in the East End', *Social Democrat*, vol. 2.

Sherman, A. V. (1960), 'Epitaph for the East End', *Commentary*, vol. 30, November.

Smith, Elaine R. (1986), 'East End Tailors, 1918-1939: An Aspect of the Jewish Workers' Struggle', *Jewish Quarterly*, vol. 34, no. 2, summer.

Smith, Elaine R. (1990), 'Jews and Politics in the East End of London, 1918-1939', in David Cesarani (ed.), *The Making of Modern Anglo-Jewry*, Oxford: Oxford University Press.

Smith, Elaine R. (1991), 'East End Jews in Politics, 1918-1939: A Study in Class and Ethnicity', PhD dissertation, University of Leicester.

Smith, Elaine R. (1992), 'Class, Ethnicity and Politics in the Jewish East End', *Jewish Historical Studies 1990-92*, vol. 32, pp. 355-69.

Tcherikower, E. (1929), 'Der Yidisher Imigrant in London in di Zibetsiker Yorn', *Yidishe Emigrantsye*, April.

Thorn, Gary (1983), 'The Politics of Trade Unionism in a Sweated Industry: Boot and Shoe Makers in Late Nineteenth Century London', PhD dissertation, Warwick University.

Wechsler, Robert Stephen (1979), 'The Jewish Garment Trade in East London, 1875-1914: A Study of Conditions and Responses', PhD dissertation, Columbia University.

White, Jerry (1980), *Rothschild Buildings: Life in an East End Tenement Block, 1887-1920*, London: Routledge & Kegan Paul.

Williams, Bill (1976), *The Making of Manchester Jewry, 1740-1875*, Manchester: Manchester University Press.

Williams, Bill (1980), 'The Beginnings of Jewish Trade Unionism in Manchester', in Kenneth Lunn (ed.), *Hosts, Minorities and Immigrants: Historical Responses to Newcomers in British Society*, Folkestone: Dawson Press.

Williams, Bill (1990), '"East and West": Class and Community in Manchester Jewry, 1850-1914', in David Cesarani (ed.), *The Making of Modern Anglo-Jewry*, Oxford: Oxford University Press.

Working Lives, 1905-1945; A People's Autobiography of Hackney (1976), London: Hackney Workers Education Association.

Young, James Douglas (1974), 'Working Class and Radical Movements in Scotland and the Revolt from Liberalism, 1866-1900', PhD dissertation, University of Stirling.

Other works

Aronsfeld, Caesar C. (1947), 'Communists in British Jewry: A Zionist

Socialist Analysis', *Jewish Monthly*, vol. 1, November.

Dale, Naomi (1985), 'Jewish Worker Circle Friendly Society, 1909-1984', *Jewish Socialist*, vol. 2.

Dobbs, Sealey Patrick (1928), *The Clothing Workers of Great Britain*, London: G. Routledge.

Eyges, T. B. (1944), *Beyond the Horizon: The Story of a Radical Emigrant*, Boston: Group Free Society.

Fox, Alan (1958), *A History of the National Union of Boot and Shoe Operatives, 1874-1957*, Oxford: Basil Blackwell.

Frumkin, Abraham (1940), *In Friling fun Yidischen Sozialism: Zichroynes fun a Zshurnalist*, New York: A. Frumkin Jubilee Committee.

Gordin, A. S. (1957), *S. Yanovsky, his Life, Struggles and Achievement, 1864-1939*, S. Yanovsky Memorial Committee, Los Angeles.

Graur, Mina (1997), *An Anarchist Rabbi: The Life and Teachings of Rudolf Rocker*, New York: St Martin's Press.

Hyman, Richard (1971), *The Workers' Union*, Oxford: Clarendon Press.

Jacobs, Joe (1978), *Out of the Ghetto: My Youth in the East End, Communism and Fascism, 1913-1939*, London: Janet Simon.

Kadish, Sharman (1992), *Bolsheviks and British Jews: The Anglo-Jewish Community, Britain and the Russian Revolution*, London: Frank Cass.

Kushner, Tony (1990), 'Jewish Communists in Twentieth-Century Britain: The Zaidman Collection', *Labour History Review*, vol. 55, autumn.

Lerner, Shirley W. (1956), 'The History of the United Clothing Workers Union', PhD dissertation, University of London.

Levenberg, Schneir (1945) *The Jews and Palestine: A Study in Labour Zionism*, London: Poale Zion.

Levenberg, Schneir (1971), '50 Yor Poalei-Tsionistis Kampf in der Britisher Arbeyter-Bavegung', *Zukunft*, vol. 78, no. 4.

Levenberg, Schneir (1974), 'The Impact of Yiddish in the Jewish Labour Movement', *Jewish Quarterly*, vol. 22, nos 1-2.

Litvinoff, Barnet (1969), *A Peculiar People*, New York: Weybright and Talley.

Litvinoff, Emanuel (1972), *Journey through a Small Planet*, London: Michael Joseph.

Orbach, Maurice (1962), 'Noah Barou and the Trades Advisory Council', Henryk F. Infield (ed.), *Essays in Jewish Sociology, Labour and Cooperation in Memory of Dr. Noah Barou, 1889-1955*, London: Thomas Yoseloff.

Piratin, Phil (1948), *Our Flag Stays Red*, London: Thames Publications (reprinted 1978, London: Lawrence & Wishart).

Pollins, Harold (1980), *A History of the Jewish Working Men's Club and Institute, 1874-1912,* Oxford: Ruskin College Library.

Reid, Hew (1986), *The Furniture Makers: A History of Trade Unionism in the Furniture Trade, 1865- 1972*, Oxford: Malthouse Press.

Rocker, Rudolf (1952), *In Shturem: Golus Yorem*, London: Fraye arbaytershtimme, [a segment of which was published in 1956 in English as *The London Years*, trans. and intro, Joseph Leftwich, London: Fraye arbeter shtime].

Shimoni, Gideon (1986), 'Poale Zion: A Zionist Transplant in Britain (1905-1945)', in Peter Y. Medding (ed.), *Studies in Contemporary Jewry II*, Bloomington, IN: Indiana University Press.

Shinwell, Emanuel (1909), 'Jewish Characteristics – by One of Them', *Clothiers' Operatives Gazette*, September.

Shinwell, Emanuel (1973), *I've Lived Through It All*, London: Gollancz.

Silberner, Edmund (1952), 'British Socialism and the Jews', *Historica Judaica*, vol. 14, April.

Srebrnik, Henry Felix (1986), 'Communism and Pro-Soviet Feeling among the Jews of East London, 1935-45', *Immigrants and Minorities*, vol. 5, no. 3, November.

Srebrnik, Henry Felix (1995), *London Jews and British Communism, 1935-1945*, Ilford: Vallentine Mitchell.

Stewart, Margaret and Leslie Hunter (1964), *The Needle Is Threaded: The History of an Industry*, London: Heinemann/Newman Neane.

Workers' Circle (1929), *The Workers' Circle Jubilee Publication, 1909-29*, London: Workers' Circle.

Workers' Circle (1959), *The Circle Golden Jubilee, 1909-1959*, London: Workers' Circle.

Workers' Circle (1969), *Diamond Jubilee: The Workers' Circle Friendly Society, 1909-1969*, London: Workers' Circle.

Yanofsky, Shaul (1948), *Ershte Yorn fun Yidishen Frayhaytlekhn Sotzializm*, New York: Fraye arbeter shtime.

Part 2: The United States

General works

Asher, Robert (1976), 'Jewish Unions and the American Federation of Labor Power Structure, 1903-1935', *American Jewish Historical Quarterly*, vol. 65.

Baum, Charlotte, Hyman, Paula and Michel, Sonya (1976), 'Weaving the Fabric of Unionism: Jewish Women Move the Movement', in *idem*, *The Jewish Woman in America*, New York: Dial Press.

Bell, Daniel (1957), 'Jewish Labor History', *Publications of the American Jewish Historical Society*, vol. 46, no. 3, March.

Berman, Hyman (1962), 'A Cursory View of the Jewish Labor Movement: An Historiographical Survey', *American Jewish Historical Quarterly*, vol. 52, no. 2, December.

Bloom, Bernard H. (1960), 'Yiddish Speaking Socialists in America, 1892-1905', *American Jewish Archives*, vol. 12, no. 1, April.

Brandes, Joseph (1976), 'From Sweatshop to Stability: Jewish Labor Between the World Wars', *YIVO Annual*, vol. 16, pp. 1-149.

Buhle, Paul (1980), 'Jews and American Communism: The Cultural Question', *Radical History Review*, vol. 23, spring.

Buhle, Paul (1983), 'The Roots of Jewish Labor: Will the Vision Be Renewed?', *Genesis II*, Boston, February.

Danish, Max D. (1948), 'The Jewish Labor Movement: Facts and Prospects', in *idem, The Jewish People Past and Present*, vol. 4, New York: Jewish Encyclopedic Handbooks.

David, Henry (1952), 'The Jewish Unions and Their Influence upon the American Labor Movement', *Publications of the American Jewish Historical Society*, vol. 41, no. 4, June.

David, Henry (1957), 'Jewish Labor History: A Problem Paper', *Publications of the American Jewish Historical Society*, vol. 46, no. 3, March.

Davidowicz, Lucy S. (1976), 'The Jewishness of the Jewish Labor Movement in the United States', in Bertram Wallace Korn (ed.), *A Bicentennial Festschrift for Jacob Rader Marcus*, New York: American Jewish Historical Society/KTAV (reprinted in *The American Jewish Experience*, ed. Jonathan D. Sarna (1986), New York: Holmes & Meier).

Dubofsky, Melvyn (1961), 'Organized Labor and the Immigrant in New York City, 1900-1918', *Labor History*, vol. 2, spring.

Epstein, Melech (1950, 1953), *Jewish Labor in the United States, 1882-1952*, vol. 2, New York: Trade Union Sponsoring Committee (reprinted 1969).

Epstein, Melech (1959), *The Jew and Communism, 1919-1941*, New York: Trade Union Sponsoring Committee.

Feingold, Henry·L. (1982), 'Matching Power and Responsibility: The Jewish Labor Movement', in *idem, A Midrash on American Jewish History*, Albany: SUNY Press.

Frager, Ruth A. (1992), *Sweatshop Strife: Class, Ethnicity, and Gender in the Jewish Labour Movement of Toronto, 1900-1939*, Toronto: University of Toronto Press.

Frankel, Jonathan (1976), 'The Jewish Socialists and the American Jewish Congress Movement', *YIVO Annual*, vol. 16.

Glanz, Rudolph (1951), 'Source Material on the History of Jewish Immigration to the U.S., 1800-1880', *YIVO Annual*, vol. 6.

Glanz, Rudolph (1976), 'Some Remarks on the Jewish Labor Movement and American Public Opinion in the Pre-World War I Era', *YIVO Annual*, vol. 16.

Glenn, Susan A. (1990), *Daughters of The Shtetl – Life and Labor in the Immigrant Generation*, Ithaca: Cornell University Press.

Goren, Arthur (1970), 'The Jewish Labor Movement and the Kehillah', in *idem, Quest for Community: The Kehillah Experiment, 1908-1922*, New York.

Hardman, J. B. S. (1952), 'The Jewish Labor Movement in the United States:

Jewish and Non-Jewish Influences', *Publications of the American Jewish Historical Society*, vol. 41, no. 4, December.

Hardman, J. B. S. (1952), 'Jewish Workers in the American Labor Movement', *YIVO Annual*, vol. 7.

Herberg, Will (1952), 'The Jewish Labor Movement in the United States', in *American Jewish Year Book*, vol. 53.

Howe, Irving (1958), 'The Significance of the Jewish Labor Movement', *The Jewish Labor Movement in America: Two Views*, New York: Jewish Labor Committee.

Howe, Irving (1976), 'Jewish Labor, Jewish Socialism', in *idem, World of Our Fathers*, New York: Simon and Schuster.

Howe, Irving and Libo, Kenneth (1979), 'Labor and Socialism', in *idem, How We Lived: A Documentary History of Immigrant Jews in America, 1880-1930*, New York: R. Marek.

Kosak, Hadassa (2000), *Cultures of Opposition: Jewish Immigrant Workers, New York City, 1881-1905*, Albany: SUNY Press.

Knox, Israel (1958), 'Jewish Labor – The Reality and the Ideal', in *idem, The Jewish Labor Movement in America: Two Views*, New York: Jewish Labor Committee.

Leviatin, David (1969), *Followers of the Trail: Jewish Working-Class Radicals in America*, New Haven: Yale University Press.

Levin, Nora (1973), 'Socialist Intellectuals Encounter Jewish Workers in America, 1881-84', *Gratz College Annual of Jewish Studies*, vol. 2.

Levin, Nora (1976), 'The Influence of the [Jewish Labor] Bund on the Jewish Socialist Movement in America', *Gratz College Annual of Jewish Studies*, vol. 5.

Levin, Nora (1977), 'The American Jewish Labor Movement', in *idem, While Messiah Tarried: Jewish Socialist Movements, 1871-1917*, New York: Schocken Books.

Liebman, Arthur (1979), *Jews and the Left*, New York: John Wiley.

McCreesh, Carolyn Daniel (1985), *Women in the Campaign to Organize Garment Workers, 1880-1917*, New York and London: Garland.

Mendelsohn, Ezra (1990), 'The Russian Roots of the American Jewish Labor Movement', *YIVO Annual*, vol. 16, 1976 (reprinted in Deborah Dash Moore (ed.), *East European Jews in Two Worlds: Studies from the YIVO Annual*, Evanston: Northwestern University Press).

Menes, Abraham (1972), 'The East Side and the Jewish Labor Movement', in Irving Howe and Eliezer Greenberg (eds), *Voices from the Yiddish*, Ann Arbor: University of Michigan Press.

Mergan, Bernard (1976), '"Another Great Prize": The Jewish Labor Movement in the Context of American Jewish History', *YIVO Annual*, vol. 16.

Perlman, Selig (1952), 'Jewish-American Unionism: Its Birth Pangs and Contribution to the General American Labor Movement', *Publication of the American Jewish Historical Society*, vol. 41, no. 4, June.

Perlman, Selig (1957), 'America and the Jewish Labor Movement: A Case of Mutual Illumination', *Publications of the American Jewish Historical Society*, vol. 46, no. 3, March.

Reich, Nathan (1952), 'Some Observations on Jewish Unionism', *Publications of the American Jewish Historical Society*, vol. 41, no. 4, June.

Rich, Jacob C. (1948), 'The Jewish Labor Movement in the United States', in *idem, The Jewish People Past and Present*, New York: Jewish Encyclopedic Handbooks.

Rich, Jacob C. (1957), 'Sixty Years of the "Jewish Daily Forward"', *New Leader*, 3 June.

Rischin, Moses (1962), *The Promised City: New York's Jews, 1870-1914*, Cambridge, MA: Harvard University Press.

Rischin, Moses (1963), 'The Jewish Labor Movement in the United States: A Social Interpretation', *Labor History*, vol. 4, fall.

Rogoff, Abraham Meyer (1945), *Formative Years of the Jewish Labor Movement in the United States, 1890-1900*, Ann Arbor: Edwards Bros.

Rosenblum, Gerald (1973), *Immigrant Workers: Their Impact on American Labor Radicalism*, New York: Basic Books.

Ruchames, Louis (1969), 'Jewish Radicalism in the U.S.', in Peter I. Rose (ed.), *The Ghetto and Beyond: Essays in Jewish Life in America*, New York: Random House.

Sanders, Ronald (1969), *The Downtown Jews: Portrait of an Immigrant Generation,* New York: Harper & Row.

Salutsky, J. B. (1916), 'The Jewish Labor Movement in the United States', *American Jewish Year Book, 1916.*

Schappes, Morris U. (1950), *A Documentary History of the Jews in the United States, 1645-1875*, New York: Citadel Press.

Schappes, Morris U., series on Jewish labour movement in *Jewish Life*, 'Socialist Traditions of Jewish Labor' (May 1950); 'Jewish Labor in the [Eighteen] Nineties' (June 1950); 'Appeal of Jewish Workingmen's Union 1885' (May 1952); 'Jewish Workers' Victory – 1890' (April 1953); 'The 1880s – Beginnings of Jewish Trade Unionism' (September 1954); 'The Nineties – Ups and Downs of Jewish Trade Unions' (October 1954); 'The New Century Opens – Jewish Labor Movement Grows' (December 1954); 'The Heroic Period of Jewish Labor, 1909-1914' (January 1955).

Seidman, Joel (1942), *The Needle Trades*, New York: Farrar and Rinehart.

Seligman, Ben B. (1953), 'Needle, Thread and Thimble: The Story of Jewish Labor in the U.S.', *Jewish Frontier*, September.

Seller, Maxine S. (1986), 'The Rising of the Twenty Thousand: Sex, Class and Ethnicity in the Shirtwaist Makers Strike of 1909', in Dirk Hoerder (ed.), *Struggle a Hard Battle: Essays on Working Class Immigrants*, Dekalb, IL: Northern Illinios University Press.

Sherman, Charles Bezalel (1954), 'Nationalism, Secularism and Religion in the Jewish Labor Movement', *Judaism*, vol. 3, fall. (Reprinted in *Voices from the Yiddish*, eds Irving Howe and Eliezer Greenberg, Ann Arbor, MI: University of Michigan Press).

Shuldiner, David Philip (1999), *Of Moses and Marx: Folk Ideology Within the Jewish Labor Movement of the United States*, Westport, CT: Bergin and Garvey.

Sorin, Gerald (1985), *The Prophetic Minority: American Jewish Immigrant Radicals, 1880-1920*, Bloomington: Indiana University Press.

Sorin, Gerald (1989), 'Tradition and Change: American Jewish Socialists as Agents of Acculturation', *American Jewish History*, vol. 59, no. 1, autumn.

Stein, Leon (ed.) (1977), *Out of the Sweatshop: The Struggle for Industrial Democracy*, New York: Quadrangle/The New York Times Book Co.

Tax, Meredith (1980), 'The Uprising of the Thirty Thousand', in *idem, The Rising of the Women*, New York and London: Monthly Review Press.

Tcherikover, Elias (1961), *The Early Jewish Labor Movement in the United States*, trans. and ed. Aaron Antonovsky, New York: YIVO.

Trunk, Isaiah (1976), 'The Cultural Dimensions of the Jewish Labor Movement', *YIVO Annual*, vol. 16.

Tyler, Gus (n.d.), *The Jewish Labor Movement: A Living Legacy*, New York: Jewish Labor Committee.

Tyler, Gus (1965), 'The Legacy of the Jewish Labor Movement', *Midstream*, March.

Wahl, Edward (1947), 'American Jewish Labor Movement', *Chicago Jewish Forum*, vol. 5, spring.

Waldinger, Roger D. (1986), *Through the Eye of the Needle: Immigrants and Enterprise in New York's Garment Trades*, New York: New York University Press.

Weinryb, Bernard D. (1946), 'The Adaptation of Jewish Labor Groups to American Life', *Jewish Social Studies*, vol. 3, no. 4.

Wertheimer, Barbara Mayer (1977), 'The Rise of the Woman Garment Worker: New York, 1909-1910' (Chapter 16), and 'Women in the Men's Clothing Trades: A New Union, 1910-1914' (Chapter 17), in *idem, We Were There: The Story of Working Women in America*, New York: Pantheon Books.

Yellowitz, Irwin (1976), 'American Jewish Labor: Historiographical Problems and Prospects', *American Jewish Historical Quarterly*, vol. 65, no. 3, March.

Yellowitz, Irwin (1981), 'Jewish Immigrants and the American Labor Movement, 1900-1920', *American Jewish History*, vol. 71, no. 2, December.

Yellowitz, Irwin (1992), 'Labor Movement', in Jack Fischel and Sanford Pinsker (eds), *Jewish-American History and Culture: An Encyclopedia*, New York and London: Garland.

Alperin, Aaron (1976), *Seventy Years of Labor Zionism in America*, New York: Labor Zionists of America.

Avrich, Paul (1988), 'Jewish Anarchism in the United States', in *idem*, *Anarchist Portraits*, Princeton: Princeton University Press.

Barbash, Jack (1968), 'The ILGWU as an Organization in the Age of Dubinsky', *Labor History*, vol. 9, special supplement, New York.

Beck, Burt (1974), *A Brief History of the Amalgamated*, New York: Amalgamated Clothing Workers of America.

Belsky, Joseph (1952), *I, The Union: Being the Personalized Trade Union Story of the Hebrew Butcher Workers of America*, Yonkers, NY: Raddock & Brothers.

Brenner, Paul (1983), 'The Formative Years of the Hebrew Bakers' Unions, 1881-1914', *YIVO Annual*, vol. 18.

Bookbinder, Hyman H. (1950), *To Promote the General Welfare: The Story of the Amalgamated*, New York: Amalgamated Clothing Workers of America.

Brooks, Tom (1957), 'The Terrible Triangle Fire', *American Heritage*, vol. 8, no. 5, August.

Budish, J. M. and George Soule (1920), *The New Unionism in the Clothing Industry*, New York: Harcourt, Brace and Howe.

Carpenter, Jesse Thomas (1972), *Competition and Collective Bargaining in the Needle Trades, 1910-1967*, Ithaca: NY State School of Industrial and Labor Relations.

Cohen, Julius Henry (1946), *They Builded Better Than They Knew*, New York: J. Messner.

Danish, Max D. (1950), *ILGWU News-History, 1900-1950*, New York: ILGWU.

Eisner, J. M. (1969), 'Politics, Legislation and the ILGWU', *American Journal of Economics and Sociology*, vol. 28.

Foner, Philip S. (1950), *The Fur and Leather Workers Union: A Story of Dramatic Struggles and Achievements*, Newark: Nordan Press.

Foner, Philip S. (1980), 'Revolt of the Garment Workers I and II', in *idem* *History of the Labor Movement in the United States*, vol. 5, New York: International Publishers.

Fraser, Steven (1986), 'Landsleit and Paesani: Jews and Italians in the Amalgamated Clothing Workers', in Dirk Hoerder (ed.), *Struggle a Hard Battle: Essays on Working Class Immigrants*, Dekalb: Northern Illinois University Press.

Green, Charles H. (1944), *The Headwear Workers: A Century of Trade Unionism*, New York: United Hatters, Cap and Millinery Workers International Union.

Hardman, J. B. S. (1960), 'The Needle Trade Unions: A Labor Movement at Fifty', *Social Research*, vol. 27, no. 3, autumn.

Hardy, Jack (1935), *The Clothing Workers*, New York: International Publishers.

Hertz, Jacob S. (1958), *The Jewish Labor Bund: A Pictorial History 1897-1957* (bilingual Yiddish/English), New York: Farlag Unser Tsait.

Hurwitz, Ariel (ed.) (1994), *Against the Stream: Seven Decades of Hashomer Hatzair in North America*, Israel: Givat Haviva Institute.

Hurwitz, Maximillian (1936), *The Workmen's Circle*, New York: Workmen's Circle.

Korman, Gerd (1986), 'Ethnic Democracy and Its Ambiguities: The Case of the Needle Trade Unions', *American Jewish History*, vol. 75, no. 4.

Korman, Gerd (1994), 'New Jewish Politics for an American Labor Leader: Sidney Hillman, 1942-1946', *American Jewish History*, vol. 82, nos 1-4, whole year.

Kopold, Sylvia and Ben M. Selekman, 'The Epic of the Needle Trades', *Menorah Journal*, vol. 15, nos 4, 5, and 6 (October, November and December 1928) and vol. 18, no. 4 (April 1930).

Laslett, John H. M. (1970), 'Jewish Socialism and the Ladies Garment Workers of New York', in *idem, Labor and the Left*, New York.

Lebowitz, Arieh (1994), 'The Jewish Labor Committee: Past and Present', in *Shofar* (Midwest Jewish Studies Association), spring.

Lebowitz, Arieh and Gail Malmgreen (eds) (1993), *Archives of the Holocaust, Vol. 14: Robert F. Wagner Labor Archives, New York University – Records of the Jewish Labor Committee*, New York: Garland.

Loft, Jacob (1940), 'Jewish Workers in the New York City Men's Clothing Industry', *Jewish Social Studies*, vol. 2, January.

Lorwin, Louis [Levine, Louis] (1924), *The Women's Garment Workers: A History of the International Ladies Garment Workers Union*, New York: B. W. Heubsch.

Malmgreen, Gail (1991), 'Labor and the Holocaust: The Jewish Labor Committee and the Anti-Nazi Struggle', *Labor's Heritage*, vol. 3, no. 4, October.

Markowitz, Ruth Jacknow (1993), *My Daughter, the Teacher: Jewish Teachers in the New York City Schools*, New Brunswick, NJ: Rutgers University Press.

Munts, Raymond and Mary Louise (1968), 'Welfare History of the ILGWU', *Labor History*, vol. 9, special supplement.

Nadel, Stanley (1985), 'Reds Versus Pinks: A Civil War in the International Ladies Garment Workers Union', *New York History*, January.

O'Neal, James (1927), *A History of the Amalgamated Ladies Garment Cutters' Union, Local 10*, New York: ALGCU.

Potofsky, Jacob (1969), 'Profile: The Amalgamated Clothing Workers of America', *American Labor*, 21-27 December.

Robinson, Donald B. (1948), *Spotlight on a Union: The Story of the United Hatters, Cap And Millinery Workers International Union*, New York:

Dial.

Schlossberg, Joseph, (ed.) (1920[?]), *Documentary History of the Amalgamated Clothing Workers of America, New York 1914-1916*, New York: ACWA.

Schappes, Morris U. (1977), 'The Political Origins of the United Hebrew Trades', *Journal of Ethnic Studies*, vol. 5, no. 1, spring.

Seidman, Joel (1942), *The Needle Trades*, New York: Farrar and Rinehart.

Seidman, Joel (1968), 'The ILGWU in the Dubinsky Period', *Labor History*, vol. 9, special supplement.

Shapiro, Judah J. (1970), *The Friendly Society: A History of the Workmen's Circle,* New York: Workmen's Circle.

Shavelson, Clara L. (1982), 'Remembering the Waistmakers General Strike, 1909', *Jewish Currents*, November.

Soyer, Daniel (1988), 'Landsmanshaftn and the Jewish Labor Movement: Co-operation, Conflict, and the Building of Community', *Journal of American Ethnic History*, vol. 7, no. 2.

Stein, Leon (1962), *The Triangle Fire*, Philadelphia: J. P. Lippincott Co. (reprinted New York: Carroll and Graf, 1985).

Stolberg, Benjamin (1944), *Tailor's Progress: The Story of a Famous Union and the Men Who Made It*, New York: Doubleday, Doran.

Stowell, Charles Jacob (1918), *The Journeymen Tailor's Union of America*, Urbana: University of Illinois Press.

Strong, Earl D. (1940), *The Amalgamated Clothing Workers of America*, Grinnell, IA: Herald-Register Publishing Co.

Taft, Philip (1974*), United They Teach: The Story of the United Federation of Teachers (of New York City)*, Los Angeles: Nash.

Tyler, Gus (1995), *Look for the Union Label: A History of the International Ladies' Garment Workers' Union*, Armonk, NY: M. E. Sharpe.

Waldinger, Roger (1987), 'Another Look at the International Ladies' Garment Workers' Union: Women, Industry, Structure and Collective Action', in Ruth Milkman (ed.), *Women, Work and Protest: A Century of U.S. Women's Labor History*, London and New York: Routledge and Kegan Paul.

Weiler, N. Sue (1981), 'The Uprising in Chicago: The Men's Garment Workers Strike, 1910-1911', in Joan M. Jensen and Sue Davidson (eds), *A Needle, A Bobbin, A Strike: Women Needleworkers in America*, Philadelphia: Temple University Press.

Zaretz, Charles Elbert (1934), *The Amalgamated Clothing Workers of America: A Study in Progressive Trades-Unionism*, New York: Ancon.

Zitron, Celia (1968), *The New York City Teachers Union, 1916-1964*, New York: Humanities Press.

Autobiographies, biographies, memoirs

Antler, Joyce (1997), 'Radical Politics and Labor Organizing' [on Emma

Goldman, Rose Pastor Stokes, Rose Pesotta and Rose Schneiderman], in *idem*, *The Journey Home: Jewish Women and the American Century*, New York: The Free Press.

Cahan, Abraham (1969), *The Education of Abraham Cahan*, trans. by Leon Stein, Philadelphia: Jewish Publication Society of America.

Cahan, Abraham (1985), *Grandma Never Lived in America*, Bloomington: Indiana University Press.

Chobanian, Peter (1994), 'Sidney Hillman: A Bibliography', *Bulletin of Bibliography*, vol. 51, no. 3, September.

Danish, Max D. (1957), *The World of David Dubinsky*, Cleveland: World Publishing Co.

Dubinsky, David and Raskin, A. H. (1977), *David Dubinsky: A Life with Labor*, New York: Simon and Schuster.

Endelman, Gary (1982), *Solidarity Forever: Rose Schneiderman and the Women's Trade Union League*, New York: Arno Books.

Epstein, Melech (1965), *Profiles of Eleven*, Detroit, MI: Wayne State University Press.

Epstein, Melech (1971), *Pages from a Colorful Life*, Miami, FL: I. Block.

Fink, Leon (1991), 'A Memoir of Selig Perlman and His Life at the University of Wisconsin', *Labor History*, vol. 32.

Fliegel, Hyman (1959), *Life and Times of Max Pine*, New York: Hyman J. Fliegel.

Fraser, Steven (1991), *Labor Will Rule: Sidney Hillman and the Rise of American Labor*, New York: The Free Press.

Gold, Ben (n.d.), *Memoirs*, New York: William Howard Publishers.

Gompers, Samuel (1984), *Seventy Years of Life and Labor: An Autobiography*, Ithaca: ILR Press – edited, by Nick Salvatore (original edition, 1925).

Goulden, Joseph C. (1982), *Jerry Wurf: Labor's Last Angry Man*, New York: Atheneum.

Hardman, J. B. S. (1948), *Sidney Hillman: Labor Statesman*, New York: Amalgamated Clothing Workers of America.

Hardman, J. B. S. (1968), 'David Dubinsky, Labor Leader and Man', *Labor History*, vol. 9, special supplement.

Haskel, Harry (1950), *A Leader of the Garment Workers: The Biography of Isidore Nagler* (intro. by David Dubinsky), New York: Amalgamated Ladies' Garment Cutters Union, Local 10, ILGWU.

Herling, John (1939), 'Baruch Charney Vladeck', *American Jewish Year Book*, vol. 41.

Hillquit, Morris (1934), *Loose Leaves from a Busy Life*, New York: Macmillan.

Jacobs, Paul (1965), *Is Curly Jewish?*, New York: Vintage.

Jeshurin, Ephim (1936), *B. C. Vladeck: Fifty Years of Life and Labor*, New York: Forward Association.

174

Josephson, Matthew (1952), *Sidney Hillman: Statesman of American Labor*, Garden City, NY: Doubleday.

Julianelli, Jane (1973), 'Bessie Hillman: Up from the Sweatshop', *Ms*, May.

Kann, Kenneth (1981), *Joe Rapoport, the Life of a Jewish Radical*, Philadelphia: Temple University Press.

Katzman, Jacob (1975), *Commitment: The Labor Zionist Life-Style in America*, New York: Labor Zionist Letters.

Kessler-Harris, Alice (1976), 'Organizing the Unorganizable: Three Jewish Women and Their Unions', *Labor History*, vol. 17, no. 1, winter.

Kessler-Harris, Alice (1987), 'Rose Schneiderman and the Limits of Women's Trade Unionism', in Melvyn Dubofsky and Warren van Tine (eds), *Labor Leaders in America*, Urbana and Chicago: University of Illinois Press.

Korman, Gerd (1994), 'New Jewish Politics for an American Labor Leader: Sidney Hillman, 1942-1946', *American Jewish History*, vol. 82.

Leeder, Elaine (1993), *The Gentle General: Rose Pesotta, Anarchist and Labor Organizer*, Albany: SUNY Press.

Lewis, Marx (1931), *Max Zaritsky at Fifty: The Story of an Aggressive Labor Leader*, New York: Max Zaritsky Fiftieth Anniversary Committee (United Hatters, Cap and Millinery Workers).

Madison, Charles A. (1949), 'Sidney Hillman: Leader of the Amalgamated', *American Scholar*, vol. 18, no. 4, autumn.

Malkiel, Theresa Serber (1910), *The Diary of a Shirtwaist Striker*, New York: Cooperative Press.

Miller, Sally (1978), 'From Sweatshop Worker to Labor Leader; Theresa Malkiel: A Case Study', *American Jewish History*, vol. 68, no. 2, December.

Mitelman, Bennie (1981), 'Rose Schneiderman and the Triangle Fire', *American History Illustrated*, July.

Newman, Pauline (1980), 'Pauline Newman', in Joan Morrison and Charlotte Fox Zabusky (eds), *American Mosaic: The Immigrant Experience in the Words of Those Who Lived It*, New York: E. P. Dutton.

Orleck, Annelise (1995), *Common Sense and a Little Fire: Women and Working-Class Politics in the United States, 1900-1965* (Fannia Cohn, Pauline Newman, Rose Schneiderman and Clara Lemlich Shavelson), Chapel Hill: University of North Carolina Press.

Pesotta, Rose (1958), *Days of Our Lives*, Boston: Excelsior Press.

Pesotta, Rose (1987), *Bread Upon the Waters*, Ithaca: ILR Press/Cornell (original edition, 1944).

Potofsky, Joseph (1948), 'Self-Portrait', in L. Kinkelstein (ed.), *American Spiritual Biographies*, New York: Harper.

Pratt, Norma Fain (1979), *Morris Hillquit, A Political History of an American Jewish Socialist*, Westport, CT: Greenwood Press.

Raskin, A. H. (1948), *Sidney Hillman, 1887-1946*, Philadelphia: Jewish Publication Society.

Raskin, A. H. (1953), 'From Gompers to Hillman; Labor Goes Middle Class', *Antioch Review*, vol. 13, pp. 191-201.

Raskin, A. H. (1968), 'Dubinsky: Herald of Change', *Labor History*, vol. 9, special supplement.

Raskin, A. H. (1982), 'David Dubinsky: 1892-1982', *The New Leader*, 4 October.

Rich, J. C. (1968), 'David Dubinsky: The Young Years', *Labor History*, vol. 9, special supplement.

Rischin, Moses (1985), *Grandma Never Lived in America: The New Journalism of Abraham Cahan*, Bloomington: Indiana University Press.

Rogoff, Harry (1930), *An East Side Epic: The Life and Work of Meyer London*, New York: Vanguard Press.

Scheier, Paula (1954), 'Clara Lemlich Shavelson', *Jewish Life*, vol. 8, no. 95, November.

Scheier, Paula (1981), 'Clara Lemlich Shavelson: 50 Years in Labor's Front Line', in *idem*, *The American Jewish Woman: A Documentary History*, New York: KTAV.

Schneiderman, Rose, with Lucy Goldthwaite (1967), *All For One*, New York: Paul S. Ericksson.

Schofield, Ann (1998), *To Do and To Be: Portraits of Four Women Activists, 1893-1986* (Gertrude Barnum, Mary Dreier, Pauline Newman and Rose Pesotta), Boston: Northeastern University Press.

Shepherd, Naomi (1993), '"I Need a Violent Strike": Rose Pesotta and American Jewish Immigrant Unionists', in *idem*, *A Price Below Rubies: Jewish Women as Rebels and Radicals*, Cambridge: Harvard University Press.

Soule, George (1939), *Sidney Hillman, Labor Statesman*, New York: Macmillan.

Stolberg, Benjamin (1944), *Tailor's Progress*, Garden City, NY: Doubleday.

Syrkin, Marie (1968), (biographical introduction to) *Hayim Greenberg Anthology*, Detroit: Wayne State University Press.

Taft, Philip (1968), 'David Dubinsky and the Labor Movement', *Labor History*, vol. 9, special supplement.

Waldman, Louis (1944), *Labor Lawyer* (autobiography), New York: E. P. Dutton.

Weinstone, William (1946), *The Case Against David Dubinsky*, New York: New Century.

Yellowitz, Irwin (1978), 'Morris Hillquit: American Socialism and Jewish Concerns', *American Jewish Historical Quarterly*, vol. 68, December.

Unpublished works

Asher, Nina Lynn (1982), 'Dorothy Jacobs Bellanca: Feminist Trade Unionist, 1884-1946', PhD dissertation, SUNY Binghamton.

Arian, Charles (1986), 'Zionism, Socialism and the Kinship of Peoples:

Hashomer Hatzair in North America', rabbinic thesis, Hebrew Union College-Jewish Institute of Religion, Cincinnati.

Beck, Burt, 'A Joining of Hands: The Story of the ACTWU', unpublished manuscript in ACTWU archives, Cornell University, Ithaca, NY.

Berlin, George (1966), 'The Anti-Nazi Activities of the Jewish Labor Committee in the 1930s', MA thesis, Columbia University.

Berman, Hyman (1956), 'Era of the Protocol: A Chapter in the History of the International Ladies Garment Workers Union, 1910-1916', PhD dissertation, Columbia University.

Brown, Howard M. (1973), 'The Communists and the Needle Trades, 1920-1928', MA thesis, Columbia University.

Brown, Howard M. (1977), 'Political Factions and the Cloakmakers Strike of 1926', MA thesis, Columbia University.

Cohen, Ricki Carole Myers (1976), 'Fannia Cohn and the International Ladies' Garment Workers Union', PhD thesis, University of Southern California.

Cohen, Martin A. (1941), 'Jewish Immigrants and American Trade Unions', MA thesis, University of Chicago.

Gurowsky, David (1978), 'Factional Disputes within the ILGWU, 1919-1928', PhD dissertation, SUNY Binghamton.

Jonas, Franklin (1972), 'The Early Life and Career of B. Charney Vladeck, 1882-1921: The Emergence of an Immigrant Spokesman', PhD dissertation, New York University.

Kram, Harriet Davis (1997), 'No More a Stranger and Alone: Trade Union, Socialist and Feminist Activism – A Route to Becoming American' (on Pauline Newman and Rose Schneiderman), PhD dissertation, City University of New York Graduate Center.

Leiserson, William (1908), 'The Jewish Labor Movement in New York', BA thesis, University of Wisconsin.

Orenstein, Eugene (1978), 'The Jewish Socialist Federation of the US (1912-1921)', PhD dissertation, Columbia University.

Prickett, James Robert (1975), 'Communists and the Communist Issue in the American Labor Movement, 1920-1950', PhD dissertation, University of California at Los Angeles.

Prudson, David (1982), 'Communism and the Jewish Labor Movement in the USA, 1919-1929', PhD dissertation, Tel Aviv University.

Spingarn, Sandra Dawn (1994), 'Trade Unionism among the Jewish Workers in the Fur Manufacturing Industry in New York City, 1912-1929', PhD dissertation, SUNY Binghamton.

Waltzer, Kenneth (1987), 'American Jewish Labor and Aid to Polish Jews during the Holocaust', paper delivered to conference of the United States Holocaust Memorial Council, Washington, DC, March (copy at Robert F. Wagner Labor Archives, New York University).

Afterword: Dresden Homecoming

Irene Wagner

It was 60 years ago that I left Dresden for good. The Nazis were searching for me, the situation absolutely impossible. I said goodbye to my parents and left Germany via Hamburg to make my temporary – as I thought – home in London. All along those 60 years Dresden made itself felt in my consciousness some way or the other. Was it the ghastly raid at the end of the war or artists making an appearance in a concert hall?

When one reaches a certain age, one feels one ought to get back to one's roots. And so it was with both myself and my husband. We decided that we would go to Budapest and Danzig first to see the places of my husband, George's youth and then make a journey to Dresden as well. The visit to Dresden was *very* short and gave me a taste for a longer visit – though I really felt a stranger all the time. And then it all happened so quickly: a journalist from Dresden came to interview me during polling day 1997. For her it was a 'scoop' to be able to see a local party in action, for me a valuable contact. And 'so it came to pass' that I received an all-expenses paid invitation from the Lord Mayor of Dresden to come as a guest of the city and 'bring a companion'. So, having secured a cat-and-flat sitter as well as a companion (Maria from Wesel, a close friend), I set forth by plane to Düsseldorf and from there by first-class train to Dresden. So very comfortable and luxurious in all creature comforts! The journey went through parts of Germany that I had never been to, but started to remind me of the nightly bombing of 'marshalling yards', munitions factories, etc. There were undulating hills, smoking chimneys, vast factories, the Harz mountains, and suddenly the twin towers of the cathedral in Meissen (where the Dresden china is made) and I knew I would be soon in the town of my birth.

Presently we arrived. Outside the station a steady stream of cars made it difficult to cross to the towering hotel in front of us, which was to be our home for a week. I arrived there bewildered on the eleventh floor, looked out of the window and saw a town, new, brash and strangely alien to me – I was completely disorientated. I so wanted to love everything immediately and had to come to terms with a different world: the complete destruction of the town centre and the rebuilding and realignment of roads made me feel absolutely alienated from this that ought to be my roots. The shock was immense. A subsequent initial walk made me wonder where in fact I was. All the lovely buildings in the immediate vicinity of the hotel have gone. There was nothing that could console me when I recalled 'Bomber Harris's' words: how important it was to flatten Dresden so as to frustrate troop movements towards the west and halt the stream of refugees. (As I write the same seems to happen in Kosovo.) We wander down the Prague Street which is twice as wide as it was before, with its modern shops and stores, and as we came to the end I saw the spectre of the couture house where I spent my apprentice-ship and I started to get a bit moist around the eyes. With a heavy heart I approached the Old Market, the scene of the death of 30,000 dead in one night of bombing. It is strange that I should have felt guilty that UK air force planes were involved and at the time there was nothing that I could do to prevent it. But rationalise I did: among the stalls with hot dogs, waffles, toys and first-class jazz band, beer, Coke. And yet the corpses that had lain on that night in the same place mixed with the fairground into a surreal picture. I was angry and it was almost impossible to keep my sadness in check. On occasions like that I used to take refuge somewhere: either in the world-famous café with coffee and luscious cakes or in the church of the Holy Cross. After the coffee I did go into the church. I heard my mother sing there so often: singing Bach and Handel and, of course, Schütz who is buried side by side with past rulers there. The reconstructed church did not prevent me from hearing all those voices of the famous choir in my mind

Homecoming? Not quite. The rebuilt opera house, the catholic cathedral and the 'Zwinger' finally did it. I felt this is *the* place I once belonged to. My cultural background made itself felt once again and the amnesia of the departure had a partial breakthrough. People were wonderfully understanding that I could not remember 90 per cent of where I was or where I was going in the coming days. It was a paradise lost forever. The evil forces of Nazism had instituted destruction in every way. Yes, I once belonged here, but this belonging has gone forever. I now know that it is not possible to go back, at least for myself. Sixty years is a long time.

Index

184